WOMEN BEFORE THE COURT

LAW AND PATRIARCHY IN THE ANGLO-AMERICAN WORLD, 1600–1800

→ Lindsay R. Moore ←

Manchester University Press

Copyright © Lindsay R. Moore 2019

The right of Lindsay R. Moore to be identified as the author of this work has been asserted by her in accordance with the Copyright, Designs and Patents Act 1988.

Published by Manchester University Press
Altrincham Street, Manchester M1 7JA
www.manchesteruniversitypress.co.uk

British Library Cataloguing-in-Publication Data
A catalogue record for this book is available from the British Library

ISBN 978 1 5261 3633 6 hardback
ISBN 978 0 5260 5171 1 paperback

First published 2019

The publisher has no responsibility for the persistence or accuracy of URLs for any external or third-party internet websites referred to in this book, and does not guarantee that any content on such websites is, or will remain, accurate or appropriate.

Typeset
by Toppan Best-set Premedia Limited

Contents

LIST OF TABLES	*page* vi
ACKNOWLEDGEMENTS	vii

Introduction: 'When Women goe to Law, the Devill is full of Businesse' 1

Part I: the courts and the law

1 The varieties of Anglo-American law: property, patriarchy and women's legal status in England and America 21

2 Women as plaintiffs and defendants: the common law, equity and ecclesiastical jurisdictions 39

Part II: the family and society

3 Masters and mistresses, servants and slaves: patriarchy and subordinate agency in the household 59

4 Wives and (unwed) mothers: women's claims for financial support 81

5 Inheritance and family feuds: the legal power of elite women 105

Part III: the economy and equity

6 Economic expansion and the erosion of patriarchy 133

BIBLIOGRAPHY	159
INDEX	171

Tables

2.1	Women acting as plaintiffs and defendants in litigation in courts of common law, 1630–90	*page* 41
2.2	Role and marital status of women involved in debt litigation in the London Mayor's Court, 1630–90	42
2.3	Sex of plaintiffs in testamentary litigation in the Essex Archdeacon's Court and the London Commissary Court, 1630–41 and 1669–87	48
2.4	Sex of defendants in testamentary litigation in the Essex Archdeacon's Court and the London Commissary Court, 1630–41 and 1669–87	48
2.5	Marital status of female plaintiffs in testamentary litigation in the Essex Archdeacon's Court and the London Commissary Court, 1630–41 and 1669–87	48
6.1	Women acting as plaintiffs and defendants in litigation in equity courts	141
6.2	Testamentary cases heard before the diocesan courts in the Archbishopric of York	153

GENDER IN HISTORY

Series editors:
Lynn Abrams, Cordelia Beattie, Pam Sharpe and Penny Summerfield

The expansion of research into the history of women and gender since the 1970s has changed the face of history. Using the insights of feminist theory and of historians of women, gender historians have explored the configuration in the past of gender identities and relations between the sexes. They have also investigated the history of sexuality and family relations, and analysed ideas and ideals of masculinity and femininity. Yet gender history has not abandoned the original, inspirational project of women's history: to recover and reveal the lived experience of women in the past and the present.

The series Gender in History provides a forum for these developments. Its historical coverage extends from the medieval to the modern periods, and its geographical scope encompasses not only Europe and North America but all corners of the globe. The series aims to investigate the social and cultural constructions of gender in historical sources, as well as the gendering of historical discourse itself. It embraces both detailed case studies of specific regions or periods, and broader treatments of major themes. Gender in History titles are designed to meet the needs of both scholars and students working in this dynamic area of historical research.

Women before the court

OTHER RECENT BOOKS
IN THE SERIES

The state as master: gender, state formation and commercialisation in urban Sweden, 1650–1780   Maria Ågren

Love, intimacy and power: marriage and patriarchy in Scotland, 1650–1850   Katie Barclay (Winner of the 2012 Women's History Network Book Prize)

Men on trial: performing emotion, embodiment and identity in Ireland, 1800–45   Katie Barclay

Modern women on trial: sexual transgression in the age of the flapper   Lucy Bland

The Women's Liberation Movement in Scotland   Sarah Browne

Modern motherhood: women and family in England, c. 1945–2000   Angela Davis

Gender, rhetoric and regulation: women's work in the civil service and the London County Council, 1900–55   Helen Glew

Jewish women in Europe in the Middle Ages: a quiet revolution   Simha Goldin

Women of letters: gender, writing and the life of the mind in early modern England   Leonie Hannan

Women and museums 1850–1914: Modernity and the gendering of knowledge   Kate Hill

The shadow of marriage: singleness in England, 1914–60   Katherine Holden

Women, dowries and agency: marriage in fifteenth-century Valencia   Dana Wessell Lightfoot

Women, travel and identity: journeys by rail and sea, 1870–1940   Emma Robinson-Tomsett

Imagining Caribbean womanhood: race, nation and beauty contests, 1929–70   Rochelle Rowe

Infidel feminism: secularism, religion and women's emancipation, England 1830–1914   Laura Schwartz

Women, credit and debt in early modern Scotland   Cathryn Spence

Being boys: youth, leisure and identity in the inter-war years   Melanie Tebbutt

Queen and country: same-sex desire in the British Armed Forces, 1939–45   Emma Vickers

The 'perpetual fair': gender, disorder and urban amusement in eighteenth-century London   Anne Wohlcke

Acknowledgements

During the years spent writing this book, I have developed quite a long list of people to thank. I am grateful to my mentors and advisors at George Washington University, especially Linda Levy Peck, who provided such important and helpful feedback during the earliest stages of this project, and who continues to give me guidance and advice. Many thanks to Marcy Norton and David Silverman for their constant encouragement, and for reading numerous early drafts this work. Keith Wrightson first introduced me to the value of legal records as a source of historical evidence in a seminar at the Folger Shakespeare Library, and helped me navigate the archives during my year of research in England. Without the help of Heather Wolfe, whose palaeographical skills are unsurpassed, I never would have survived the archives. I am also grateful to Tim Stretton for his insightful and close readings of portions of this work.

This work would not have been possible without funding from many different sources and institutions. The Mellon Foundation and the Council on Library and Information Resources provided a year-long grant that funded a year of research in English archives. I am grateful to the staff and archivists at the Huntington Library and the Massachusetts Historical Society, whose wonderful collections rounded out so much of the research presented here. I would also like to thank the North American Conference on British Studies, the Coordinating Council for Women in History and the Cosmos Club for their generous contributions to my research.

Portions of this work have been published in the following volumes: 'Single women and sex in the early modern Atlantic world', *Early Modern Women: An Interdisciplinary Journal*, 5 (2010), pp. 223–8; 'Women and property litigation in seventeenth-century England and North America', in Tim Stretton and Krista Kesselring (eds), *Married Women and the Law: Coverture in England and the Common Law World* (Montreal: McGill-Queen's University Press, 2013), pp. 113–38; and 'Women, property, and the law in the Anglo-American world, 1630–1700', *Early American Studies: An Interdisciplinary Journal*, 14:3 (2016), pp. 537–67.

As I wrote this book, at times I felt that I was giving more time and attention to women and men of the past rather than to the people surrounding me in the present. Luckily for me, my friends and family have borne it well. I thank Betty Medearis, whose vivacity and fun helped me leave the archives behind outside of working hours. I thank my family, especially Phil and Donna Moore, who have never stopped encouraging me. I am grateful for my daughter, Edie, who I hope one day will be inspired by the fierce women of the past. Finally, I thank my most ardent supporter, my husband Ken Marshall. He doubts many things, but he has always believed in my ability to accomplish great things. Without him, I never would have undertaken this journey in the first place.

Introduction: 'When Women goe to Law, the Devill is full of Businesse'

In the Jacobean tragicomedy *The Devil's Law-Case: or When Women goe to Law, the Devill is full of Business* (1623), the widow Leonora takes her son, Romelio, to court. Her design was ostensibly to deprive Romelio of his inheritance in favour of her daughter, whom she much preferred over her son. When her servant Winifred tries to persuade her to settle her family business privately, out of the public eye, Leonora retorts: 'Privacie? It shall be given him / In open Court, Ile make him swallow it / Before the Judges face.'[1] According to her critics in the play, widow Leonora had too much power and independence, reflected in her ability to bequeath the family property to her daughter rather than her son, and her transgression of patriarchal laws of inheritance. She had overstepped the boundaries of patriarchy by using the law as a mode of female empowerment, a move that contravened the social order ordained by God and upheld by man. One character in the play reviles Leonora for her litigious behaviour, saying that such women 'have more need / Of a Physician then a Lawyer', and that their frivolous 'vile suits / Disgrace our Courts'.[2] Though playwright John Webster set the play in Spain, the trope of the overly bold, independent and litigious widow would have resonated with English audiences. Webster and other seventeenth-century playwrights consistently depicted women as remarkably tenacious defenders of their interests in the law courts. Far from being excluded from the courtroom, women occupied central roles in litigation concerning property and inheritance.[3]

The litigious women depicted in seventeenth-century dramas had a basis in reality. From the 1580s onwards, more women entered the courtroom than ever before as they prosecuted cases, presented petitions or testified on behalf of another party. The rising number of women appearing before the courts in England was part of the growing litigiousness of English society as a whole. Between the 1580s and 1670s, the number of cases heard in the central courts of Common Pleas and King's Bench more than doubled.[4] Women comprised an increasing percentage of litigants before the courts: during the reign of Elizabeth I, 17 per cent of all plaintiffs in the English Court of Chancery were female, a number which rose to 26 per cent in the early seventeenth century.[5] In the English Court of Requests, the percentage of female litigants rose from about 12 per cent in 1562 to 18 per cent in 1624.[6] The ecclesiastical courts also saw an increasing number of female litigants. While female plaintiffs brought a little over half of defamation actions in the York Consistory Court in the 1590s, by the 1690s this number had risen to 76 per cent.[7] The same was true of ecclesiastical courts in the south-east. Based on a sampling of cases between 1630 and 1699 from the court of the Archdeaconry of Essex, the Diocese of London Commissary Court and the London Consistory Court, women accounted for 84 per cent of the plaintiffs named in slander cases before the courts, and 52 per cent of the plaintiffs named in inheritance litigation.[8]

This rising volume of litigation, and women's participation in it, indicates the increasing role played by law and legal institutions in the everyday lives of English women and men. Over the course of the seventeenth and eighteenth centuries, more and more people turned to the law to arbitrate disputes that they could not resolve outside of the courtroom. Since legal suits involving women frequently concerned disputes between family members, especially over inheritance and marriage agreements, the law often pierced right into the heart of the patriarchal family itself. Legal suits between mothers and sons, sisters and brothers, and even between husbands and wives reflected that the patriarchal ideals of reciprocity and mutual obligation sometimes failed to provide adequate remedies for both men and women.

Women and the law in a period of transition

The centuries between the founding of Britain's North American colonies and the dissolution of the empire after the success of the American Revolution was a period dominated by momentous changes in nearly every aspect of life. In England, bitter political and religious disputes led to a bloody civil war in the 1640s and the temporary dissolution of the monarchy in the 1650s. It was, in fact, during these years that men, women and children left England in droves, seeking to escape the political turbulence they faced at home and establish new communities in a vast and remote land.

The English monarchy was restored in 1660 but was not yet capable of exercising full control over the empire actively taking shape in North

America. The constitutional and political crises of the second half of the seventeenth century barred any consistent attempts by the Crown to bring the colonies under a single, uniform system of English law and religion. As a result, the colonies were left to fend for themselves, and developed in ways that served the interests and preferences of the colonists rather than the English government. The eighteenth century brought a reassertion of royal power and a more intentional approach by the Crown to colonial administration in North America. After the Glorious Revolution of 1688 the English government implemented new fiscal policies that increased royal revenue and helped to build a strong military that safeguarded the expanding empire. Concurrently with this process, a new commercial economy took shape; trade knitted Britain and its Atlantic colonies together more closely than ever before.[9]

These momentous changes between the years 1600 and 1800 had a profound impact on the history of Britain and America, and on the legal status of women in the Anglo-American world. The lack of royal oversight during the seventeenth century meant that the legal regimes of the American colonies took different trajectories, the southern colonies falling more in line with the multi-jurisdictional English example and the northern colonies privileging the common law jurisdiction. The legal systems in England and the southern colonies generally supported women's ability to inherit property, and the expansion of the equity jurisdiction in these areas gave married women increasing financial independence. The legal culture of the New England colonies, however, provided no such independence for women. New England patriarchs upheld the right of men, whether fathers, husbands, sons or brothers, to own and manage property; even widows, who under common law could own property outright, had to seek the permission of magistrates before selling or bequeathing family property.

During the eighteenth century, women's roles in the legal regimes of Anglo-America changed as they contributed to the expansion of the commercial economy as traders, borrowers, lenders, rentiers and financiers; these roles inevitably drew them into the courtroom as they prosecuted and defended legal suits concerning debt, mortgages, inheritance and property. New developments in English equity law underpinned this expansion of the market economy through the creation of principles that ensured the payment of creditors and the equitable protection of borrowers. At the same time, the English Chancery adopted new principles that expanded married women's ability to own property separately from their husbands. Colonies with strong equity jurisdictions, such as Maryland, Virginia and South Carolina, adopted these principles; as a result, women appeared frequently in the equity courts as they prosecuted and defended cases concerning their property.

One of the reasons the English legal system was effective at home and worthy of emulation in the colonies is that it had the capability to meet the needs of different populations. It provided a number of different avenues for legal recourse for the rich and the poor, for men and women, and operated at both national and local levels. While there is no doubt that the English legal system was complex, costly and sometimes dilatory, it was at the same time a remarkably effective tool for the promotion of social order and the administration of justice. The common law, embodied in the central royal courts in London and in the local administration of justice by Justices of the Peace, had jurisdiction over criminal matters involving life and limb, as well as civil actions concerning debt, trespass and assumpsit.

Operating alongside the common law, the ecclesiastical courts possessed jurisdiction in a wide range of spiritual and temporal affairs, including the important task of probating wills. Equity law provided a further avenue for legal redress. The High Court of Chancery in London and the lower equity courts throughout the country had special jurisdiction over performance of contract, the deployment of trusts and uses, and marriage settlements. Complex though it was, the English legal system functioned extraordinarily well and garnered wide support across English society.[10]

The colonists who emigrated from England to America in the seventeenth century had been steeped in this English legal tradition. In the 1630s and 1640s, newly arrived colonists quickly founded courts and laws modelled on the English legal system. These courts were the foundation of law and order in fledgling colonial societies, and magistrates were the sanctioned arbiters of civil disputes between parties and the enforcers of punishments for criminal offenders from the earliest days of settlement. Even in Puritan Massachusetts Bay, where a communal, harmonious society was the ideal, colonists resorted to the law in ever-increasing numbers throughout the seventeenth century.[11] The religious diversity of other colonies such as Maryland, which included Catholics, Anglicans, Quakers and Puritans, made the establishment of legal courts necessary to ensure some degree of religious toleration and social cohesion.[12] The women and men who emigrated from England to America in the seventeenth century would thus have found colonial laws and legal institutions to be familiar.

Yet the adoption of English legal principles and procedures in the colonies was uneven and irregular; some colonies attempted to replicate

English courts, principles and procedures as closely as frontier conditions would allow.[13] The southern colonies of Maryland, Virginia and South Carolina adopted common law principles and procedures, and also established strong jurisdictions in equity law that became pivotal in protecting women's ability to own and control property. Other colonies were more selective, adopting certain features of English law while eschewing others. The legal systems of Massachusetts and Connecticut embraced the common law almost exclusively: while New England magistrates had the authority to dispense justice according to the principles of equity, the equity jurisdiction itself was never embodied in a permanent court structure. None of the American colonies established ecclesiastical courts, although for different reasons. Puritans in New England viewed the ecclesiastical courts as a distasteful relic from England's days as a Catholic country. In the southern colonies, a high degree of religious diversity made common adherence to canon law nearly impossible. This piecemeal adoption of different aspects of English law throughout the colonies had a profound impact on colonial women's legal rights and status under the law.

The English legal system, composed of a variety of legal jurisdictions, offered women more varied and robust avenues for pursuing legal redress than the legal systems of the colonies. The advantage of this system for English women was that the law of coverture, which applied only in courts of common law, could be circumvented or even ignored in other legal jurisdictions. Coverture mandated that women surrendered their legal independence when they married: unlike single women and widows, a married woman could not initiate or defend a suit in a common law court unless her husband appeared as a co-party with her. Given that the vast majority of women in the seventeenth and eighteenth centuries were married, the law of coverture was a major obstacle for women's legal action. However, other legal jurisdictions allowed women more flexibility and freedom in pursuing redress before the courts. Over the course of the seventeenth and eighteenth centuries the equity jurisdiction developed a sophisticated body of precedents that allowed married women to own property separately from their husbands. In the ecclesiastical jurisdiction, married women regularly initiated litigation to secure their inheritance.

While colonial women's relationship with the law varied by colony, the overarching trend is that the simplicity of colonial law circumscribed women's legal capabilities. Colonial women lacked the benefits of the multi-jurisdictional and sophisticated legal system that protected women's property in England. This was especially the case in New England, where common law continued to be the dominant legal jurisdiction throughout the seventeenth and eighteenth centuries, and where colonists never established equity and ecclesiastical jurisdictions. However, southern colonies, especially Maryland, Virginia and South Carolina, adhered more closely to the multi-jurisdictional model. These colonies adopted many facets of the English legal system in the first few decades of settlement, including robust jurisdictions in equity that became an integral part of protecting married women's property.

By the eighteenth century, new legal devices that allowed women more control over their property increased the number of women participating in the commercial economy as traders, borrowers, lenders and rentiers. The English equity jurisdiction increasingly supported married women's separate estates, property which wives could control and profit from independently of their husbands. Colonies that developed equity jurisdictions on the English model bestowed these same benefits on women. The result was an uneven but steady advancement of women's legal and economic activities over the course of the eighteenth century.

Women's legal status in England and America: a comparison

The legal systems of England and the North American colonies were adapted to suit the unique demographic, social, political and religious conditions of each area. But what impact did the development of these distinctive legal systems have on women? The argument advanced in this book – that England's multi-jurisdictional legal system enhanced rather than hindered women's legal capabilities – runs contrary to decades of scholarship on the legal status of women in Britain and America. Many scholars have viewed the legal status of colonial women as much superior to that of their English counterparts, connecting what they see as the greater empowerment of colonial women in the seventeenth century to a corresponding decline in the eighteenth century, as the colonial economy, law and society became more anglicised.[14] Colonies dominated by Protestant Dissenters, so these scholars have argued, streamlined and simplified English legal procedures, making them more accessible to a wide sector of society, including women. This more egalitarian legal climate enhanced social participation and made the law more available to the average person by 'eliminating absurd formalities'.[15] The legal system established by Puritans in New Haven, for example, treated women more equitably than English common law because of its emphasis on lay-pleading and more simplified procedures. Puritan jurisprudence, according to this view, encouraged women's testimonies and countermanded English legal traditions. It was only after 1700, when New England courts began to embrace English legal procedures, that the number of women appearing before the courts began to decline.[16] Scholars of the colonial Chesapeake Bay region have argued that women's greater empowerment in the tobacco colonies was a product of the unique demography of the region. Because men vastly outnumbered women and mortality rates were high, women often had the opportunity to marry up the economic ladder; if left a widow, a woman might also have control over a substantial amount of property.[17]

Though many scholars have argued that colonial women possessed increasing control over property and a more accessible legal system compared to their English sisters, their arguments do not square with decades of scholarship on the legal capabilities of English women. Far from being bound by outdated rules and arcane legal procedures, these scholars have shown that English women inherited, owned and managed property throughout the seventeenth and eighteenth centuries, and also took legal action to defend it.[18] While acknowledging the real restrictions women faced under the common law, these scholars have noted that other legal jurisdictions gave women the ability to exercise some independent control over property, and the flexibility to pursue litigation if that property was threatened.[19]

Both equity and ecclesiastical law allowed married women to circumvent some of the harsher restrictions of the common law: equity law allowed women to retain control over real property even after their marriages through the use of trusts, while ecclesiastical law protected women's inheritance and moveable property.[20] Manorial law and local customs gave women an additional avenue for legal redress in English towns and villages. Trusts negotiated by manorial courts allowed women to control and inherit property in spite of common-law restrictions.[21] Moreover, even common law courts could be flexible in their view of coverture when it came to the legal status of married female traders in English cities; English law granted married businesswomen the status of feme sole traders, which allowed them to make contracts, and borrow or lend money in their own names, even while under coverture.[22]

While scholars of American and British women have explored many of the same themes, including the impact of the doctrine of coverture, and the ability of women to inherit and bequeath property, there has been surprisingly little dialogue between them.[23] One of the central aims of this book is to put these works on women and the law into conversation with one another. By setting women's experiences before the law in a comparative perspective, we can see how women in England and North America adapted to changing legal landscapes, and created new strategies to secure the best outcomes in court for themselves and for their families.

Given the variety of laws, legal institutions and procedures, making generalisations about women's legal status across the Anglo-American world is difficult. However, two patterns do emerge that help us interpret women's legal status and their ability to use the law to seek redress. First, the increasing adoption of anglicised legal procedures in the colonies did not alienate women from the colonial courtroom, just as they had never alienated women from the English courtroom. Second, over the course of the seventeenth and eighteenth centuries, equity law gave married women increasing financial independence that ultimately helped to undermine the role of patriarchy as the foundation of familial relationships. As new legal devices, enforceable in courts of equity, expanded the ability of married women to manage their own property, wives relied less and less on their husbands for financial support and legal representation.

Women's legal power in an age of (eroding?) patriarchy

Women often appeared before the courts when patriarchal relationships, which were supposed to ensure justice and tranquillity between family members, had broken down. In the ideal version of the patriarchal family, ultimate authority was vested in the male head of household, who acted as the benevolent yet supreme leader of the family. He was responsible for caring for and protecting his family members, which included not only a wife and children but servants and other dependents as well. In return for the master's support and protection, the subordinates of the household owed him respect, deference and submission to his commands.[24] This was the ideal version of patriarchy but it was one that very few early modern households lived up to. In reality, men often shirked their responsibilities to provide for their families and sometimes abused the subordinates that they had been charged to protect. Conversely, women, children and servants could be unruly, outspoken and subversive of patriarchal authority.

There are many examples in this study which show that women's words before the court directly confronted household hierarchies. Female servants challenged their masters legally for a range of offences, including breach of contract, debt, rape, murder and theft. Wives petitioned for marital separation and the payment of financial support from husbands who abandoned, abused or neglected them. Widows sued their sons and step-sons for control of their widow's portions. According to religious teaching and social custom, the patriarchal family remained the ideal, yet these relationships were always contested between members of the household. One of the arguments of this book is that individuals negotiating these relationships increasingly used the law to assert their power and gain more leverage within their households.[25]

As this book will show, some women did possess a great deal of freedom and latitude in pursuing their own legal affairs; but how do we square women's exercise of power in the courtroom with the constraints they faced under the law and in society at large? One of the central issues in this question is how limiting the doctrine of coverture really was for married women. In theory at least, coverture meant that a married woman's legal identity was subsumed within her husband's. Upon her marriage, she surrendered all rights to property as well as her ability to pursue legal action independently. Some scholars have argued that coverture remained remarkably persistent across the medieval, early modern and modern periods, leading two scholars to remark that, as far as their legal status was concerned, 'a typical wife in New England in 1750 had much in common with a typical wife in England in 1250'.[26] These scholars point out that while laws, legal institutions and court procedures could vary drastically in different areas of the Anglo-American world, women's subordination within the patriarchal order remained a basic fact of life for most women, whether married or not. However, on the other hand, some scholars have emphasised that women had a remarkable degree of legal and economic agency, and that both women and men could adapt, or even ignore, the doctrine of coverture when it was convenient to do so.[27]

In my view, there is no fundamental disagreement between these scholars on the status of women under the law: they merely emphasise different sides of the same coin. As this book shows, married women certainly felt the limitations imposed by coverture in common law courts, and some undoubtedly had husbands who asserted to the greatest extent their legal dominance over their wives. However, there are also many examples of women who found brilliant ways to navigate the legal systems, and actively sought to gain what was rightfully theirs under the law. Women's legal power, then, was Janus-faced; there were real limitations and restrictions women faced under the law and in society at large, but also extraordinary opportunities for women to pursue cases in which their persons or the property were at stake. Some women found ways to work around difficult husbands; some husbands were often happy to leave the management of time-consuming litigation to their capable wives; and in further examples some husbands and wives actively partnered in pursuing legal action. As many of the examples in this book suggest, women were active participants in guiding their cases through the courts, and many of them possessed a detailed understanding of the law that they used quite skilfully.

However, to see women's pursuit of legal redress as a straightforward expression of agency or a resistance of patriarchy would be to obscure the complexity of their goals and motivations, and to overlook the critical role many women played in supporting the structures of patriarchy. When initiating litigation or presenting a petition to the courts, women were not always rebelling against patriarchy but finding practical and sometimes ingenious methods of working within it. The idea of 'agency', as a mode of self-directed action, was certainly not how women in the seventeenth and eighteenth centuries would have understood their actions before the courts.[28] The notion of autonomy of the individual that underpinned the women's movement in the nineteenth century was still inconceivable in the seventeenth and eighteenth centuries.

In the early modern period, women's reasons for engaging with the courts were often linked to the nexus of family relationships of which they formed an integral part: their roles as mothers, wives and daughters spurred them to action as they sought to provide for, and to protect, their family's interests. Moreover, most women who initiated litigation or testified before the courts did not explicitly reject patriarchy, although the actions of some women directly contradicted contemporaries' most basic assumptions about women's inferior status. Some women who appeared before the court were even actively involved in supporting the patriarchal structures of the law. Midwives, for example, helped police prosecute sexual immorality in early modern communities, and were actively involved in bringing criminal charges against women and men for sexual offences. In other words, women's legal activity was not always subversive or representative of a desire for autonomy. Rather, women's engagement with the courts was embedded within and defined by social networks in which patriarchy was the norm.[29]

Looking at women's legal activities across a broad time and space, the picture that emerges is one of complexity and variation. While early modern women generally accepted patriarchy as the status quo, they still went to law to secure and protect their own interests. Women had a robust understanding of the law's protection of their persons and their property and were often actively involved in seeking legal redress when they felt these protections had been unlawfully violated. However, other women felt the restrictions imposed on them by law, society and family dynamics. To centre our focus on one group or the other would be misleading, and would distort our understanding of the variety of women's experiences in the early modern world.

In each of the following chapters, there are examples of women who endured the worst abuses and found little recompense in the courts.

Others brilliantly navigated their way through complex legal cases and successfully secured their own advantage. Certainly, all women did not have the same opportunities or resources to seek justice in the courts, and any number of factors might influence their decisions to pursue legal action. One of the goals of this book is to look at the variations in women's circumstances, and to uncover the different strategies and methods that women used to engage with the law.

Sources: opportunities and limitations

Depositions, petitions, bills of complaint and other texts that comprise the historical legal record make this study of women's lives in early modern England and the American colonies possible. The bulk of the evidence for this book is based on nearly six thousand legal cases and over five hundred petitions drawn from courts on both sides of the Atlantic. These legal records form the basis of my quantitative analysis in tracking the number of female litigants and petitioners before the courts and provide the rich material for the qualitative portions of the book that analyse women's experiences of the law and litigation.

While this book draws extensively from the records produced by legal institutions in England and the American colonies, it takes seriously the limitations of using these sources as straightforward evidence of women's words, actions and opinions. The depositions, petitions and other legal records are as much a product of the legal institutions that created them as they are a reflection of the 'voices' of the litigants, witnesses and petitioners before the court. Clerks who took down the depositions of court witnesses routinely edited and streamlined the words actually spoken by the witnesses or petitioners in order to clarify the most important elements in the case. Lawyers who worked in the English church courts, for example, advised scribes recording the depositions of witnesses to eliminate any 'vain talk' or information not relevant to the case.[30] Additionally, what we hear in court records may also be an attempt by legal professionals to persuade a magistrate or judge to a particular point of view more than a straightforward recording of women's words, motivations and opinions. In other words, court records give us a treasure trove of detail about life in the early modern world, but we must remember that these records were produced with certain goals in mind. So, how can we be sure who contributed what?[31]

While court records should be evaluated critically and read against the grain, I think it is rather self-defeating to discredit the possibility of hearing traces of women's voices in the legal record. Interspersed throughout the following chapters are cases in which the recorded depositions and testimonies of women are written in the first person rather than the third, suggesting that the court clerks working in these cases may have hastily recorded the spoken words of the women without bothering to stop and edit them. Some women personally wrote and signed their own depositions before the court. While it is of course impossible to recreate the specific circumstances of each woman's testimony, it is worth noting when these instances arise in the court records and what these depositions might reveal about how women shaped their narratives, and to what purpose.

Additionally, whenever possible, this book draws from evidence outside of the legal record. Women's letters and correspondence, many written in their own hands to lawyers and legal advisors, augment our perspectives on women's voices in legal matters. While depositions, testimonies and petitions were generally drawn up by court clerks and filtered through formulaic legal language, letters and correspondence give us a more unmediated and distilled understanding of women's legal knowledge and their strategies in pursuing legal action. Joanne Bailey has noted that letters, correspondence and other documents written by lawyers and litigants provide a unique glimpse into the issues at stake in the case. Because these documents were not meant for public consumption, they allow us to move past the legalese of official court documents and hear the voices of individuals.[32]

This book analyses legal records with care and special attention to the social and institutional contexts in which they were written. Court processes and procedures, the intervention of lawyers and legal advisors, and even the *raison d'etre* of the legal institutions themselves shaped women's words before the court. Rather than focusing on uncovering the 'truth' of the particular event discussed in a case, this book focuses on the strategies women used to seek redress from the courts and how they shaped their narratives to secure the most beneficial outcome in their cases.[33] Whether the narratives told by women before the court were objectively true or not, what is important is that women crafted accounts of events that they considered believable by their courts and communities.

Overview

The overall aims of this book are to show how women used the legal systems of Anglo-America to secure their own benefit, and to examine how women's use of the law increasingly undermined the patriarchal family structure. Part I begins with a comparative analysis of women's legal status in England and the American colonies in the seventeenth century. Examining women as plaintiffs, defendants and petitioners before a variety of courts, it focuses especially on married women's use of the legal system to protect and defend their property. Chapter 1 defines women's legal status in a variety of jurisdictions across the Anglo-American world, and examines how English law was adopted and modified by colonists in the earliest decades of colonisation. Chapter 2 offers a quantitative analysis of female litigants in courts across three jurisdictions during the seventeenth century. Though the percentages of female litigants in common law courts remained low, an increasing number of women sought legal redress in the equity jurisdiction in England and in those colonies that established courts of chancery. Remarkably, women appeared as plaintiffs and defendants in more than half of the cases heard before the English ecclesiastical courts, a percentage that far surpasses women's participation in any court in the colonies.

While Part I offers a quantitative analysis of women's legal activities, Part II takes a qualitative approach. Drawing from petitions, depositions, testimonies, letters and inventories, Part II shows that women on both sides of the Atlantic were remarkably knowledgeable about their legal affairs and that many of them were actively involved in their legal cases. Women's legal competence was not necessarily linked to social status: both elite women and women lower on the social scale possessed a detailed knowledge of what they were entitled to under the law. Chapter 3 examines how the legal status of female servants and slaves evolved over the course of the seventeenth century. While female servants had a relatively wide spectrum of legal rights and routinely petitioned the courts for breach of contract, slaves had no legal standing before the courts. The legal relationship between a master and a female servant depended on a contract that stipulated the amount of time to be served and the payment the woman would receive for her labour. Masters owned the labour of the servant while she was under contract, but not the servant herself. The legal relationship between a master and a slave, however, was not subject to the terms of a contract. Masters owned not only the labour of their slaves but also their persons; this made it legally impossible for slaves to bring any grievances against their masters to court.

Chapter 4 assesses the legal power of wives, midwives and mothers in the legal regimes of Anglo-America. Though under coverture, wives clearly had a right to petition the courts to compel neglectful husbands to give them financial maintenance. Husbands had a patriarchal responsibility to provide for their wives and children, and magistrates had an interest in holding men to their obligations to care for their families. Laws regarding divorce and marital separation differed by location. In England and the southern colonies, authorities granted full divorces in very few instances. Instead, these areas preferred separation of bed and board. Under this agreement the couple was still legally married and a wife could claim financial support from her husband even if she lived separately from him. The New England colonies, however, permitted couples who could not live harmoniously together to divorce; this agreement dissolved the marriage and negated any obligation of the husband to provide for his wife. Remarkably, in all areas of the Anglo-American world, a man who fathered children out of wedlock still had a patriarchal responsibility to provide financial support to his family. Mothers of these children, supported by midwives, could legally claim financial support from the men they named as the fathers even if the fathers denied the women's accusations.

While the women examined in chapter 4 are mostly of middling and lower status, those studied in chapter 5 are drawn from the English and colonial elite. This chapter draws from women's letters and correspondence to lawyers and family members to examine the depth of women's legal knowledge and how they participated in litigation even while they were under coverture. Different demographic patterns and inheritance laws across England and the colonies affected how elite women managed and protected their property, and defined the legal conflicts between women and their male relatives. In England the relative shortage of land and the likelihood of parents to live into old age often resulted in family feuds: widows who sought to gain their widow's portions came into conflict with heirs eager to receive their full inheritance. In the colonies, on the other hand, land was more abundant, a factor that released some of the pressure between generations. However, the longer life-spans of people in New England compared with those of people in the Chesapeake had a significant impact on elite women's control of property. In colonies such as Maryland the frequency of death and remarriage gave men an incentive to grant their widows wide authority over family property. Because widows usually remarried, this property was often placed in trust for the benefit of widows and children to prevent it from being squandered by a greedy step-father.

Part III takes us into the economic expansion and the increasing development of the equity jurisdiction in the eighteenth century. The legal regimes of England and the southern colonies gave women a wide latitude to pursue investment and trade and allowed married women greater financial independence than ever before. In urban areas of England and America the expansion of the use of feme sole trading status allowed married women to make contracts in their own names for transactions pertaining to their trade. The increasing appearance of women in cases concerning mortgages, foreclosure, debts and contracts, all matters heard before the courts of equity, reveal women's wide participation in the economy as investors, renters, borrowers and lenders. Equity law also expanded married women's ability to retain control of their own property during marriage through the creation of new legal devices such as the simple agreement, equity to a settlement and restraint upon anticipation. Because of these economic and legal changes in the eighteenth century, family relationships came to be more defined by legal notions of contract rather than the mutual obligations that underpinned the patriarchal family.

Notes

1 John Webster, *The Devil's Law-Case: or When Women goe to Law, the Devill is full of Businesse* (London, John Grismand: 1623), G 3.
2 Webster, *The Devil's Law-Case*, G 5–6.
3 For a discussion of women's portrayal in Jacobean and Restoration satires and dramas, see Tim Stretton, *Women Waging Law in Elizabethan England* (Cambridge: Cambridge University Press, 1998), pp. 55–69.
4 Christopher Brooks, *Lawyers, Litigation, and English Society Since 1450* (London: Hambledon, 1998), p. 68.
5 Amy Erickson, 'Common law versus common practice: the use of marriage settlements in early modern England', *Economic History Review*, 43:1 (1990), p. 28; Amy Erickson, *Women and Property in Early Modern England* (London: Routledge, 1993), p. 115. Wilfrid Prest estimates that women accounted for 40 per cent of all complainants before the Chancery court in 1625. See Wilfrid R. Prest, 'Law and women's rights in early modern England', *Seventeenth Century*, 6:2 (1991), p. 182.
6 Stretton, *Women Waging Law*, p. 39.
7 J. A. Sharpe, *Defamation and Sexual Slander in Early Modern England: The Church Courts at York* (York: Borthwick Institute of Historical Research, 1980), pp. 27–8.
8 Based on a sampling of a total of 241 cases from English ecclesiastical courts. Essex Record Office, Chelmsford, UK, Archdeaconry of Essex Depositions, D/AE/D8; London Metropolitan Archives, London Commissary Court and London Consistory Court, D/CL. These sources are discussed in more detail in chapter 2. See also Laura Gowing, *Domestic Dangers: Women, Words, and Sex in Early Modern London* (Oxford: Oxford University Press, 1996), pp. 35–7.
9 Major works on Britain's establishment of and increasing control over the American colonies include James Horn, *Adapting to a New World: English Society in the Seventeenth-century Chesapeake* (Chapel Hill: University of North Carolina Press, 1994); Alan Taylor, *American Colonies: The Settling of North America* (London: Penguin, 2002); Nicholas Canny (ed.), *The Origins of Empire: British Overseas Enterprise to the Close of the Seventeenth Century* [vol. 1 of William Roger Louis (ed.), *The Oxford History of the British Empire*] (Oxford: Oxford University Press, 1998). On Britain's increasing economic control over the colonies, see John Brewer, *The Sinews of Power: War, Money, and the English State, 1688–1783* (London: Unwin Hyman, 1989); David Hancock,

Citizens of the World: London Merchants and the Integration of the British Atlantic Community, 1735–1785 (Cambridge: Cambridge University Press, 1995).

10 Cynthia Herrup, *The Common Peace: Participation and the Criminal Law in Seventeenth-century England* (Cambridge: Cambridge University Press, 1987); J. H. Baker, *An Introduction to English Legal History*, 3rd edn (London: Butterworths, 1990), pp. 113–14, 147–52; Stretton, *Women Waging Law*, pp. 26–7.

11 David Thomas Konig, *Law and Authority in Puritan Massachusetts: Essex County, 1629–1692* (Chapel Hill: University of North Carolina Press, 1979), pp. 109–13, 156–7.

12 Horn, *Adapting to a New World*.

13 Christopher Tomlins and Bruce Mann (eds), *The Many Legalities of Early America* (Chapel Hill: Omohundro Institute of Early American History and Culture, 2001), Introduction.

14 See the arguments made by John Murrin, including 'The legal transformation: the bench and bar of eighteenth-century Massachusetts', in Stanley Katz and John Murrin (eds), *Colonial America: Essays in Politics and Social Development* (Boston: Little, Brown, 1971).

15 William M. Offutt, Jr., *Of 'Good Laws' and 'Good Men'; Law and Society in the Delaware Valley, 1680–1710* (Urbana: University of Illinois Press, 1995), pp. 16–17, 30.

16 Cornelia Hughes Dayton, *Women Before the Bar: Gender, Law, and Society in Connecticut, 1639–1789* (Chapel Hill: University of North Carolina Press, 1995), pp. 10–11; Cornelia Hughes Dayton, 'Was there a Calvinist type of patriarchy? New Haven colony reconsidered in the early modern context', in Tomlins and Mann (eds), *The Many Legalities of Early America*, p. 346. The origin of this thesis seems to come from Richard Morris, *Studies in the History of American Law: With Special Reference to the Seventeenth and Eighteenth Centuries* (New York: Octagon Books, 1930), pp. 126–8, 200. It has a strong presence in work on colonial women undertaken in the 1970s and 1980s. See Joan R. Gundersen and Gwen Victor Gampel, 'Married women's legal status in eighteenth-century New York and Virginia', *William and Mary Quarterly*, 3rd series, 39:1 (1982), pp. 114–34; Nancy Cott, 'Divorce and the changing status of women in eighteenth-century Massachusetts', *William and Mary Quarterly*, 3rd series, 33:4 (1976), pp. 586–614; Sheldon Cohen, 'What man hath put asunder: divorce in New Hampshire, 1681–1784', *Historical New Hampshire*, 41:3 (1986), pp. 118–41. For more recent works, in addition to the works by Offutt and Dayton, see Elizabeth Reis, *Damned Women: Sinners and Witches in Puritan New England* (Ithaca: Cornell University Press, 1997), pp. xi–xii; Irmina Wawrzyczek, 'The women of Accomack versus Henry Smith: gender, legal recourse, and the social order in seventeenth-century Virginia', *Virginia Magazine of History and Biography*, 105:1 (1997), p. 6.

17 Lois Green Carr and Lorena S. Walsh, 'The planter's wife: the experience of white women in seventeenth-century Maryland', *William and Mary Quarterly*, 3rd series, 34:4 (1977), p. 543; Linda Sturtz, *Within Her Power: Propertied Women in Colonial Virginia* (New York: Routledge, 2002), pp. 6–7, 11.

18 The following list is not exhaustive but will give the reader a sense of the trend of this historiography. In addition to the works discussed in the text, see Maria Cioni, *Women and the Law in Elizabethan England, with Particular Reference to the Court of Chancery*

(New York: Garland, 1985); Maria Cioni, 'The Elizabethan Chancery and women's rights', in D. J. Guth and J. W. McKenna (eds), *Tudor Rule and Revolution* (Cambridge: Cambridge University Press, 1982), p. 160; Prest, 'Law and women's rights in early modern England', pp. 169–87; Christine Churches, 'Putting women in their place: female litigants at Whitehaven, 1660–1760', in Nancy Wright, Margaret Ferguson and A. R. Buck (eds), *Women, Property, and the Letters of the Law in Early Modern England* (Toronto: University of Toronto Press, 2004), pp. 50–65; David Lemmings, 'Women's property, popular cultures, and the Consistory Court', in Wright, Ferguson and Buck (eds), *Women, Property, and the Letters of the Law in Early Modern England*, pp. 66–94; Joanne Bailey, 'Favoured or oppressed? Married women, property, and "coverture" in England, 1660–1800', *Continuity and Change*, 17:3 (2002), pp. 351–72; Margaret Hunt, 'Wives and marital "rights" in the Court of Exchequer in the early eighteenth century', in Paul Griffiths and Mark Jenner (eds), *Londinopolis: Essays in the Cultural and Social History of Early Modern London* (Manchester: Manchester University Press, 2000), pp. 111–12; Margot Finn, 'Women, consumption, and coverture in England, c. 1760–1860', *Historical Journal*, 39:3 (1996), p. 703; Bronach Kane and Fiona Williamson (eds), *Women, Agency, and the Law, 1300–1700* (London: Pickering and Chatto, 2013); Tim Stretton and Krista Kesselring (eds), *Married Women and the Law: Coverture in England and the Common Law World* (Montreal: McGill-Queen's University Press, 2013).

19 Pearl Hogrefe, 'Legal rights of Tudor women and the circumvention by men and women', *Sixteenth Century Journal*, 3:1 (1972), pp. 97–105; Ruth Kittel, 'Women under the law in medieval England, 1066–1485', in Barbara Kanner (ed.), *The Women of England: Interpretive Bibliographical Essays* (Hamden: Archon, 1979), pp. 131–2; Patricia Crawford, 'From the woman's view: pre-industrial England, 1500–1750', in Patricia Crawford (ed.), *Exploring Women's Past: Essays in Social History* (London: George Allen & Unwin, 1984), pp. 61–3.

20 Stretton, *Women Waging Law*; Erickson, *Women and Property*, pp. 27, 32–5, 156–71; Erickson, 'Common law versus common practice', pp. 21–39; Susan Staves, *Married Women's Separate Property in England, 1660–1833* (Cambridge, MA: Harvard University Press, 1990).

21 Christine Churches, 'Women and property in early modern England: a case-study', *Social History*, 23:2 (1998), pp. 165–80.

22 Craig Muldrew, '"A mutual assent of her mind"? Women, debt, litigation, and contract in early modern England', *History Workshop Journal*, 55:1 (2003), pp. 47–71. See also Marjorie K. McIntosh, 'The benefits and drawbacks of *femme sole* status in England, 1300–1630', *Journal of British Studies*, 44 (2005), pp. 410–38.

23 Two notable exceptions are worth mentioning here. First, see the cluster of articles on gender, sexuality and family in the early modern Atlantic world, which begins to explore some of the benefits of a transnational approach to women's history, especially the article by Karin Wulf, 'Women and families in early (North) America and the wider (Atlantic) world', in 'Rethinking gender, family and sexuality in the early modern Atlantic world', *History Compass*, 8:3 (2010), pp. 238–47. Also, although her analysis is focused on a comparison of elite women in Britain and America in the eighteenth

century, see Rosemary O'Day, *Women's Agency in Early Modern Britain and the American Colonies* (London: Pearson, 2007).
24 Carole Shammas, 'Anglo-American household government in comparative perspective', *William and Mary Quarterly*, 3rd series, 52:1 (1995), pp. 104–44.
25 On the contested nature of patriarchy, see Terri Snyder, *Brabbling Women: Disorderly Speech and the Law in Early Virginia* (Ithaca: Cornell University Press, 2003); Anthony Fletcher, *Gender, Sex, and Subordination in England, 1500–1800* (New Haven: Yale University Press, 1995).
26 Stretton and Kesselring, *Married Women and the Law*, p. 5.
27 Cordelia Beattie and Matthew Stevens (eds), *Married Women and the Law in Premodern Northwest Europe* (Woodbridge: Boydell Press, 2013).
28 Walter Johnson, 'On agency', *Journal of Social History*, 37:1 (2003), pp. 115–16.
29 Cornelia Hughes Dayton, 'Rethinking patriarchy, recovering voices', *American Historical Review*, 109:3 (2004), pp. 842–43; Dana Wessell Lightfoot, *Women, Dowries and Agency: Marriage in Fifteenth-Century Valencia* (Manchester: Manchester University Press, 2013), pp. 2–8.
30 R. H. Helmholz, *The Canon Law and Ecclesiastical Jurisdiction from 597 to the 1640s* [vol. 1 of *The Oxford History of the Laws of England*] (Oxford: Oxford University Press, 2004), pp. 339–40.
31 Frances Dolan, *True Relations: Reading, Literature, and Evidence in Seventeenth-Century England* (Philadelphia: University of Pennsylvania Press, 2013), p. 122.
32 Joanne Bailey, 'Voices in court: lawyers' or litigants'?', *Historical Research*, 74:186 (2001), pp. 393–4.
33 One of the pioneers of this approach of 'unlocking' legal records by focusing on the presentation of women's arguments in court was Stretton, *Women Waging Law*, pp. 10–19.

Part I

The courts and the law

1

The varieties of Anglo-American law: property, patriarchy and women's legal status in England and America

The English legal system was the subject of much controversy and debate in the seventeenth century. Some contemporary writers decried the dilatory proceedings, high costs and obscure language which characterised litigation and legal procedures, while others believed that the legal system had become so cumbersome and labyrinthine as to make it all but inaccessible to the average person seeking justice and legal redress in the courts.[1] According to contemporary critics, abuses of the law were rampant: judges were too easily bought off by the wealthier party, and lawyers were too eager to line their own pockets by taking advantage of laypeople's ignorance.[2] The multiplicity of jurisdictions within the English legal system (according to Sir Edward Coke, there were sixteen) also made the decision of what court had proper jurisdiction over a case confusing to those unversed in the law.[3]

Complex though it was, at base the English legal system garnered wide support from across English society, and was an effective tool for the promotion of social order and the administration of justice.[4] This legal system, which in England had grown up piecemeal over centuries, provided the foundation of society and government in British America. The colonists who left England for America in the seventeenth century were well versed in English law, and colonial leaders quickly moved to establish law and order according to the traditions of their homeland.[5] A simplified version of English common law became the foundation of law and order, and the basis of civil and criminal codes, in all of the American colonies.[6]

However, colonial attitudes towards the legal jurisdictions outside of the common law were more varied, and some colonies adhered more closely to the English model than others. Maryland, for example, established an equity jurisdiction by creating a court of chancery modelled on the High Court of Chancery in London, while other colonies, especially in

New England, vehemently rejected the creation of chancery courts.[7] Additionally, the ecclesiastical jurisdiction was virtually eliminated in the colonies, although some colonies such as Maryland, South Carolina and New York established more limited, quasi-ecclesiastical prerogative courts whose task was to oversee the probate of wills and to hear any litigation that arose over estate administration.[8] The result was that some colonies developed intricate and complex legal systems that embraced the various legal jurisdictions found in England, while others created a more streamlined legal system centred exclusively on the common law.[9]

It was the very complexity of the English legal system that gave English women a decisive advantage over some of their colonial counterparts. While married women were limited in common law courts by the doctrine of coverture, other legal jurisdictions provided women with alternative avenues for legal redress. The two most important jurisdictions for English women were equity law and ecclesiastical law, which both provided some remedy for the common law's severity towards women. Equity law recognised the ability of married women to own property independently of their husbands, and allowed them to pursue litigation to protect that property if necessary.[10] The ecclesiastical courts, which oversaw the process of probate and any litigation that concerned testamentary matters, ignored the doctrine of coverture altogether. Unlike common law courts, the ecclesiastical justices recognised married women as legal actors who could act independently of their husbands, and allowed married women to appear in litigation without their husbands' presence or consent.[11]

Whether the leaders of a colony adopted or rejected the complex, multi-jurisdictional English legal model had important implications for colonial women. Some colonial scholars have argued that the simplicity of the colonial common law provided women with a unique opportunity for legal action. Focusing on New England and Pennsylvania, these scholars have argued that the common law in these colonies in the seventeenth century had not yet been encumbered by the formal procedures that made the English legal system largely inaccessible to anyone untrained in the law. Women and others unlearned in the law could therefore plead before the magistrates in their own words without the fear of making a technical or procedural error. As the legal systems in these colonies fell more in line with the English model after 1689, however, women's presence in the courts declined.[12]

What these studies have overlooked is that the complexity of the English system may have actually worked in women's favour. Women in England, and in the colonies that adopted the English equity and quasi-ecclesiastical model, had a variety of legal avenues open to them outside of the common law for legal redress. South Carolina, Maryland and Virginia had courts of common law but also established alternative avenues of legal redress in the equity and prerogative courts that gave women more avenues for economic independence and legal agency.[13] In contrast, the New England and mid-Atlantic colonies focused primarily on the establishment of courts of common law, in which coverture imposed real restrictions on the legal and economic independence of married women.

Patriarchy, coverture and Anglo-American common law

While many aspects of English jurisprudence changed in the transition to the colonies, one facet of English law that proved remarkably enduring across the Anglo-American world was the common law doctrine of coverture. In England, in the Law French of the twelfth century, a married woman was a feme covert as opposed to a feme sole, and her husband was her baron, or lord. In other words, in the eyes of the common law, the husband and wife were one person, the wife being 'covered' by her husband. Practically speaking, this meant that married women could not draw up their own wills without the consent of their husbands, enter into binding contracts, or initiate or defend a legal suit without their husbands' assistance. A husband legally controlled and reaped the profits of his wife's wages or property during their marriage.[14] According to the legal concept of unity of person, the legal identities of the husband and wife were merged; this concept arose from the customary treatment of women as inferiors and the subordinate status of the wife under the husband outlined in the Old and New Testaments.[15] While Protestant theology granted women a spiritual status equal with men, it also rigidly upheld men's duty to act as spiritual and temporal leaders both within the household and without.

The patriarchal family was the model for household life and the foundation of government authority in the early modern period. Women, children and servants were under the dominion of the father, who acted as the family's guardian and representative to the institutions of the state. Religious and secular authorities alike expected male heads of household to be the first line of defence against the potential social disruption of insubordinate dependants. This structure of household government remained remarkably similar across the Anglo-American world in spite of differences in religious outlooks, demographic circumstances and political authorities. Catholics, Dissenters and orthodox members of the Church of England all upheld the duty of fathers to oversee the economic, spiritual and social affairs of the family. Especially in New England, authorities placed a great deal of importance on the power of fathers during the early decades of colonisation while the institutions of government were still weak and in development.[16]

While Anglo-American common law imposed some real limitations on women's economic and legal independence, it also steadfastly preserved the right of a woman to inherit a portion of her husband's land after his death. Under English common law, a widow could claim her dower rights, which meant she was entitled to the management and profits of one-third of the freehold property her husband had held at any time during their marriage. Widows held their dower lands as a life tenant only, which meant the estate would pass to the husband's next heir after his death. A widow therefore could not legally bequeath her dower lands to heirs of her choice. In England the ecclesiastical courts had jurisdiction over the descent of personal property, or moveable goods, including money, debts, clothing, household utensils and furniture, and food. For most of the seventeenth century, ecclesiastical law ensured that a widow received one-third of her husband's moveable property upon his death, although he could leave her more in his will if he chose. However, by a series of statutes set out between 1692 and 1724 it became legal for a husband to bequeath all of his personal property to an heir of his choice.[17]

The majority of colonies followed English precedent in protecting the rights of widows to a portion of their husbands' estates. As in England, a man could not legally bequeath land reserved for his wife's dower, although inheritance laws regarding lineal descendants varied between colonies. A widow's right to a one-third share of her husband's land was upheld by statute in the seventeenth century by several colonies.[18] A Maryland law of 1642, for example, guaranteed a widow the use of at least one-third of her husband's real estate; if her marriage had been childless, she would receive the use of the entire estate upon her husband's death.[19] For most of the seventeenth century, a widow's third also entailed the use of her husband's personalty, although this practice became more restricted in England and the colonies by the early eighteenth century. Only in Maryland and Virginia did widows continue to receive a right to personalty throughout the eighteenth century.[20]

While the common law concepts of coverture were well defined in the early modern period, common law rules regarding women were not always consistently applied in practice. Coverture was, in particular, difficult to enforce absolutely. It was in men's interest to allow some limited exceptions to the law of coverture while upholding the doctrine in general. Husbands needed their wives' help in provisioning households and maintaining the family businesses, and it was both useful and necessary for them to allow their wives some degree of independence over purchasing goods and accepting contracts in their stead.[21] In large trading centres such as London, local courts sometimes recognised married female traders not as feme coverts but as feme soles. This granted a tradeswoman the right to make contracts with suppliers, accept purchases from customers on credit, contract her own apprentices and represent herself independently of her husband in a court of law. Magistrates presiding over cases involving a married businesswoman often gave her the option of appearing as a feme covert (in which case her husband was legally responsible for her contracts and debts) or as a feme sole (in which case the woman herself would be responsible for paying her debts).[22]

Exceptions to the doctrine of coverture were also recognised by common law courts in the colonies. In Virginia, travelling businessmen sometimes granted power of attorney to their wives, who were given full power to act as their husbands' local agents during their absences. Power of attorney allowed a married woman to administer her husband's business interests while he was away, including paying and collecting debts. However, these powers had to be outlined in the letter of attorney granted by a woman's husband and could be as broad or as limited as he saw fit.[23]

The exceptions to the doctrine of coverture recognised by Anglo-American common law courts allowed *some* married women *some* flexibility and economic independence. But the impact of these loopholes in the seventeenth century should not be overstated. Coverture did not govern women absolutely, but it did continue to set the parameters for married women's legal existence until at least the eighteenth century. In the vast majority of cases, early modern common law courts closely adhered to and enforced coverture. Additionally, while there is no doubt that women with shrewd business sense and legal foresight could work these legal loopholes to their benefit, these loopholes were not designed to increase women's legal and economic independence.[24] Indeed, moralists and prescriptive writers on both sides of the Atlantic underscored that a wife who kept her property interests separate from her husband only sowed discord and disunity.

Alternatives to common law: equity in the Anglo-American world

Like the common law, equity law was part of the legal regime colonists brought with them when they established colonies in British America. The equity jurisdiction was important in the expansion of Anglo-American women's legal and economic independence in the early modern period:

while coverture imposed restrictions on married women's ability to own and manage property, beginning in the early seventeenth century, equity law allowed married women some freedoms to circumvent the harsher aspects of the common law.[25] In England the equity jurisdiction had evolved in the late fourteenth century as a 'court of conscience' to hear cases in which the common law could not provide adequate remedy. The preeminent equity court in England was the Court of Chancery, in which the Lord Chancellor or his deputy decided cases according to moral and equitable grounds rather than the strict letter of the common law.[26] Other equity courts, such as the Court of Requests and the equity side of the Court of Exchequer, arose in the sixteenth century as the caseload of Chancery expanded.[27]

The equity courts had special jurisdiction over matters pertaining to land held in trust and over any disputes arising over marriage settlements. If a jointure was included as part of a marriage settlement, it was actionable only in the equity jurisdiction.[28] Jointure agreements stipulated that upon the death of one of the partners, the other would receive full control of the land designated in the agreement or be paid an annuity arising from the rents of the land. Jointure became common in England because it was often easier for a widow to claim than common law dower rights. While a dower entitled a widow to one-third of the land her husband had held during his lifetime, it excluded any land he had held under copyhold or leasehold, or lands subject to entail. Jointure agreements, however, guaranteed a widow the use of any lands stipulated in the marriage contract.[29]

While common law was the basis of the colonial legal system, colonists recognised that equity provided useful precedents in cases that fell outside of the strict letter of the common law and in cases in which the common law did not have jurisdiction. As in England, colonial equity law mitigated some of the harsher aspects of common law and allowed for more flexible procedures.[30] In the early decades of colonisation, equity cases and common law cases were often heard by the same magistrates in the same courts. For example, the Maryland Provincial Court, created in 1634, had the power to hear cases concerning common law and equity, as well as matters concerning probate, in the first few decades after the colony's founding. Virginia common law courts exercised a broad jurisdiction in equity that embraced the practices and procedures of the English Court of Chancery. The Virginia General Court heard equity cases from the earliest days of the settlement's founding, while the county courts heard cases in equity from the 1640s onward.[31] A litigant appearing before the county courts could decide whether she wanted the case heard on the common law side or the equity side.[32]

Jointures and marriage settlements became important mechanisms by which women in England and colonial America controlled and managed property. Although these measures were not used by all, or even most, women contemplating marriage, they do represent a trend towards the greater protection of women's property over the course of the seventeenth century. Amy Erickson estimates that about 10 per cent of couples in seventeenth-century England drew up a settlement prior to the marriages.[33] The overall percentage of colonial couples with marriage settlements was probably lower than in England. Marylynn Salmon estimates that 1–2 per cent of marrying couples in eighteenth-century South Carolina arranged for a marriage settlement.[34] However, individual cases from the colonial courts indicate that jointures and marriage contracts were an option available to women in the colonies and that colonial courts upheld English equity practices from the earliest days of colonial settlement. A jointure agreement appears in the court records of York County, Virginia, as early as 1645 when Ralph Wormley agreed to a prenuptial contract placing land in trust for the use of his future wife, Agatha, if she should become a widow.[35]

Colonial courts exercised concurrent jurisdictions in common law and equity in the first decades of settlement; men who had been educated in the law were scarce, and the hardships of early settlement made it both impossible and unnecessary to establish two separate jurisdictions. However, by the mid-seventeenth century separate Chancery courts emerged in the colonies. The establishment of these courts was important because they maintained close ties with the High Court of Chancery in London, and adopted English rules and procedures that protected women's property.[36] Founded in 1669, the Maryland Court of Chancery upheld premarital contracts and jointure agreements, and also maintained the right of married women to have land held in trust.[37] It followed the English example closely, adopting new rules and precedents as they developed in the home country. For example, prior to her marriage to Nathaniel Utye in 1669, Elizabeth Carter agreed to a jointure agreement in the Maryland Court of Chancery in which she would have the choice between receiving one-third of her husband's property at his death or £600 of English money. The agreement stipulated that she would have one whole year after Nathaniel's death to decide whether she would choose the land or the money.[38]

The New England colonies and Pennsylvania were the most resistant to the establishment of courts of chancery based on the English model, although they did incorporate equity practices into their common law courts and legislatures. The Massachusetts Bay General Court acted as a limited court of equity throughout most of the seventeenth century, having the power to hear petitions and decide cases that fell outside of the common law, as well as appeals from the lower courts.[39] The Pennsylvania common law courts sometimes upheld the terms of jointures and marriage settlements, although without a chancery court the colony never developed a sophisticated and consistently applied body of law that protected women's property.[40]

The absence of a separate equity jurisdiction in Massachusetts, Connecticut and Pennsylvania meant that women in these colonies lacked an important tribunal for the defence of their property rights. One reason for the absence of chancery jurisdictions in Massachusetts, Connecticut and Pennsylvania was ideological. These colonies, established by Dissenter Puritans and Quakers, had been founded on the very idea of social, religious, legal and political reform. In their minds, the English Chancery was associated with the broad, sweeping powers of the Lord Chancellor and his appointed justices, in contradiction to the common law tradition of trial by jury. These Puritans, who in England had opposed the increasing exercise of the prerogative powers of the monarchy in the late sixteenth and early seventeenth centuries, had a long tradition of support for the common law and trial by jury, which they saw as a bulwark against the growth of arbitrary royal power. The heirs to the legal reformers of the English Civil War and Interregnum, the Puritans and Quakers who settled New England and Pennsylvania envisioned legal systems designed to make the law equitable and accessible for the average person. Thus, William Penn and other leading Quakers who founded the colony in 1682 implemented a comprehensive set of legal reforms that sought to simplify and streamline the complicated English system of law: all legal proceedings and records were carried on in English, laymen were allowed to plead their own causes, and common law and equity cases were heard in the same courts.[41]

While magistrates in Massachusetts, Connecticut and Pennsylvania adopted some of the principles of equity in their administration of the common law, without a separate equity jurisdiction that recognised exceptions to the doctrine of coverture, married women's ability to go to law to protect their property was more limited. Unlike their counterparts in England, Maryland and later South Carolina and Virginia, married women in Massachusetts, Connecticut and Pennsylvania were more strictly bound by the common law doctrine of coverture. These colonies were also less willing to uphold married women's separate estates. Connecticut refused to recognise them altogether, while in Massachusetts the laws regarding separate estates were not precisely defined until the early nineteenth century.[42]

Alternatives to the common law: ecclesiastical law and colonial prerogative courts

Women comprised a greater percentage of litigants before the English ecclesiastical courts than any other jurisdiction in England and the colonies. The ecclesiastical jurisdiction in England emerged gradually over the course of the thirteenth century as a way to govern the clergy and to help create an orderly, Christian society. Their jurisdiction developed based on the power of the archbishops and bishops to hear and settle disputes within their dioceses, a function which resulted in the development of formal and professionally staffed archbishops' courts as well as the bishops' consistory courts. At the top of the ecclesiastical court hierarchy were the courts of the archbishops of Canterbury and York. Both archbishoprics also had special courts that handled only probate, the Prerogative Court of Canterbury for the south and the Exchequer Court in the North, which had special jurisdiction over testators who died leaving property in more than one diocese.[43] Sitting below them were the bishops' consistory courts, presided over by chancellors learned in canon law. Bishops were vested with the power to probate the wills of a decedent who had been a resident of his diocese.[44] The archdeacons' courts were the lowest level and operated within limited localities.[45] While this machinery of ecclesiastical law was interrupted temporarily during the Interregnum, when probate was placed under a single, secular court, at the restoration of the monarchy in 1660 probate administration was returned to the ecclesiastical jurisdiction.

The English church courts are typically associated with the prosecution of moral offences such as fornication, drunkenness and adultery. This disciplinary jurisdiction of the church courts was known as the 'office' side of the courts because an ecclesiastical judge initiated the cases based on the power of his office. The English church courts did not have the power to administer corporal punishment, although they did have the power to excommunicate offenders and also commonly used social shaming rituals to enforce compliance.[46] However, the vast majority of the business of the church courts concerned the settlement of estates, including the disbursement of legacies, the division of moveable property and the appointment of estate administrators.[47] These cases were heard on the 'instance' side of the church courts, which heard litigation between parties, or at 'the instance' of individuals seeking redress for a specific wrong.

Ecclesiastical jurisdiction over property extended only to moveable goods such as cash, household goods, farm tools and furniture. Land was never at issue in a case heard before the ecclesiastical courts, although sometimes leases for land were included in inventories of moveable property bestowed by a testator to a legatee.[48]

This jurisdiction of the ecclesiastical courts touched the lives of a large percentage of the English population, and was a critical component of the nation's legal system until the mid-nineteenth century, when probate and testamentary matters were subsumed by the government. The power of the ecclesiastical jurisdiction over the administration of estates was justified on the basis of honouring the requests of the deceased set out in their wills. While the landed property of an estate was always decided in a court of common law, moveable property, bequests and disputes over who was the rightful executor of the estate fell within the purview of the ecclesiastical jurisdiction.[49]

The ability of married women to sue independently of their husbands in the ecclesiastical jurisdiction is significant: these were the only courts in the Anglo-American world that completely disregarded the common law assumption that wives must be legally represented by their husbands. Instead, English ecclesiastical judges recognised the ability of a married woman to act as her own legal representative, a fact that had important implications for women's access to and control of property.[50] Several explanations have been given for why the English ecclesiastical courts departed so drastically from the practices of common law regarding married women's legal status. One explanation stems from the Christian belief that all souls are equal before God, and therefore all persons, including married women, should have equal access to the justice provided by religious authorities and their agents.[51] Other scholars have emphasised that the ability of married women to sue and be sued in the English ecclesiastical courts had its roots in the tradition of Roman civil law, under which wives were allowed to keep the property they had prior to their marriages and also were allowed to appear in a legal suit independently of their husbands. English canonists in the Middle Ages drew from this tradition, as well as the decrees of successive popes and Lateran councils, when they formulated and codified the law of the English church.[52]

The rationale for allowing married women to make wills stemmed from the church's jurisdiction over marriage: since the church had jurisdiction over marital affairs, it also claimed to have jurisdiction over the division of property between spouses when the marriage was terminated, either through death or separation. Another historian has theorised that the ecclesiastical authorities defended married women's ability to make wills so that they could protect women's ability to bequeath money to the church. Whatever the explanation for it, the practice of allowing married women to represent their own interests before the ecclesiastical courts was a remarkable component of the English legal system.[53] Since women often acted as administrators and executors of estates, the ecclesiastical courts became important avenues by which women could go to law to defend property they considered rightfully theirs.[54]

The English ecclesiastical courts, which were so important to women in England, had a complicated history in the colonies. In some colonial territories, religious diversity made such courts all but impossible. The population of seventeenth-century Maryland, for example, included Puritans, Baptists, Presbyterians, Anglicans and Quakers, a fact which obviously eliminated the option of a unified ecclesiastical jurisdiction.[55] Colonies like Massachusetts, on the other hand, did not replicate the ecclesiastical legal jurisdiction of England, which they saw as being connected to the corruption of the Church and the expansion of royal authority in England. Churches in Massachusetts did sometimes arbitrate disputes between members and, like those in England, provided public censure for moral offences such as fornication, adultery and drunkenness. However, Massachusetts churches rarely resolved disputes concerning debt, trespass or estate administration. Women who appeared before Massachusetts churches did so much more often as a person accused of a moral offence rather than an advocate of her property rights.[56]

Although there was no formal ecclesiastical court structure in the colonies, individual colonial churches played important roles in enforcing standards of morality.[57] As in England, churchmen in the colonies did not have legitimate power to administer corporal punishment for misbehaviour; they referred offenders to the secular authorities for punishment. This seems to have been the case in colonies that embraced the established Anglican Church and those who eschewed it. In Anglican Virginia, for example, the men who served on the church vestry were often the same who served on the bench, and there was very little distinction between the duties of the parish official and the county magistrate.[58] Much the same was true for Puritan Massachusetts: church leaders and justices of the peace shared a vision for the creation of a godly society, and churchmen relied on Justices of the Peace to enforce morally upstanding behaviour through corporal punishment.[59]

However, a few colonies did have prerogative courts, modelled on the English Prerogative Court of Canterbury, which drew extensively from the practices and procedures of the church courts in England.

Maryland (1670), New York (1686) and South Carolina (1692) established prerogative courts that probated wills, granted letters of administration and heard disputes regarding bequests, legacies and the inheritance of moveable property. Unlike its English counterpart, which was part of the archbishopric of Canterbury, the administration of these colonial prerogative courts was secular: the colonial governor or his commissary acted as chief justice in probate, and the jurisdiction of the court was limited to testamentary matters only.[60]

In other ways colonial prerogative courts drew from the legal heritage of England's ecclesiastical jurisdiction. In Maryland, politicians debated whether to create a colonial bishopric by uniting the office of the commissary general (who acted as chief judge in the Maryland Prerogative Court) and the ecclesiastical commissary (who acted as the deputy to the bishop of London). Proponents of the idea made the argument that both offices were clearly ecclesiastical in origin, and that the profits made from the Prerogative Court would be enough to support the dignity of a full bishop.[61] The Prerogative Court of Maryland handled much of the testamentary business of the colony, including probate, the hearing of disputes concerning the validity of wills and the disbursement of legacies and bequests; it performed this function from the court's founding in 1670 up to the establishment of the Register of Wills in 1776. The founders of Maryland modelled the jurisdiction of their prerogative court on the English Prerogative Court of Canterbury, which was part of the ecclesiastical legal jurisdiction of the Archbishop of Canterbury. However, the Maryland Prerogative Court, unlike its English counterpart, was a civil court overseen by an officer of the colonial government rather than a church official.[62]

The New York Prerogative Court took the symbol of a bishop's mitre as the emblem on its seal, and the Crown vested each royal governor with the same testamentary powers exercised by bishops in England. The New York Prerogative Court also followed English ecclesiastical procedures when the validity of a will was contested. In these cases, 'solemn form proof' was needed, which meant that the widow or next of kin was obliged to appear before the court to hear the testimonies of witnesses concerning the circumstances under which the will was executed. As in English practice, a caveat would be filed by the party wishing to contest the will's validity, followed by a formal petition from the will's executor explaining why he should rightly administer the estate.[63]

While colonial prerogative courts adopted many of the practices and procedures of the ecclesiastical courts in England, they seem to have departed significantly from the English practice of allowing married women to enter into litigation independently of their husbands. In Maryland, New York and South Carolina, widows did appear frequently in prerogative court records to file wills and inventories for the estates of their late husbands. Widows were also sometimes involved in litigation over the estate. However, if the litigation involved a married woman who was the beneficiary of an estate, either as a former widow who had since remarried or as a legatee of the will, she always appeared as a joint party with her husband. Of the sixteen estate administration cases heard by the Maryland Prerogative Court between 1677 and 1682, three involved a woman. In all three of these cases, the woman was married and appeared before the court as a joint party with her husband.[64] The same seems to be true of the prerogative court in South Carolina, called the Court of Ordinary. Married women were sometimes given power of attorney to act as an estate administrator on their husband's behalf, but these were rare instances. Married women nearly always acted as joint parties with their husbands.[65]

Conclusion

The equity and ecclesiastical courts provided women with important alternative avenues for legal redress. While the doctrine of coverture limited women in courts of common law in England and the colonies, equity law, and especially ecclesiastical law, gave women the opportunity to pursue legal redress in jurisdictions in which the law of coverture did not strictly apply. In England, women had access to the equity and ecclesiastical jurisdictions, and, as the next chapter shows, used them frequently to pursue litigation concerning property and debt collection. The colonies that established separate equity jurisdictions, such as Maryland, New York and South Carolina, provided women with many of the same opportunities to pursue litigation as their counterparts across the Atlantic. However, the absence of a formal ecclesiastical court structure in British America meant that women lacked this important forum for the legal protection of their property. The following chapter reveals that women acted as plaintiffs or defendants in over half of the litigation cases brought before the English ecclesiastical courts, a percentage that far surpasses that of any other legal jurisdiction in the colonies.

Notes

1 Barbara Shapiro, 'Law reform in seventeenth-century England', *American Journal of Legal History*, 19:4 (1975), pp. 280–312.

2 Christopher Brooks, *Pettyfoggers and Vipers of the Commonwealth: The 'Lower Branch' of the Legal Profession in Early Modern England* (Cambridge: Cambridge University Press, 1986).
3 Tim Stretton, *Women Waging Law in Elizabethan England* (Cambridge: Cambridge University Press, 1998), p. 25.
4 Cynthia Herrup, *The Common Peace: Participation and the Criminal Law in Seventeenth-century England* (Cambridge: Cambridge University Press, 1987).
5 George Haskins, *Law and Authority in Early Massachusetts, A Study in Tradition and Design* (New York: Macmillan, 1960); James Horn, *Adapting to a New World: English Society in the Seventeenth-century Chesapeake* (Chapel Hill: University of North Carolina Press, 1994).
6 William M. Offutt, Jr., *Of 'Good Laws' and 'Good Men': Law and Society in the Delaware Valley, 1680–1710* (Urbana: University of Illinois Press, 1995); David Thomas Konig, *Law and Society in Puritan Massachusetts: Essex County, 1629–1692* (Chapel Hill: University of North Carolina Press, 1979); William Nelson, *The Common Law in Colonial America*, 2 vols (Oxford: Oxford University Press, 2008, 2013).
7 Stanley Katz, 'The politics of law in colonial America: controversies over chancery courts and equity law in the eighteenth century', in Donald Fleming and Bernard Bailyn (eds), *Perspectives in American History*, vol. 5 (Cambridge, MA: Harvard University Press, 1971), pp. 262–65.
8 Vernon Skinner (ed.), *Abstracts of the Testamentary Proceedings of the Prerogative Court of Maryland*, vol. 4: *1677–1682, 1702–1704* (Baltimore: Clearfield Company, 2006), pp. iii–iv; Edith E. MacQueen, 'The commissary in colonial Maryland', *Maryland Historical Magazine*, 25 (Baltimore: Maryland Historical Society, 1930), pp. 190–206; Herbert Alan Johnson, 'The Prerogative Court of New York, 1686–1776', *American Journal of Legal History*, 17:2 (1973), p. 97–105; A. S. Salley, 'Abstracts from the records of the Court of Ordinary of the province of South Carolina, 1692–1700', *South Carolina Historical and Genealogical Magazine*, 8:3 (1907) p. 164.
9 For the variety of legal traditions in the colonies, see Christopher Tomlins and Bruce Mann (eds), *The Many Legalities of Early America* (Chapel Hill: Omohundro Institute of Early American History and Culture, 2001); Marylynn Salmon, *Women and the Law of Property in Early America* (Chapel Hill: University of North Carolina Press, 1986).
10 Stretton, *Women Waging Law*; Maria Cioni, *Women and the Law in Elizabethan England, with Particular Reference to the Court of Chancery* (New York: Garland, 1985); Maria Cioni, 'The Elizabethan Chancery and women's rights', in D. J. Guth and J. W. McKenna (eds), *Tudor Rule and Revolution* (Cambridge: Cambridge University Press, 1982), p. 160; Wilfrid Prest, 'Law and women's rights in early modern England', *Seventeenth Century*, 6:2 (1991), pp. 169–87; Margaret Hunt, 'Wives and marital "rights" in the Court of Exchequer in the early eighteenth century', in Paul Griffiths and Mark Jenner (eds), *Londinopolis: Essays in the Cultural and Social History of Early Modern London* (Manchester: Manchester University Press, 2000), pp. 111–12; Margot Finn, 'Women, consumption, and coverture in England, c. 1760–1860', *Historical Journal*, 39:3 (1996), p. 703; Amy Erickson, 'Common law versus common practice: the use of marriage settlements in early modern England', *Economic History Review*, 43:1 (1990).

11 Amy Erickson, *Women and Property in Early Modern England* (London: Routledge, 1993); Lloyd Bonfield, 'Testamentary causes in the Prerogative Court of Canterbury, 1660–96', in Christopher Brooks and Michael Lobban (eds), *Communities and the Courts in Britain, 1150–1900* (London: Hambledon, 1997).

12 Richard Morris, *Studies in the History of American Law: With Special Reference to the Seventeenth and Eighteenth Centuries* (New York: Octagon Books, 1930), pp. 126–8, 200; Cornelia Hughes Dayton, *Women Before the Bar: Gender, Law, and Society in Connecticut, 1639–1789* (Chapel Hill: University of North Carolina Press, 1995), pp. 10–11; Offutt, *Of 'Good Laws' and 'Good Men'*, pp. 16–17, 30; Linda Sturtz, *Within Her Power: Propertied Women in Colonial Virginia* (New York: Routledge, 2002), pp. 6–7, 11. On anglicisation, see John Murrin, 'The legal transformation: the bench and bar of eighteenth-century Massachusetts', in Stanley Katz and John Murrin (eds), *Colonial America: Essays in Politics and Social Development* (Boston: Little, Brown, 1971).

13 This point draws from the work of Marylynn Salmon in her *Women and the Law of Property*, but goes beyond her emphasis on equity by also drawing in the influence of the ecclesiastical jurisdiction in the colonies.

14 See the discussion of the role of coverture under Anglo-American law in Tim Stretton and Krista Kesselring, 'Introduction: coverture and continuity', in Stretton and Kesselring (eds), *Married Women and the Law: Coverture in England and the Common Law World* (Montreal: McGill-Queen's University Press, 2013), p. 5; Stretton, *Women Waging Law*, pp. 22–3; Barbara Harris, *English Aristocratic Women, 1450–1550: Marriage and Family, Property and Careers* (Oxford: Oxford University Press, 2002), pp. 17–18; J. H. Baker, *An Introduction to English Legal History*, 3rd edn (London: Butterworths, 1990), p. 551

15 Sara Mendelson and Patricia Crawford, *Women in Early Modern England* (Oxford: Clarendon Press, 1998), pp. 31–4.

16 Carole Shammas, 'Anglo-American household government in comparative perspective', *William and Mary Quarterly*, 3rd series, 52:1 (1995), pp. 104–44; Mary Beth Norton, *Founding Mothers and Fathers: Gendered Power and the Forming of American Society* (New York: Knopf, 1996), pp. 38–9; Karin Wulf, *Not All Wives: Women in Colonial Philadelphia* (Ithaca: Cornell University Press, 2000), pp. 1–5.

17 Baker, *Introduction to English Legal History*, pp. 308–9; Erickson, *Women and Property*, pp. 23–5, 170.

18 Norton, *Founding Mothers and Fathers*, pp. 111–12; Carole Shammas, 'English inheritance law and its transfer to the colonies', *American Journal of Legal History*, 31:2 (1987), pp. 156–9.

19 William Hand Browne (ed.), *Proceedings and Acts of the General Assembly, January 1637/8 – September 1664*, vol. 1 (Baltimore: Maryland State Archives, 1883), pp. 156–7, accessed 11 October 2018 through http://aomol.msa.maryland.gov/000001/000001/html/am1-156.html.

20 Shammas, 'English inheritance law and its transfer to the colonies', p. 158.

21 Joanne Bailey, 'Favoured or oppressed? Married women, property, and "coverture" in England, 1660–1800', *Continuity and Change*, 17:3 (2002), pp. 351–72; Finn, 'Women, consumption, and coverture in England', p. 703–22.

22 Marjorie K. McIntosh, 'The benefits and drawbacks of *femme sole* status in England, 1300–1630', *Journal of British Studies*, 44:3 (2005), pp. 410–13.
23 Linda L. Sturtz, '"As though I my self was pr[e]sent": Virginia women with power of attorney', in Tomlins and Mann (eds), *The Many Legalities of Early America*, p. 251–2.
24 Suzanne Lebsock, *The Free Women of Petersburg: Status and Culture in a Southern Town, 1784–1860* (New York: Norton, 1984), pp. 57–8; Linda Kerber, *Women of the Republic: Intellect and Ideology in Revolutionary America* (Chapel Hill: University of North Carolina Press, 1980), pp. 9–10.
25 For the English context, the most notable are Cioni, *Women and Law in Elizabethan England*; Stretton, *Women Waging Law*; Erickson, *Women and Property*; Susan Staves, *Married Women's Separate Property in England, 1660–1833* (Cambridge, MA: Harvard University Press, 1990). For the American context, see Mary Beard, *Woman as a Force in History: A Study in Traditions and Realities* (New York: Macmillan, 1946); Salmon, *Women and the Law of Property*; Lebsock, *The Free Women of Petersburg*.
26 J. H. Baker, *The Oxford History of the Laws of England*, vol. 6: *1483–1558* (Oxford: Oxford University Press, 2003), pp. 173–4; William Searle Holdsworth, *A History of English Law*, 18 vols (London: Methuen, 1903–72), vol. 1, pp. 446–7.
27 Stretton, *Women Waging Law*, pp. 70–6.
28 Stretton, *Women Waging Law*, pp. 109–10.
29 Baker, *Introduction to English Legal History*, p. 309; Stretton, *Women Waging Law*, p. 27.
30 Katz, 'The politics of law in colonial America', pp. 262–5.
31 William Hamilton Bryson, 'English common law in Virginia', *Journal of Legal History*, 6:3 (1985), pp. 250–3.
32 Sturtz, *Within Her Power*, pp. 20–1.
33 Erickson, 'Common law versus common practice', p. 35.
34 Marylynn Salmon, 'Women and property in South Carolina: the evidence from marriage settlements, 1730–1830', *William and Mary Quarterly*, 3rd series, 39:4 (1982), p. 663.
35 Sturtz, *Within Her Power*, p. 21.
36 Salmon, *Women and the Law of Property*, p. 185.
37 J. Hall Pleasants, 'First century of the court of chancery', in Pleasants (ed.), *Proceedings of the Court of Chancery of Maryland, 1669–1679* (Baltimore: Maryland Historical Society, 1934), pp. xxxv–xxxvii, xlv, accessed 11 October 2018 through http://aomol.msa.maryland.gov/000001/000051/html/am51p-35.html. The establishment of a chancery court in South Carolina had been discussed as early as 1671 but did not come fully into existence as a functioning court until 1720. Anne King Gregorie (ed.), *Records of the Court of Chancery of South Carolina, 1671–1779* (Binghamton: Vail-Ballou Press, 1950), pp. 5–7, 25–6, 30–6; Salmon, 'Women and property in South Carolina', p. 659; Katz, 'The politics of law in colonial America', p. 273; Joseph Smith and Leo Hershkowitz, 'Courts of equity in the province of New York: the Cosby controversy, 1732–1736', *American Journal of Legal History*, 16:1 (1972), pp. 6–10. North Carolina also had a chancery court, but it acted as an appellate jurisdiction and its practices and procedures bore little resemblance to the English Court of Chancery. Nelson, *The Common Law in Colonial America*, vol. 2, pp. 88–9. Virginia established a separate

chancery court in 1777; see Marvin Singleton, 'The chancery side of Virginia's evolution to statehood', *Journal of American Studies*, 2:2 (1968), pp. 151–3.

38 Pleasants (ed.), *Proceedings of the Court of Chancery of Maryland, 1669–1679*, pp. 4–6, 37, 449, accessed 11 October 2018 through https://msa.maryland.gov/megafile/msa/speccol/sc2900/sc2908/000001/000051/html/am51-4.html.

39 Barbara Black, 'Judicial power and the General Court in early Massachusetts, 1634–1686' (unpublished PhD Thesis, Yale University, 1975), pp. 162–3.

40 Salmon, *Women and the Law of Property*, pp. 11–12, 82–3.

41 Shammas, 'English inheritance law and its transfer to the colonies', p. 157; Salmon, *Women and the Law of Property*, pp. 120–1, 188; Offutt, *Of 'Good Laws' and 'Good Men'*, pp. 15–20; Marylynn Salmon, 'The court records of Philadelphia, Bucks, and Berks counties in the seventeenth and eighteenth centuries', *Pennsylvania Magazine of History and Biography*, 107:2 (1983), pp. 251–6; Spencer Liverant and Walter Hitchler, 'A history of equity in Pennsylvania', *Dickinson Law Review*, 37:156 (1933), pp. 156–183; Roscoe Pound, *The Formative Era of American Law* (Boston: Little, Brown, 1938), p. 155; William J. Curran, 'The struggle for equity jurisdiction in Massachusetts', *Boston University Law Review*, 31:3 (1951), pp. 270–3.

42 Salmon, *Women and the Law of Property*, pp. 82–3, 120.

43 R. H. Helmholz, *The Canon Law and Ecclesiastical Jurisdiction from 597 to the 1640s* [vol. 1 of *The Oxford History of the Laws of England*] (Oxford: Oxford University Press, 2004), pp. 396–7, 428.

44 Johnson, 'The Prerogative Court of New York', p. 97.

45 Baker, *Introduction to English Legal History*, pp. 146–52; Martin Ingram, *Church Courts, Sex and Marriage in England, 1570–1640* (Cambridge: Cambridge University Press, 1988), pp. 35–7.

46 Erickson, *Women and Property*, p. 32; Helmholz, *The Canon Law and Ecclesiastical Jurisdiction*, pp. 207–28, 285, 398; Ingram, *Church Courts, Sex and Marriage in England*, pp. 43–4. For the church court's jurisdiction over matrimonial affairs, defamation and moral offences, see Laura Gowing, *Domestic Dangers: Women, Words, and Sex in Early Modern London* (Oxford: Oxford University Press, 1996).

47 Bonfield, 'Testamentary causes in the Prerogative Court of Canterbury', p. 145.

48 Erickson, *Women and Property*, pp. 32–4.

49 Helmholz, *The Canon Law and Ecclesiastical Jurisdiction*, pp. 387–8.

50 Erickson, *Women and Property*, p. 32; Helmholz, *The Canon Law and Ecclesiastical Jurisdiction*, pp. 207–28, 285, 398; Ingram, *Church Courts, Sex and Marriage in England*, pp. 43–4.

51 Helmholz, *The Canon Law and Ecclesiastical Jurisdiction*, p. 403.

52 Helmholz, *The Canon Law and Ecclesiastical Jurisdiction*, p. 87; James Brundage, *The Medieval Origins of the Legal Profession: Canonists, Civilians, and Courts* (Chicago: University of Chicago Press, 2008), p. 75; Linda Briggs Beimer, *Women and Property in Colonial New York: The Transition from Dutch to English Law, 1643–1727* (Ann Arbor: UMI Research Press, 1983), pp. 1–2.

53 Erickson, *Women and Property*, pp. 139–40. See also Michael Sheehan, 'The influence of canon law on the property rights of married women in England', in James Farge

(ed.), *Marriage, Family, and Law in Medieval Europe: Collected Studies* (Toronto: Toronto University Press, 1997), pp. 16–30.

54 Bonfield, 'Testamentary causes in the Prerogative Court of Canterbury', p. 145. For women's involvement in defamation suits, see Gowing, *Domestic Dangers*; James Brundage, 'Juridical space: female witnesses in canon law', *Dumbarton Oaks Papers*, 52 (1998), p. 147–56.

55 Though the Church of England was established as the state religion after the Glorious Revolution in 1689, these groups remained. Michael Graham, 'Meetinghouse and chapel: religion and community in seventeenth-century Maryland', in Lois Green Carr, Philip D. Morgan and Jean B. Russo (eds), *Colonial Chesapeake Society* (Chapel Hill: University of North Carolina Press, 1988), pp. 257–62.

56 For example, while church authorities in Massachusetts charged thirty-three women with fornication between 1620 and 1689, there are no recorded cases in the same period of a woman bringing a case concerning trespass, debt or estate administration. See Emile Oberholzer, *Delinquent Saints: Disciplinary Action in the Early Congregational Churches of Massachusetts* (New York: Columbia University Press, 1955), Appendix, Table V, pp. 200–13.

57 Oberholzer, *Delinquent Saints*, Appendix, Table V, pp. 200–13; Dayton, *Women Before the Bar*, p. 163.

58 John Kendall, *A Blessed Company: Parishes, Parsons, and Parishioners in Anglican Virginia, 1690–1776* (Chapel Hill: University of North Carolina Press, 2001), pp. 14–15, 35.

59 Konig, *Law and Society in Puritan Massachusetts*, chapter 1.

60 Skinner (ed.), *Abstracts of the Testamentary Proceedings of the Prerogative Court of Maryland*, vol. 4, pp. iii–iv; MacQueen, 'The commissary in colonial Maryland', pp. 190–206; Johnson, 'The Prerogative Court of New York', pp. 97–105; Salley, 'Abstracts from the records of the Court of Ordinary', p. 164.

61 MacQueen, 'The commissary in colonial Maryland', pp. 190, 198.

62 Elizabeth Hartsook and Gust Skordas (eds), *Land Office and Prerogative Court Records of Colonial Maryland* (Annapolis: Hall of Records Commission, 1946), p. 81, accessed 11 October 2018 through https://msa.maryland.gov/megafile/msa/speccol/sc2900/sc2908/000001/000415/html/am415-81.html; Skinner (ed.), *Abstracts of the Testamentary Proceedings of the Prerogative Court of Maryland*, vol. 4, pp. iii–iv.

63 Johnson, 'The Prerogative Court of New York', pp. 95–7, 119–22.

64 Skinner (ed.), *Abstracts of the Testamentary Proceedings of the Prerogative Court of Maryland*, vol. 4, pp. 189, 198–9. In New York the picture is not as clear because the records of litigation heard in the Prerogative Court of New York have not survived prior to the late eighteenth century. Johnson, 'The Prerogative Court of New York', p. 126.

65 Salley, 'Abstracts from the records of the Court of Ordinary', p. 207.

2

Women as plaintiffs and defendants: the common law, equity and ecclesiastical jurisdictions

Although women acted as plaintiffs and defendants in common law, equity and ecclesiastical courts, their levels of participation were not at all uniform across these jurisdictions. Coverture imposed major restrictions on women's ability to pursue legal redress in common law courts, a fact that is reflected in the low percentage of women acting as plaintiffs and defendants in this jurisdiction. However, the greater percentage of women appearing as litigants in the equity and ecclesiastical jurisdictions show that these courts allowed women, especially married women, some relief from the severity of the common law. Remarkably, over half of the plaintiffs and defendants that appeared in litigation before the church courts were women, many of whom were wives engaging in litigation independently from their husbands.

English women had an advantage over their colonial counterparts because they had access to the equity and ecclesiastical jurisdictions. As the last chapter discussed, only Maryland, New York and South Carolina followed the English model by establishing separate equity jurisdictions and quasi-ecclesiastical prerogative courts. However, even in these colonies, women's level of involvement in these courts did not match the levels of their counterparts in England.

Female plaintiffs and defendants in courts of common law

Under English and colonial common law, married women could not draw up their own wills without the consent of their husbands, enter into binding contracts or initiate or defend a legal suit without their husbands' assistance. The colonial formulation of coverture was much like its English counterpart: though inheritance practices varied between colonies, under colonial common law married women could still not own or manage property, and could not initiate or defend a suit in a common law court without their husbands' assistance.[1]

The low percentages of women appearing as litigants in common law courts demonstrate that coverture had a significant impact on women's ability to initiate or defend suits at law. Table 2.1 offers a comparison of the numbers of women acting as plaintiffs or defendants in debt, trespass and detinue cases heard in the London Mayor's Court, the Quarterly Courts held at Salem and Ipswich in Massachusetts Bay, and the Maryland Provincial Court.[2] While the jurisdictions of these courts were somewhat different, they provide a good basis of comparison for women's involvement in common law litigation because their records span several decades consecutively, and because they heard similar kinds of cases concerning property. The London Mayor's Court had jurisdiction over debt and trespass cases within the city, as well as a limited jurisdiction in actions of debt against executors of estates. The Essex county courts, established at Boston, Cambridge, Salem and Ipswich by an act of 1636, heard a wider range of cases than the London Mayor's Court: they had jurisdiction over cases concerning debt, trespass, estate administration and non-capital criminal offences. The Maryland Provincial Court, based in St. Mary's City, also heard cases concerning debt, trespass and detinue. Until 1677, when a separate equity jurisdiction was established in the Maryland Court of Chancery, the Maryland Provincial Court also had a jurisdiction in equity that allowed it to decide in cases concerning trusts and estate administration.[3]

Women appeared as either plaintiffs or defendants in the London Mayor's Court in only 10–11 per cent of cases in the seventeenth century, while in Massachusetts Bay women appeared in only 6–9 per cent of litigation heard before the Essex County Quarterly Courts. These figures are consistent with other research on women in common law courts in England and the colonies. One study found that English women appeared as plaintiffs in 11 per cent of cases heard before the Great Yarmouth Borough Court between 1677 and 1678, and in 16 per cent of cases before the Exeter Mayor's court between 1690 and 1692.[4] Similarly, a study of colonial women found that women made up 10 per cent of plaintiffs in the New York Mayor's Court in the early eighteenth century.[5]

Marital status was a defining factor in women's legal capabilities, and the lack of married women acting as parties independently of their husbands is a real indication of how seriously the law of coverture applied in common law courts. Table 2.2 shows the marital status of women who appeared before the London Mayor's Court. The married women who are named as either plaintiffs or defendants in these suits always appeared as co-parties alongside their husbands. In both England and the colonies, the majority of women who appeared before courts of common law were widows,

Table 2.1 Women acting as plaintiffs and defendants in litigation in courts of common law, 1630–90

	Number of female plaintiffs	Number of female defendants	Number of cases with a female plaintiff or defendant	Number of suits sampled
London Mayor's Court, England				
1630–51	31	34	65 (11%)	611
1660–90	50	25	75 (10%)	739
Court total	81	59	140	1,350
Essex County Quarterly Courts, Massachusetts				
1656–62	7	4	11 (6%)	170
1668–70	11	4	15 (8%)	200
1678–82	8	8	16 (9%)	169
Court total			42	539
Maryland Provincial Court				
1666–70	21	30	51 (25%)	200
1681–83	48	15	63 (13%)	470
Court total				670
Total cases examined				2,559

Sources: London Metropolitan Archives, Mayor's Court Original Bills, CLA/024/02, 1630–1690; George Francis Dow (ed.), *Records and Files of the Quarterly Courts of Essex County, 1636–1686*, 9 vols (Salem: Essex Institute, 1911), vols 2, 4, 7, 8, accessed 12 October 2018 through http://salem.lib.virginia.edu/Essex/index.html; J. Hall Pleasants (ed.), *Proceedings of the Provincial Court, 1666–1670* (Baltimore: Maryland Historical Society, 1940), accessed 12 October 2018 through http://aomol.msa.maryland.gov/000001/000057/html/index.html; Elizabeth Merritt (ed.), *Proceedings of the Provincial Court, 1681–1683* (Baltimore: Maryland Historical Society, 1964), accessed 12 October 2018 through http://aomol.msa.maryland.gov/000001/000070/html/index.html.

many of whom were drawn into litigation as the administrators of their late husbands' estates. Widows who acted as estate administrators were charged with paying and collecting any outstanding debts; though these cases could be heard in equity courts in that they involved land or money held in trust, most suits concerning the recovery of a simple debt owing to an estate were heard at common law.

Table 2.2 Role and marital status of women involved in debt litigation in the London Mayor's Court, 1630-90

	Number of cases
Women initiating or responding to suits as estate administrators	68 (48%)
Widows	59
Married	7
Single	2
Women initiating or responding to suits in other capacities	72 (52%)
Widows	44
Married	3
Single	7
Unknown	18
Total	140

Source: London Metropolitan Archives, Mayor's Court Original Bills, CLA/024/02, 1630-1690.

In the London Mayor's Court, widows accounted for 73 per cent of the women acting as either plaintiffs or defendants.[6] In one case in 1640, Margaret Powell, widow and executor of the estate of David Powell, brought suit against Robert Hall in the Mayor's Court for the recovery of a £47 debt due to Powell's estate. To ensure the payment of the debt, Margaret entered the suit as a case of foreign attachment, under which she could recover the debt through the seizure of Hall's goods even if they were in the possession of a third party. Margaret had the court appraise a large portion of Hall's household possessions to be valued against the debt. The extensive list included a variety of expensive household items, including 'one cipress chest, six backstooles of Russia leather, six Turkey cushions, and twoe leather cushions guilt'.[7]

Margaret Powell's case is representative of many of the other cases heard before the London Mayor's Court and in similar jurisdictions during the seventeenth century. Widows who acted as executrixes to their husbands' estates frequently appeared before the courts as they paid or collected their husbands' debts, and they clearly had an interest in seeing that the estate was settled with skill and care. While they were charged with ensuring that all debts owing from the estate were paid, they also had an incentive to retain as much as possible for themselves and their children. As feme soles, widows clearly had the legal power and authority to safeguard their own interests at law and to ensure they had sufficient maintenance to support themselves during their widowhood.

Colonial widows appeared in courts of common law in roles similar to those of their English counterparts. While their demographic, social and religious circumstances might have changed when women crossed the Atlantic, the practice of widows presenting their husbands' wills for probate, and settling the estates' accounts, was a common practice for colonial widows throughout the seventeenth and eighteenth centuries.[8] In the county courts of Massachusetts Bay, widows accounted for 69 per cent of the women who appeared as litigants.[9] Widow Elizabeth Blesdale, for example, sued Edward Gyllman in June 1653 in the Salem Quarterly Court for the collection of £3 which he had promised to pay to her late husband, Ralfe Blesdale. The court ruled in Elizabeth's favour and, remarkably, she offered to remit some of the debt due if Gyllman promised never to challenge her in court concerning the matter again.[10] In a case from 1678, Elizabeth Price entered a suit against John Wincoll in the Salem Quarterly Court as the widow of Captain Walter Price and the executor of his estate. She sued Wincoll for the payment of a debt of over £400 worth of pine boards that he had contracted to pay Captain Price in the early 1660s. The court found for Elizabeth and ordered Wincoll to pay the debt due to her. Because the sum was so large, the court also required him to put up his land as security for the debt.[11]

In Maryland, women acted as plaintiffs or defendants in 25 per cent of cases heard between 1666 and 1670, a percentage that is significantly higher than that of women in England or Massachusetts (see Table 2.1). The greater percentage of women appearing as litigants before the Maryland common law courts is in part due to the high mortality rates among men in the Chesapeake Bay region in the seventeenth century, and the tendency for women to quickly remarry. A Maryland woman might be widowed two or three times during her lifetime, each time appearing before the courts to present her husband's will for probate and settle his accounts.[12] Since most Maryland widows remarried within a year of their husbands' deaths, it was common for these former widows to appear as co-parties with their new husbands. About 60 per cent of female plaintiffs and defendants in the Maryland Provincial Court were widows; the remaining 40 per cent were married women appearing as co-parties alongside their husbands.[13]

As in England and Massachusetts, widows in Maryland ensured that their husbands' estates were settled with attention to their future maintenance and to safeguard the inheritance of any children born to the marriage. In one case, Rebecca Burton, widow of Edmond Burton and executor of his estate, entered a suit against Henry Hudson in the Maryland Provincial Court in 1668. She informed the court that 'her late husband

Edmond Burton, of whose goods and chattles she is administatrix', had during his lifetime obtained an attachment against Hudson's goods for the repayment of a debt, and that 'she prayes a continuance of the said attachment to her as administatrix'. At the same time, she sued Hudson for the collection of the debt that he had owed to her husband. Burton stated that she was suing Hudson 'in a plea that hee render unto her seven thowsand five hundred seventy fowre pounds of tobacco which hee oweth her and unjustly doth detaine'.[14] She won on both counts.

Table 2.1 reflects one of the unique aspects of women's experience of the law in the Chesapeake. Between the years 1666 and 1670, 25 per cent of cases heard before the Maryland Provincial Court included at least one female litigant. This percentage far outstrips the percentage of cases including a female litigant in England and Massachusetts, which for the same period stayed at around 10 per cent or slightly below. There are two reasons for this higher percentage of women appearing before the Maryland Provincial Court. Firstly, life-spans in Maryland were shorter than in England or Massachusetts, a fact that resulted in more widows with more estates to settle in court. The second reason is that prior to 1677, when the Maryland Court of Chancery was established, the Maryland Provincial Court had the power to adjudge in common law and equity cases.[15] Since equity law had jurisdiction over marriage settlements and property given to women in trust or by jointure, Maryland women brought their suits over these matters to the Provincial Court. After the establishment of the Chancery, women pursued cases concerning marriage settlements in that jurisdiction. The decrease in the number of women appearing before the Maryland Provincial Court in the 1680s is probably because women began to have their cases heard in Chancery rather than in the Provincial Court.

Female plaintiffs and defendants in courts of equity

The equity jurisdiction was fundamental in the protection of women's property, and also in their ability to go to law if that property was threatened. The English Court of Chancery, which was the model for colonial chancery courts, is foundational for understanding the later development of the equity jurisdiction and its importance for women in the colonies. England's Court of Chancery relied on the summary justice of judges who examined parties and witnesses, and then decided cases according to equitable and moral grounds rather than the strict letter of the law.[16] Other courts of equity – including the Court of Requests and the equity side of the Court of Exchequer – arose later as the caseload of Chancery grew.

The equity jurisdiction gave women distinct legal advantages by allowing married women to circumvent some of the restrictions that coverture imposed on them. Before her marriage, a woman might transfer the ownership of her title to property to a trustee who was then obliged to act on her behalf by managing lands and passing on the rents. According to the terms of the trust, lands that had been placed in trust before a woman's marriage could not later come under the control of her husband. Such legal devices were only defendable in a court of equity. Additionally, the equity jurisdiction technically allowed wives to sue independently of their husbands; some married women sued their husbands for maintenance and alimony in courts of equity. Although these instances are rare, they do show that equity courts recognised the ability of married women to sue independently of their husbands. The procedures of equity were also more flexible: a litigant could sue whether or not she had the bond, deed or contract to prove her title to the property.[17]

The more flexible procedures of the equity courts, and their unique jurisdiction in upholding the terms of marriage settlements, meant that women appeared in these courts more frequently than in courts of common law. Since equity was the only jurisdiction that upheld jointures, trusts and marriage settlements, many of the cases heard in this jurisdiction inevitably concerned property in which a woman had an interest. In England, women were named as either plaintiffs or defendants in 26 per cent of cases heard before the Court of Chancery between 1613 and 1714, and in almost one-third of cases in the Court of Requests in the early seventeenth century.[18]

Colonies that established an equity jurisdiction modelled on the English Court of Chancery provided women with an important alternative to the common law. Maryland was the first colony to establish a separate equity jurisdiction in the Court of Chancery in 1677, followed by New York in 1701 and South Carolina in 1720.[19] However, while Maryland and South Carolina established chancery courts that followed the English example closely, adopting new rules and precedents as they developed in the home country, New York's Chancery operated more as an appellate jurisdiction. As in England, chancery courts in these colonies adopted the use of jointures, trusts and marriage settlements that provided protection for women's property. These trusts functioned in the same way as they did in England, and were only enforceable in courts of equity, not in common law courts.[20]

In Maryland, women's participation in the Court of Chancery accelerated steadily. While women accounted for only 8 per cent of the plaintiffs and defendants before the Maryland Court of Chancery between 1681 and 1685, by the late 1690s this had rather dramatically increased to 17 per cent.[21] While this percentage still remains relatively low compared to the English Court of Chancery, it does reveal that the equity jurisdiction in Maryland was gaining in popularity and perhaps in accessibility to women.

Taking one example, Anne Avery, as the widow of John Avery and the executor of his estate, entered a breach of trust case in Chancery in 1678 against her son-in-law, Benjamin Granger, for the recovery of £24 in cash and over 3,000 lb of tobacco. According to the court records, Anne had entered the case in Chancery because she had no case 'by the strict rules of the comon law to enforce a discovery of such clandestine frauds & transaccons & trusts' that she alleged against Granger, which had been a 'great hindrance of the execucon of the deceaseds last will and testament'. Further, Anne had no written records to prove that her late husband had entrusted the sums to his son-in-law. The summary of the case further states that, 'not being able to make such proofe of the perticuler goods & sumes of money to him delivered by the said John Avery & intrusted with him as the law requires', Anne therefore had 'noe other ways to be releived save in this honoble court'. Acting as a joint party with her new husband, John Hasslewood, Anne filed a bill of complaint against Granger for repayment of the sums so that John Avery's debts could be paid and his estate settled. In her bill, Anne alleged that Granger and his wife, who was Anne's daughter, had accompanied John Avery on a business trip to England and that Granger had taken control of a large sum of Avery's money after he unexpectedly died on the voyage home. Anne stated: 'John Avery dyed before he came on shore leaving all his money & goods in the possession of the said Benjamin Granger.' Anne demanded 'an account of the said money & goods or satisfaccon for the said sume & to acquaint her with what other goods or money he have in his custody', but 'he absolutely refused'. Though Granger 'did positively deny that he had or received of the said John Avery any of his goods', in the end the court decided in Anne's favour. The court ordered that John Avery 'did lend to & entrust the same Benjamin Granger with severall quantities of goods & divers sumes of money', and ruled that Granger give Anne the cash and tobacco, as well as pay costs of suit.[22]

Female plaintiffs and defendants in the English ecclesiastical courts and the colonial prerogative courts

While women in England, and women in colonies with established equity jurisdictions, had an advantage over their counterparts elsewhere by having access to courts of chancery, English women had an additional benefit that all colonial women lacked: access to the ecclesiastical courts. The percentage of female litigants in the English ecclesiastical courts far surpassed any other legal jurisdiction in the Anglo-American world. Women appeared frequently in the ecclesiastical courts to present wills for probate, and as parties in litigation if any dispute arose concerning the will or the administration of an estate. Though most women did not make wills themselves, about 70 per cent of all people filing accounts in the province of Canterbury were women, usually the widow of the deceased. A woman's right to probate her husband's estate was seen as a natural outgrowth of her investment in the estate during her lifetime, and her guardianship of any young children produced by the marriage. Widows who acted as executors had nearly complete control over their late husbands' estates, and were charged with arranging and paying for funeral and burial expenses, paying the legacies specified in the will and discharging the deceased's debts and collecting his credits. As executors of an estate, a widow received not only the bequests her husband gave her in his will (or her dower thirds, whichever was greater) but also the use of the portions of any of her children during their minorities.[23]

The church courts were unique in allowing married women to appear as litigants independently of their husbands: women could, and very often did, bring suits against other parties in the ecclesiastical courts for the collection of an unpaid legacy or for the right to act as executrix of an estate, most often of a deceased husband or relative.[24] The percentage of women appearing as either plaintiffs or defendants in these courts suggests that they took full advantage of the legal freedom that ecclesiastical law allowed them. The number of women acting as parties to ecclesiastical litigation far outstrips the level of women participating in common law courts or even courts of equity. Tables 2.3 and 2.4 show the percentage of cases that named a male or female as the primary plaintiff or defendant in cases heard before the Essex Archdeacon's Court and the London Commissary Court. This sample of cases shows that women initiated 56 per cent of the testamentary cases in the period 1630–41, and 57 per cent of cases between 1669 and 1687.

Table 2.5 shows the marital status of female plaintiffs in the Essex Archdeacon's Court and the London Commissary Court. Of the women who appeared before these courts, 48 per cent were widows acting as the administrators or executors of the late husbands' estates. English men frequently named their wives the executors of their estates, a role which could draw women into a variety of different legal disputes as they disbursed legacies, submitted inventories of the estate, and paid and collected debts.

Table 2.3 Sex of plaintiffs in testamentary litigation in the Essex Archdeacon's Court and the London Commissary Court, 1630–41 and 1669–87

	1630–41	1669–87	Total cases examined
Male	24 (42%)	32 (40%)	56
Female	32 (56%)	45 (57%)	77
Unknown	1 (2%)	2 (3%)	3
Total	57	79	136

Sources: Essex Record Office, Archdeaconry of Essex Depositions, D/AE/D8; London Metropolitan Archives, Guildhall Manuscripts, 9065a, vol. 8, Depositions of the London Commissary Court.

Table 2.4 Sex of defendants in testamentary litigation in the Essex Archdeacon's Court and the London Commissary Court, 1630–41 and 1669–87

	1630–41	1669–87	Total cases examined
Male	24 (42%)	38 (48%)	62
Female	24 (42%)	26 (33%)	50
Unknown	9 (16%)	15 (19%)	24
Total	57	79	136

Sources: Essex Record Office, Archdeaconry of Essex Depositions, D/AE/D8; London Metropolitan Archives, Guildhall Manuscripts, 9065a, vol. 8, Depositions of the London Commissary Court.

Table 2.5 Marital status of female plaintiffs in testamentary litigation in the Essex Archdeacon's Court and the London Commissary Court, 1630–41 and 1669–87

Marital status	Number of cases
Widowed	33 (43%)
Married	29 (38%)
named as sole plaintiff	24
named as co-party with husband	5
Single	6 (7%)
Unknown	9 (12%)
Total	77

Sources: Essex Record Office, Archdeaconry of Essex Depositions, D/AE/D8; London Metropolitan Archives, Guildhall Manuscripts, 9065a, vol. 8, Depositions of the London Commissary Court.

Because widows were also the primary beneficiaries of their husbands' wills, they often had to go to law to protect their claims to administer the estate against adult children or step-children.[25]

What is perhaps most remarkable about this sampling of women involved in litigation in the ecclesiastical jurisdiction is the high percentage of married women acting as sole parties in disputes. Over one-third (38 per cent) of female plaintiffs before the ecclesiastical courts were noted as married, most of them acting independently of their husbands who are not named as parties in the suit.[26]

One example from the Essex Archdeacon's court is representative of the experiences of married women in the ecclesiastical courts. Bennett Bowles Moss, a married woman from the town of Boreham in Essex, appeared in the Archdeacon's court in 1632 to prosecute a case against her brother Peter Bowles for control of the estate of her recently deceased mother, Alice Bowles. Though the court documents say that Bennett was married, her husband was not mentioned as a party to the case. The legal point at issue was the validity of the will that Alice allegedly made on her deathbed, which named Bennett the sole executor of her estate in lieu of her brothers. Bennett claimed that her mother had named her, not her brothers, as the executor, a position that would have given Bennett nearly complete control over the estate's assets and the legacies to be paid to other persons specified in the will. Witnesses who spoke on Bennett's behalf, including the scrivener who made Alice's will, his wife and his female servant, upheld Bennett's claim to be the rightful executor of the estate, and testified that they had seen Alice sign and seal the will on her deathbed. Margaret Bragg, the 20-year-old maidservant of the scrivener who wrote Alice's will, testified that she had heard Alice say that Bennett 'had bene a true and faithfull childe to her and therefore she would not have any of her brothers or sisters to domyneere over her, but should rather be beholding to her, then she to them'.[27] While the outcome of Bennett's case is not recorded, it is clear that though she was a married woman, she independently prosecuted the case against her brother for control of her mother's estate.

Another example from a later period reflects that married women continued to use the ecclesiastical courts independently of their husbands. In 1681 Elizabeth Summers Emberson sued the executor of the estate of her former sweetheart in the Essex Archdeacon's court for a £100 legacy she claimed was due to her under the terms of the will. Though the court documents state that Elizabeth had recently married John Emberson, Elizabeth is named as the only plaintiff in the case and it is clear that she prosecuted the case independently of her husband. Elizabeth claimed that the legacy left to her by Robert Greene had been spelled out in his will, and witnesses who spoke on her behalf emphasised that Elizabeth and Robert Greene had always been very close. Elizabeth Turner, one of the witnesses who spoke on behalf of Elizabeth, testified that Greene 'whilst he lived and for some yeares before he dyed did bear a great love and affection towards the said Elizabeth ... and did severall times declare that he did intend to marry her'. Elizabeth, however, had refused Robert's offer because he 'being a Quaker would be married after the manner and according to the usual way of the Quakers marrying, which she the said Elizabeth thought illegall and contrary to the law'.[28] Though Elizabeth apparently refused Greene's proposal of marriage, her status as the wife of John Emberson when she did finally marry posed little threat to her ability to sue for her unpaid legacy.

Given the high percentage of women appearing before the ecclesiastical courts, it is not surprising that women sometimes sued each other. Elizabeth Britten brought suit against her mother-in-law, Christian Britten, in the London Commissary Court in 1674 for the right to administer the estate of her late husband, William. The dispute arose between the parties because William had devised a nuncupative will, or an oral will, on his deathbed, leaving the details of the will – and the circumstances under which it was made – subject to dispute. Elizabeth's case turned upon the testimony of the witnesses present at the time the will was made. Sara Haddon, a female servant in the Brittens' household, testified that she was a witness to the verbal will that William had made on his deathbed. Haddon stated that she had lived with Britten 'as his servant for above two yeares' and was 'cald up into the sayd deceased's chamber to make a fire', where she heard William state from his deathbed who would receive legacies from his estate. According to Haddon's testimony, William had related that he would give 'my mother (meaning Christian Britten, widow) six pounds, and if shee doe not like that it should continue in my wives hands'. However, Sara also reported that Britten had said that he would give 'all the rest of my estate ... to my wife (meaining the sayd Elizabeth Britten)'. Sara's statement before the court was corroborated by another female witness, Mary Campe, who had apparently been sent for to read to William 'out of a prayer book' during his sickness. Campe testified that she was also present when William made his last will 'by word of mouth' and that he had given his wife 'all of his estate'.[29] Both Elizabeth Britten and Christian Britten, as the widow and mother of the deceased, had an interest in gaining control of the execution of William's estate and in seeing that the property was managed according to their interests.

As in England, colonial women acted as executors and administrators of estates, and were charged with presenting the will to the court, drawing up an inventory of land and moveable goods, and collecting the bonds, receipts and accounts of debt due to the estate. As the mediators between the heirs, creditors and the courts, administrators were also charged with the task of keeping track of inventoried perishable goods consumed by the family, any wages earned by family members and all debts contracted in the course of maintaining the family.[30] While these duties could be burdensome for some women, others seem to have taken on probate responsibilities very willingly. Acting as an executor or administrator of a decedent's estate gave women at least temporary control of a substantial amount of property, and allowed them to manage the division of the estate to their own benefit.

Maryland, New York and South Carolina established separate courts of probate modelled on the ecclesiastical courts in England. Because the English ecclesiastical courts provided the model for the Prerogative Court in Maryland, it would seem that married women would be able to appear in this jurisdiction independently of their husbands, but this was not the case. In the sixteen estate administration cases heard by the court between 1677 and 1682, three involved a husband and wife as joint plaintiffs or defendants. There are no cases of a married woman appearing independently, even if her property interest was the issue at stake in the case. For example, William Wilkinson initiated a case in the Maryland Prerogative Court in 1682 on behalf of his wife Elizabeth, who was one of the beneficiaries of the estate of her parents, Abraham and Sarah Clarke.[31] In England such a case could have been initiated by Elizabeth Wilkinson herself, but in the colonies married women were bound to appear alongside their husbands.

Massachusetts Puritans privileged the common law over other legal jurisdictions when they established their court system in the 1630s, declining to replicate the ecclesiastical court structure that was present in England. The county courts in Massachusetts retained exclusive jurisdiction over cases concerning wills, bequests and probate.[32] Since the county courts were courts of common law, married women were barred from appearing independently of their husbands. As Table 2.1 shows, women appeared infrequently in the Massachusetts county courts as parties to litigation; the majority of those who did so were widows, and married women who did appear always did so as joint parties with their husbands.

The English ecclesiastical legal jurisdiction was an important and frequently used forum in which women could initiate litigation concerning estate settlement. Moreover, it was unique within the Anglo-American world in its willingness to ignore the doctrine of coverture by allowing married women to appear independently of their husbands. Given that most women were, at some point in their lives, involved in the probate and administration of an estate, their ability to pursue litigation if their claim to property was threatened is significant.

Conclusion

Anglo-American women, especially married women, faced very real restrictions under English and colonial common law. The small percentages of women appearing in courts of common law reflect the power of coverture in limiting women's legal activities. However, legal jurisdictions that recognised exceptions to the doctrine of coverture, or disregarded it altogether, gave women an important alternative to the common law. The equity jurisdiction was one important and frequently used method by which women could initiate legal action against another party. However, the English ecclesiastical jurisdiction, which allowed married women to initiate litigation independently of their husbands, gave women in England a decisive advantage over their colonial counterparts. Over half of the plaintiffs appearing before the English ecclesiastical courts in testamentary disputes were women, a level of participation unparalleled in any other legal jurisdiction in the Anglo-American world. In comparison to their English counterparts, colonial women's options were more limited. While colonies such as Maryland, New York and Pennsylvania had courts of equity that protected married women's separate estates, none of the colonies established an ecclesiastical jurisdiction that allowed married women complete freedom to initiate litigation in their own names.

The variety of different legal jurisdictions in England made the English legal system more complex than those of the colonies, but it was also more capable in meeting the challenges that women's complicated relationship to property entailed. Far from suppressing women's legal activity, the English legal system provided a number of methods by which women could control property, and a variety of avenues via which women could pursue legal redress if that property was threatened.

Notes

1 Mary Beth Norton, *Founding Mothers and Fathers: Gendered Power and the Forming of American Society* (New York: Knopf, 1996), pp. 72–5; Karin Wulf, *Not All Wives: Women in Colonial Philadelphia* (Ithaca: Cornell University Press, 2000), pp. 1–5.

2 The cases in tables 2.1 and 2.2 include a sampling of the debt, trespass, detinue and probate administration cases heard before the courts in the years listed. For the London Mayor's Court, I examined all the cases heard before the court in the years 1630–31, 1640 and 1650–51. For the Essex County Quarterly Courts, I counted all of the debt, trespass, detinue and probate administration cases heard between the years listed. For the Maryland Provincial Court, I counted all of the debt, trespass, detinue and probate administration cases heard before the court in the years listed.
3 J. H. Baker, *The Oxford History of the Laws of England*, vol. 6: *1483–1558* (Oxford: Oxford University Press, 2003), pp. 265–72, 281–83; Joseph Smith, *Colonial Justice in Western Massachusetts, 1639–1702* (Cambridge, MA: Harvard University Press, 1961), pp. 66–76; George Haskins, *Law and Authority in Early Massachusetts, A Study in Tradition and Design* (New York: Macmillan, 1960), pp. 32–3; J. Hall Pleasants (ed.), *Proceedings of the Provincial Court, 1663–1666*, vol. 49 (Baltimore: Maryland Historical Society, 1932), pp. ix, xv–xvi, accessed 12 October 2018 through https://msa.maryland.gov/megafile/msa/speccol/sc2900/sc2908/000001/000049/html/am49p-9.html; J. Hall Pleasants, 'First century of the court of chancery', in Pleasants (ed.), *Proceedings of the Court of Chancery of Maryland, 1669–1679*, vol. 51 (Baltimore: Maryland Historical Society, 1934), pp. xxxvi–xxxvii, accessed 11 October 2018 through http://aomol.msa.maryland.gov/000001/000051/html/am51p-36.html; David Newbold, *Notes on the Introduction of the Equity Jurisdiction into Maryland, 1634–1720* (Baltimore: Curlander, 1906), p. 31.
4 Craig Muldrew, '"A mutual assent of her mind"? Women, debt, litigation, and contract in early modern England', *History Workshop Journal*, 55:1 (2003), pp. 54–5.
5 Debra Rosen, *Courts and Commerce: Gender, Law, and the Market Economy in Colonial New York* (Columbus: Ohio State University Press, 1997), pp. 96–7.
6 In the London Mayor's Court widows accounted for 103 out of 140 cases (73 per cent) in which a woman appeared as either a plaintiff or a defendant between 1630 and 1690. London Metropolitan Archives (hereafter LMA), Mayor's Court Original Bills, CLA/024/02, 1630–1690.
7 LMA, Mayor's Court Original Bills, CLA/024/02/102, fl. 74, Margaret Powell v. Robert Hall (1640).
8 Vivian Bruce Conger, *The Widow's Might: Widowhood and Gender in Early British America* (New York: New York University Press, 2009), chapter 2.
9 In the Essex county courts, widows accounted for twenty-nine out of forty-two cases (69 per cent) in which a woman appeared as either a plaintiff or defendant between 1656 and 1682. George Francis Dow (ed.), *Records and Files of the Quarterly Courts of Essex County, 1636–1686*, 9 vols (Salem: Essex Institute, 1911), vol. 2, accessed 11 October 2018 through http://salem.lib.virginia.edu/Essex/vol2/index.html, vol. 4, accessed 11 October 2018 through http://salem.lib.virginia.edu/Essex/vol4/index.html, vol. 7, accessed 11 October 2018 through http://salem.lib.virginia.edu/Essex/vol7/index.html, vol. 8, accessed 11 October 2018 through http://salem.lib.virginia.edu/Essex/vol8/index.html.
10 Dow (ed.), *Records and Files of the Quarterly Courts*, vol. 1, p. 281, accessed 11 October 2018 through http://salem.lib.virginia.edu/Essex/vol1/images/essex281.html.

11 Dow (ed.), *Records and Files of the Quarterly Courts*, vol. 7, pp. 23, 154, accessed 11 October 2018 through http://salem.lib.virginia.edu/Essex/vol7/images/essex023.html.
12 Lois Green Carr and Lorena S. Walsh, 'The planter's wife: the experience of white women in seventeenth-century Maryland', *William and Mary Quarterly*, 3rd series, 34:4 (1977).
13 In the Maryland Provincial Court, widows accounted for 69 of the 114 cases (60 per cent) in which a woman appeared as either a plaintiff or defendant between 1666 and 1683. Pleasants (ed.), *Proceedings of the Provincial Court, 1666–1670*, accessed 11 October 2018 through https://msa.maryland.gov/megafile/msa/speccol/sc2900/sc2908/000001/000057/html/index.html; Elizabeth Merritt (ed.), *Proceedings of the Provincial Court, 1681–1683*, vol. 70 (Baltimore: Maryland Historical Society, 1964), accessed 11 October 2018 https://msa.maryland.gov/megafile/msa/speccol/sc2900/sc2908/000001/000070/html/index.html.
14 Pleasants (ed.), *Proceedings of the Provincial Court, 1666–1670*, pp. 379, 415, accessed 11 October 2018 through https://msa.maryland.gov/megafile/msa/speccol/sc2900/sc2908/000001/000057/html/am57-379.html.
15 J. Hall Pleasants, 'The first century of the court of chancery of Maryland', in Pleasants (ed.), *Proceedings of the Court of Chancery, 1669-1679*, vol. 51 (Baltimore: Maryland Historical Society, 1934), p. xxxvi–xxxvii, accessed 11 October 2018 through https://msa.maryland.gov/megafile/msa/speccol/sc2900/sc2908/000001/000051/html/am51p-36.html; Newbold, *Notes on the Introduction of the Equity Jurisdiction into Maryland*, p. 31.
16 Baker, *Oxford History of the Laws of England*, vol. 6, pp. 173–4; William Searle Holdsworth, *A History of English Law*, 18 vols (London: Methuen, 1903–72), vol. 1, pp. 446–7.
17 Susan Staves, *Married Women's Separate Property in England, 1660–1833* (Cambridge, MA: Harvard University Press, 1990); Tim Stretton, *Women Waging Law in Elizabethan England* (Cambridge: Cambridge University Press, 1998), pp. 25–6, 138–9, 143–4; Amy Erickson, *Women and Property in Early Modern England* (London: Routledge, 1993), pp. 26, 102–7, 115.
18 Erickson, *Women and Property*, p. 115. See also Stretton, *Women Waging Law*, pp. 7, 39.
19 Newbold, *Notes on the Introduction of the Equity Jurisdiction into Maryland*, p. 28; Henry Wilson Scott, *The Courts of the State of New York: Their History, Development, and Jurisdiction* (New York: Wilson, 1909), p. 366; Marylynn Salmon, 'Women and property in South Carolina: the evidence from marriage settlements, 1730–1830', *William and Mary Quarterly*, 3rd series, 39:4 (1982), p. 659.
20 Marylynn Salmon, *Women and the Law of Property in Early America* (Chapel Hill: University of North Carolina Press, 1986), p. 82.
21 These percentages are based on an examination of the forty-nine cases drawn from the Maryland Court of Chancery between 1681 and 1685, and a sampling of 240 cases between 1695 and 1700. Between 1681 and 1685 only three suits out of forty-nine named a woman as either a plaintiff or a defendant. Between 1695 and 1700, 39 suits out of 240 named a woman as a plaintiff or defendant. Pleasants (ed.), *Proceedings of*

the *Court of Chancery, 1669-1679*, accessed 11 October 2018 through http://aomol.
msa.maryland.gov/000001/000051/html/index.html; Maryland State Archives, *Chancery Court, 1671-1712* (Baltimore: Maryland Historical Society, 2008), accessed 11 October 2018 through http://aomol.msa.maryland.gov/megafile/msa/speccol/sc2900/sc2908/000001/000748/html/index.html.

22 Pleasants (ed.), *Proceedings of the Court of Chancery, 1669-1679*, pp. 526-31, accessed 11 October 2018 through https://msa.maryland.gov/megafile/msa/speccol/sc2900/sc2908/000001/000051/html/am51-526.html.
23 Erickson, *Women and Property*, pp. 27, 32-5, 156-71.
24 While my focus is on women involved in testamentary litigation, the percentage of slander and defamation cases in the sixteenth and early seventeenth centuries initiated by women before the London Consistory Court rose from 25 per cent in 1572 to 54 per cent in 1633. See Laura Gowing, *Domestic Dangers: Women, Words, and Sex in Early Modern London* (Oxford: Oxford University Press, 1996), p. 33.
25 Amy Erickson has estimated that between 63 and 89 per cent of English men between the fourteenth and eighteenth centuries named their wives as the executors of their estates. See Erickson, *Women and Property*, pp. 156-7, 162.
26 Essex Record Office (hereafter ERO), Archdeaconry of Essex Depositions, Chelmsford, England, D/AE/D8; LMA, Guildhall Manuscripts, 9065a, vol. 8, Depositions of the London Commissary Court.
27 ERO, Archdeaconry of Essex Depositions, D/AE/D8, 25 July 1632.
28 ERO, Archdeaconry of Essex Depositions, D/AE/D9, Elizabeth Emberson v. John Greene, 20 January 1681.
29 LMA, Guildhall Manuscripts, 9065a, vol. 8, Depositions of the London Commissary Court, Elizabeth Britten v. Christian Britten, 1674.
30 Toby L. Ditz, *Property and Kinship, Inheritance in Early Connecticut, 1750-1820* (Princeton: Princeton University Press, 1986), pp. 144-5; Debra Meyers, *Common Whores, Vertuous Women, and Loveing Wives: Free Will Christian Women in Colonial Maryland* (Bloomington: Indiana University Press, 2003), pp. 128-31. Meyers notes that while both Free Will Christian and Predestinarian Christian men named their wives as executrixes in their wills, Predestinarian women were six times more likely to relinquish control of the estate to a male representative. See Meyers, *Common Whores, Vertuous Women, and Loveing Wives*, pp. 170-1.
31 Vernon Skinner (ed.), *Abstracts of the Testamentary Proceedings of the Prerogative Court of Maryland*, vol. 4: *1677-1682, 1702-1704* (Baltimore: Clearfield Company, 2006), pp. 189, 198-9.
32 Dow (ed.), *Records and Files of the Quarterly Courts*, vol. 1, p. v, accessed 11 October 2018 through http://salem.lib.virginia.edu/Essex/vol1/images/intros/essex006.html.

Part II

The family and society

3

Masters and mistresses, servants and slaves: patriarchy and subordinate agency in the household

Like wives, the patriarchal order defined servants, both male and female, as dependents within the larger family. Male heads of household were obliged to provide for, instruct and protect their servants, just as they were with respect to their wives and children. In return, servants owed their masters deference, submission and obedience. However, this ideal vision of patriarchy, whereby benevolent masters lovingly cared for obedient and submissive dependents, was often not matched by reality. Maidservants made complaints before the local magistrates, arguing that their masters had shirked their patriarchal responsibilities, such as failure to provide household necessaries or to instruct them in a trade, and sometimes alleging severe abuse. When the mutual obligations between masters and servants broke down, female servants turned to the law to find the justice that the patriarchal household had failed to supply them.[1] The legal systems of both England and America recognised the rights of servants to bring their complaints against their masters before the court; when the patriarchal relationship between masters and servants failed, the law stepped in to provide legal redress.

Most women in the Anglo-American world spent a good portion of their teens and early twenties working in domestic service. Spending some years in service was a rite of passage for women in England and the colonies; it was common for young women of all social backgrounds to take up employment with another family to learn household management, and to save money to establish households of their own.[2] In addition to providing young women with the opportunity to earn and save money, this system of service and apprenticeship was a part of maintaining social order; the disorder and unruliness posed by 'masterless' young people was a common anxiety in the early modern period. Young men were considered too riotous and wild without a master to restrain them, while young women were believed to be vulnerable to falling into prostitution without the protection of a master. Service and apprenticeship provided young people with opportunities for financial and social advancement, and afforded a means of exercising social control under the authority of a master.[3]

Colonial slavery was an entirely different institution, both in terms of its function in society and in terms of the legal rights of those who became slaves. The goal of service and apprenticeship was to give young people the resources to eventually become independent householders and begin families of their own; young men and women who had once acted as servants in another household would someday be the masters and mistresses of the next generation of young people. This was not the case with slavery. Slaves were bonded to their masters for life, and could not look forward to the day when they would become free and independent householders. Slaves were never released from the gridlock of patriarchy: masters expected slaves, whether young or old, male or female, to be obedient and submissive to their authority. In return, masters were bound to provide their slaves with adequate food, housing and clothing that allowed them a baseline of health. While it was well within the power of servants to bring legal action against their masters or mistresses, slaves had no legal standing under Anglo-American law. Since slaves were the property of their masters, they were the legal equivalent of other chattels that a master might own. Unlike servants, slaves had no service contracts that outlined wages, length of tenure or the obligations of the master to provide for them.

The legal capabilities of women in servitude, whether bonded or free, thus could vary drastically depending on their location, their race and, unless they were slaves, the terms of their service contracts. The Chesapeake Bay region colonies were unique in the Anglo-American world because of the greater number of indentured servants and slaves, and the relative lack of traditional patriarchal households that acted as the foundation of the social order in England and New England. Men vastly outnumbered women in the colonies, and most young immigrants came as singletons rather than as part of a family group. The relative weakness of patriarchy in colonies such as Maryland led to a greater reliance on the law to act as the arbitrator of disputes. Female servants in the Chesapeake developed a more robust sense of their legal rights, and were vociferous defenders of these rights in the courtroom. However, slaves in the Chesapeake colonies had none of the legal protections afforded to servants.

The legal rights of servants and slaves

William Blackstone, the eighteenth-century lawyer and jurist, stated the differences between the legal status of servants and slaves. Blackstone maintained that 'pure and proper slavery does not, nay cannot, subsist in England'. While other nations might claim the right to make slaves by taking captives in war, or recognise the validity of selling oneself as a slave, or being born into bondage, in England no person had absolute or unlimited power over the life and fortune of another. 'A slave or negro, the instant he lands in England, becomes a freeman,' wrote Blackstone. 'The law will protect him in the enjoyment of his person, his liberty, and his property.' Although a master owned the labour of his servants, he could not own the servant himself. Blackstone maintained that English law only upheld contractual obligations between masters and servants. He wrote that 'the property that every man has in the service of his domestics' is 'acquired by the contract of hiring, and purchased by giving them wages'. The relationships between masters and servants had to be based on a mutually beneficial contract whereby the servant exchanged his labour for the wages, housing and food provided by the master. Blackstone, however, did recognise the possibility that slaves brought onto English soil from elsewhere, and who were in 'perpetual service' for their masters, would remain in the 'same state of subjection for life, which every apprentice submits to for the space of seven years, or sometimes for a longer term'.[4] The ambiguous status of slaves in England would not be decided until the beginning of the nineteenth century, when an act of Parliament ended the slave trade in British territories.

English law thus recognised servants, whether apprentices, laborers or domestic servants, as viable legal actors who fell under the protection of the law. Though female servants were defined as dependents within the early modern household, they possessed the ability to bring legal action against their masters or mistresses, and any other person they saw fit to bring before the law. Unmarried female servants had the same legal status under the law as anyone else within the realm – they could initiate litigation in a court of law, petition the magistrate for legal redress or testify against another person in court. Servants also had an additional layer of legal protection based on the terms of their service contracts. These contracts were legally binding for both masters and servants, and either party could take action against the other if the terms of the contract were violated. Contracts of apprenticeship, which were most common in urbanised areas such as London, ensured that young women would be taught a specialist trade and would be provided with adequate food, housing and clothing. It was crucial for an apprentice to retain a copy of her contract: it was necessary to prove the number of years she was entitled to serve, as well as the terms under which she would be instructed in her trade. Upon completion of their apprenticeships, these young women had the opportunity to trade freely within the city under their own name as long as they remained single, and also could take on their own apprentices to pass their skills along to a new generation.[5]

Although some women served as apprentices, it was far more common for them to act as domestic servants, positions that required more short-term contracts with employers. Contracts for domestic servants tended to be shorter than apprenticeship contracts; they were usually for the duration of one year, although either party could legally cancel the arrangement by giving three-months' notice. As early as 1563 the Statute of Artificers stated that masters and servants must not cancel their contract with one another 'without one quarter warning given before the end of his said term, either by the said master, mistress, or dame or servant the one to the other'.[6] Masters who terminated a servant's contract before its expiry would be fined 40s, unless they were able 'to prove by two sufficient witnesses such reasonable and sufficient cause of putting away of their servant or servants during their term'. The law further stipulated that any disputes arising between masters and servants should be heard before a justice of the peace of the county or the mayor of the town in which the master resided.[7] Domestic service contracts also detailed the wages the servant would earn, as well as the type of work she was expected to perform for the household. Unlike apprentices, maidservants who disliked their masters or who had been mistreated in some way had the flexibility to leave a household and search for another.[8] Apprenticeship contracts and contracts for domestic service provided young women with a solid foundation for legal action when the terms of their contracts had been violated by a master or mistress.

Some young women looking for employment set sail for the colonies, where the high demand for labour and the prospect of upward mobility provided an attractive opportunity for social advancement.[9] Indentured servitude was one of the possible methods by which a young woman could travel to the colonies. In exchange for food, shelter and rite of passage, the servant would agree to work for a master or mistress for a stipulated number of years. In some cases, these indenture contracts were drawn up before the servant even left England – English investors would pay for the servant's passage across the Atlantic, and then recoup their investments by selling the indenture contract upon arrival in the colonies.

Similar to apprenticeship contracts, indenture contracts were legally binding agreements for both parties: masters or mistresses were charged with providing food, clothes and shelter for their servants, and in return the servant was bound to perform labour until their term of service was completed. The law obliged masters to release a servant who had completed her term of service and pay her whatever freedom dues the original contract had stipulated. While indenture contracts granted a master the legal right to the value and produce of his servant's labour, it did not give him ownership of her person. Indentured servants always had recourse to the law, and could bring complaints against their masters or mistresses if the terms of their contract were violated, or if they had been mistreated in some way.

In contrast to servants, slaves had no legal standing under colonial law, and no opportunity for legal recourse if they had a complaint against their master or any other person. Masters owned not just the labour of his slaves but also their bodies and their offspring. Colonial law defined slaves as the moveable property, or chattel, of their masters, and masters were at liberty to use their slaves as they saw fit. While slaves resisted this system of bondage in a variety of ways, unlike indentured servants they were barred from seeking legal redress in the courts.[10] In the seventeenth century the legal distinction between servants and slaves was defined not only by skin colour but also by whether the labourer had arrived in the colony voluntarily or had been forcibly brought to the colony as an enslaved captive. An African brought to America as a slave would always be legally classified as a slave, and would therefore have no power to bring complaints before the magistrate. However, black or mixed race indentured servants had the same legal status as white indentured servants, including the right to seek legal redress when they had been wronged.

In the seventeenth century it was possible for slaves to appear as witnesses, although colonial magistrates permitted their testimonies on a case-by-case basis. Slaves might sometimes be compelled by the court to give evidence against their masters, especially if they were the only other person present at the time a crime was committed. However, it was not possible for them to gain their freedom by testifying, and they would be forced to return to their masters even if they had testified against them. But even the practice of admitting the evidence of slaves in court began to decline in the early eighteenth century. A Virginia statute of 1705 excluded some witnesses of colour on account that they were not Christians, and were therefore thought incapable of making a binding oath to tell the truth. The law deemed 'negroes, mulattoes, and Indian servants, and others, not being Christians', as 'persons incapable in law' and banned them from acting as witnesses 'in any cases whatsoever'. The loophole in this statute was easy to detect: if it could be shown that the witness was a Christian, their testimony would then be permissible in the court. This must have been a common mechanism to allow persons of colour to appear before the court, since an additional statute of 1732 banned even slaves or free blacks who professed to be Christians from acting as witnesses, except in trials of slaves. The statute stated that it had become common practice to allow 'negroes, mulattoes, and Indians' to give lawful testimony before the court 'when they had professed themselves to be Christians'. However, it went on to say that these people were of such 'base and corrupt natures, that the credit of their testimony cannot be certainly depended upon'.

For people of colour, the legal basis for their inability to act as credible witnesses thus shifted from one based on religion to one based on race in only a few decades.[11] By the early eighteenth century, the only cases in which the evidence of a slave was considered legally valid were cases concerning other slaves and people of colour. This was meant to ensure that any slaves who knew of a slave conspiracy or rebellion would be compelled to provide evidence before the court; if they gave false evidence, they risked having both of their ears nailed to a pillory and then cut off, as well as receiving lashes.[12]

Servant petitions for breach of contract

Petitioning was a common form of legal action for female servants, who frequently submitted petitions to the courts because they could appeal directly to a magistrate for summary justice rather than taking the time and expense of a formal trial. While litigation could be costly and time consuming, petitioning the court was a simpler, speedier and inexpensive means of legal redress. In their petitions female servants often emphasised their subordinate status, commonly referring to themselves as 'poor' or 'distressed', and calling on the magistrates to be merciful and equitable in their administration of justice. As a practice rooted in the equity tradition, magistrates recognised petitioning as a way to address injustices that fell outside of the administration of common law: petitions were decided not according to the letter of the law, but on the basis of what was considered to be fair and equitable.[13] The language of petitions reflected the language of prayer – just as a religious devotee requested God's mercy, so petitioners 'humbly prayed' that the magistrate would find compassion for their causes. Both male and female petitioners commonly appealed to the magistrate's 'wisdom' and 'tender consideracons' for their plights, and emphasised their 'sad and deplorable condicon'.[14]

In spite of their subordinate status within the household, servants were well aware of their rights under the law, and petitioned the courts when they felt they had a legitimate grievance against their masters. Servants often submitted petitions when their masters failed to uphold the terms of their service contracts, or when masters eluded their patriarchal responsibilities to protect, instruct and provide for them. It is clear from their petitions that London's female apprentices expected the terms of their contracts to be upheld: they regularly petitioned the court when their masters or mistresses failed to teach them the trade for which they had been contracted, and many also claimed that they had been abused in some way. Gertrude Kirby, who petitioned the justices at the Middlesex Quarter Sessions in January 1692, related that she had been apprenticed to Angela Patilla for a term of five years to learn to wash lace. Upon beginning her term as an apprentice, she had been given £6 by her brother Thomas, as well as two new suits of clothes. In her petition, Gertrude explained that her mistress 'hath very much abused her in not allowing her necessary apparel', and had refused to 'instruct her in her trade'. When Gertrude also complained that she had been turned out of the house 'without any just cause' and had received 'a great damage in her brest by a bruise shee received from John Patilla her Mistress' husband', she was alleging that her master and mistress had violated her service contract as well as their patriarchal obligations to care for and instruct her.[15] The magistrates who heard Gertrude's petition discharged her of her apprenticeship, and ordered John Patilla to return £3 to her within one week so that she could begin a new contract with another person.[16] In Gertrude Kirby's case, the magistrates who heard her petition recognised the failure of her master and mistress to uphold the terms of the apprenticeship contract and found it fair and equitable that she be released from it.

It was well within the legal purview of masters to use 'moderate' corporal punishment on their household subordinates; it was the duty of the master to instruct those in his household, and to ensure that everyone within the household acted according to their expected roles. However, magistrates did not condone a master who was immoderate or overzealous in his physical correction of his servants; and servants' allegations of abuse and maltreatment were taken seriously by the courts. Grace Hearle explained in her petition dated September 1696 that she had been bound as an apprentice to John Dayle and his wife Elizabeth of Cripplegate parish in February 1688 to learn to make hoods and scarves. At the time she began her service she had '7 s[hillings] in money, halfe dozens of all sorts of linnen, double apparell and a feather bedd'. Under the terms of her indenture, she would be allowed the use of all of her personal items and would be instructed in her trade. However, her petition explained that since she had been apprenticed to the Dayles, she had not been taught a trade, nor had she been given adequate clothing. She had also been 'misused and immoderately beaten' by her master so that she had become 'infirm in her limbs & especially in her neck & shoulders being soe weakened that [she] cannot scarce go upright'. The justice who heard Grace's petition ordered that she be discharged from John Dayle's household and service because of his 'immoderate correction', and that she be found another household to accept her as an apprentice.[17] The Dayles had not only failed to uphold the specific terms of her contract by withholding her personal items but had also transgressed the patriarchal responsibility to care and provide for their servant.

The apprenticeship contracts held by young female apprentices gave them solid legal grounds for bringing grievances against their masters and mistresses. Yet women who worked in domestic service, performing the regular duties of the household like cooking, washing and childcare, also had the legal protection of a contract. In September 1690 Hannah Brandon petitioned the Middlesex justices for payment of wages from her master. Her petition stated that, according to her service contract, she had been a 'hired servant to Joseph Short Esquire att four pounds and tenn shillings per annum', and that each party had agreed to give a quarter's warning and a quarter's wages if they desired to dissolve the contract. Hannah explained that she decided to leave her position after about six weeks, and gave notice that she would leave at the end of the quarter. However, in the end she stayed seven weeks past the end of the quarter so that her master had time to hire another servant. When the new servant finally took up residence, Hannah alleged that Short immediately dismissed her and 'refused to pay her the Quarters wages according to the said agreement'. She took the bold step of putting out a warrant for his arrest 'for his nonpayment of her wages'; however, Short beat her to the punch and had her committed to Bridewell prison. She entreated the justices of the court to compel Short to pay her the outstanding wages in addition to the prison fees she paid while in Bridewell.[18]

The ambiguous status of those of African descent who travelled to England is reflected in the petition of Katherine Auker, 'a black', who petitioned the Middlesex court in February 1690 for her freedom. Katherine was a slave who had been bought by Robert Rich, a plantation owner in Barbados. However, when Katherine travelled from Barbados to England in 1684 with her master and mistress, it was unclear whether she retained her status as a slave or if she had the legal rights afforded to other servants in the realm. In her petition she argued that she was a 'servant' to Robert Rich and had been baptised at St Katharine's near the Tower of London in 1688. Her baptism was an important part of her bid for freedom since it was unclear whether Christians could legally be enslaved. Katherine alleged that, after her baptism, her master and mistress severely abused and mistreated her: according to her account, they 'tortured her and turned her out of doors'. Her master had since returned to Barbados, leaving her with no maintenance or place to live, but at the same time threatening to sue any person who employed her. After the examination of witnesses, the justices of the Middlesex court concluded that Robert Rich had 'neglected to provide a service' for Katherine 'or to allow her necessary relief and maintenance' as her master. Although Katherine was of African descent and a slave, the magistrates upheld the obligation of a master to provide housing, food and shelter for those within their households. While they did not ultimately grant Katherine her freedom, they did order that she be 'at liberty to serve any person' until Robert Rich returned from Barbados and provided her with the 'necessary apparel and maintenance' that was due from a master to his servant.[19]

The decision of the Middlesex magistrates in Katherine Auker's case shows that the legal status of slaves in England was complicated. English magistrates were reticent to grant such slaves their freedom upon arrival in England: such an action would have caused an uproar in the colonies that depended on slave labour. Yet at the same, English magistrates interpreted the responsibilities of the master of a slave in the same way that they did the master of a servant; in each case, masters were bound to care for their dependents and provide them with necessities. Though Katherine was a slave and therefore had no contract with her master, the magistrates clearly recognised her entitlement to certain basic necessities and humane treatment.

The high percentage of contracted workers in the Chesapeake meant that female servants often appeared before the courts to sue their masters for breach of contract. Women both black and white were in the minority in the colony, a fact that undermined the stability of the patriarchal family and loosened the mutual obligations between masters and servants. White men outnumbered white women at a ratio of three to one in colonial Maryland, while the number of black men was nearly twice that of black women in Virginia.[20] For female indentured servants, the ability to bring grievances to the magistrates was an essential right and privilege that assured them protection from predatory or negligent masters. Because of their scarcity, female indentured servants were more highly sought after than male servants, and masters sometimes tried to unduly detain or deny them their freedom dues at the expiry of their contracts. This was especially true for indentured servants of colour, whether African, mixed race or Native American. While indentured servants of colour were allowed the same legal standing as their white counterparts, masters were more likely to abuse these servants, detain them past their contracted terms and deny them the dues owed to them. As with white indentured servants, magistrates in the Chesapeake nearly always sided with the servant rather than the master in these cases.[21]

Elizabeth Cannee, a white indentured servant to Mark Cordea, petitioned the Maryland Provincial Court in February 1680, explaining that her master had sent her to serve his son-in-law John Lecompt. It was common practice for indentured servants like Elizabeth to be 'loaned out' by their masters to other householders; since a master owned the servant's labour, it was within his right to send his servant to work in another household. In this case, Lecompt was also acting as attorney for Cordea, which gave him the legal right to manage Cordea's estate. According to Elizabeth's petition, she and Lecompt had made an agreement that if she sold him 'her corne and cloathes' that were due to her at the end of her time of service, 'she should bee then free' six months prior to the expiry of her contract. Elizabeth had readily agreed to this, and Lecompt had given her a note of discharge 'which she hath here ready to produce in court'. However, Elizabeth explained that when she attempted to leave Lecompt's service, Cordea had raised a 'hugh and cry' against her and threatened to make her serve ten days for every one day she had been absent. Elizabeth had presumably been tricked by Lecompt and Cordea into giving up her freedom dues in exchange for release from her indenture. While the magistrates ordered Elizabeth to serve out the remainder of her contract according to her original indenture, they also ordered that Cordea could not force Elizabeth to serve extra time because of the agreement she had made with Lecompt.[22] Elizabeth complied with the order and served out her contract. In May 1680 she produced her indenture in court to prove her term of service was up and asked that the magistrates order Cordea to release her. The magistrates decreed that she was now free and instructed Cordea pay Elizabeth her dues upon her release.[23]

It was common in the Chesapeake for servants' indenture contracts to be bought and sold between masters; since the masters owned the servant's labour for the time specified in the contract, it was legally within their bounds to sell the rights to that labour to another master. An indentured servant whose contract had been sold several times was at increased risk of being detained past the time specified in their service contracts: if a servant did not carefully retain a copy of the original indenture, the length of her servitude may come into dispute in the courts. The magistrates in the Chesapeake were well aware of this problem and the Maryland Provincial Court had decided as early as 1663 that the terms of a servant's original contract should always be upheld even if the contract was bought and sold several times.[24]

Irish indentured servant Mary Strattle had her contract sold on three separate occasions: originally drawn up in Dublin, Mary's contract was first sold to a Mr Addison upon her arrival in Maryland, the second time to William Calvert and the third time to Daniel Devine. In her petition to the Maryland Provincial Court in May 1682, Mary stated that her original contract had bound her to service for four years. However, when Addison had sold her indenture to Calvert he apparently had to give up his copy of Mary's original indenture contract. Mary petitioned the court that Addison be forced to produce the original document. After hearing her petition, the court ordered 'the said Mary Strattle be freed and acquitted from her time of servitude limited by her said indenture'.[25]

Female servants and slaves as witnesses: coercion, abuse and violence

Female servants were important legal witnesses because they had intimate knowledge of the families with which they served, and were often privy to the happenings within their own households as well as those of nearby neighbours. Large households could possibly include not just a master and mistress but also children, step-children, grandparents, aunts, uncles, cousins, apprentices and servants, meaning that families lived closely together, and it was often the case that everyone knew everyone else's business. Female servants whose domestic tasks drew them towards the home possibly knew the family's business better than anyone.

Female servants or slaves who testified against their masters and mistresses were in precarious positions. Contracted servants who brought allegations of abuse or other crimes committed by their masters had the chance of being legally released from their contracts if the magistrates thought they were in mortal danger. Servants who had witnessed a crime, or who had endured it themselves, might therefore have an incentive to bring the crime to the attention of a magistrate. At the same time, a servant who provided testimony against her master or mistress and hoped to gain her freedom might have to wait weeks before the courts dissolved her contract and granted her permission to physically leave the master's house. This gave masters and mistresses ample time to coerce, threaten or bribe a servant into silence. However, these women understood their rights and privileges, and provided information on a range of issues that came before the courts, including abuse, murder and rape.

Anglo-American magistrates generally allowed female servants to be admitted as credible witnesses in civil and criminal litigation, provided that the woman met the qualifications of age and mental competency.[26] However, the fact that servants were household dependents complicated their credibility as witnesses. Servants were dependent upon their masters and mistresses for their bed and board, and had an obligation to be obedient and respectful to their commands. Maidservants who testified against their household superiors also risked provoking their revenge, since the servants would in all likelihood be required to return to their masters' households according to the terms of their service contracts. For all of these reasons, the dependent status of female servants was interpreted as hindering their ability to give a true account of the facts in court.[27] Yet female servants could, and did, testify against their masters and mistresses in a range of different cases. Their testimonies were pivotal in many cases because they were the only witnesses to the event in question.

Whether a female servant's testimony was taken seriously by the magistrate depended upon the woman's social status, her reputation within the community and the testimonies of other witnesses in the case. Sarah Taylor, a 19-year-old servant to Thomas and Mary Bradnox of Maryland, appeared before the Kent County Court on four separate occasions between October 1659 and August 1661 to accuse her master and mistress of abuse. Sarah Taylor came from a high-status lineage: her mother was Jane Fenwick Smith Taylor Eltonhead, who was the daughter of a gentlemen and sister to Cuthbert Fenwick, who sat as a justice of the peace in St. Mary's County and owned a two-thousand-acre tobacco farm.[28] Sarah's mother appeared before the court no fewer than eighteen times during the 1650s, and given her mother's frequent engagements with the law it seems likely Sarah would have been familiar with the atmosphere of the court as a child. After Jane Eltonhead died in 1658 and Sarah went to live as an apprentice in the Bradnox household, it did not take her long to bring her own legal action. In October 1659 she testified before the Kent County Court of the 'divers wrongs & abuses given her by her Master & Mistress Captain Thomas Bradnox & Mary his wife'. Witnesses who spoke on Sarah's behalf noted the bruises on her back and arms, and one recounted that he had heard Mistress Bradnox give Sarah 'som bad words'.

Even Joseph Wickes, one of the magistrates who heard Taylor's testimony, reported that he had seen Mary Bradnox shamelessly 'strikeinge her sarvant before him' with the end of a large rope 'when the said sarvant was there to make her complaint'.²⁹

Only two months after she lodged her initial complaint against the Bradnoxes, Sarah went to court again complaining of abuse and maltreatment. In December 1659 she deposed before the Kent County Court that her mistress had given her 'abuses & stripes ... without cause' and 'doth frequently beate & abuse' her. She also came prepared to prove her allegations by calling witnesses to speak on her behalf, saying that 'her complaint will suffitiently appeare either by the rest of the said sarvants of the house [and] the remarkable signes [she] saith will appeare upon her body'. Mary Bradnox maintained that she had only punished Sarah for laziness, and her correction was within the bounds of the law. She even produced the stick in court that she had used to beat Sarah with as evidence that her correction of Sarah was legal.³⁰ Nicholas Bradway testified that 'Mistress Bradnox sued to her the said Sarah to be friends' but 'that shee would not, she scornd it after shee was abused'. Instead of returning her to the Bradnox household, the court allowed Sarah to stay with another family until they could investigate the matter further.³¹

Sarah Taylor's testimonies went beyond accusing her master and mistress of abuse in the Kent County Court. In July 1660 Sarah testified before the Provincial Court in St. Mary's that Thomas and Mary Bradnox had beaten their servant Thomas Watson so mercilessly that he died. In her testimony Sarah reported that Watson in the 'tyme of his sicknes had very bad usage which was not fitt for a Christian in his weake condicon', and that her mistress had forbidden the other servants 'from carrying the said Watson either victualls or drink' for seven days 'soe that he drunck his owne water in yur deponents sight'. Sarah also claimed that about three weeks before Watson's death Thomas Bradnox had pulled Watson 'out of the corner and struck him soe violently with his hand on the brest and face that the blood issued out of his mouth and nose'. Sarah reported to the magistrates that in the last days of Watson's life he repeatedly told her that he believed his master and mistress were the causes of his death. Two of Sarah's fellow servants, John White and Thomas Southerne, deposed a few months later that they believed Sarah was especially determined to see her mistress brought to justice for the abuse of Thomas Watson. They reported that they heard 'Sarah Taylor tell [them] that if shee should not gett the upper hand or day of her mistress in the seate which she hop't she should, that she would run a knife into her mistres bowells and also in her owne before the face of the Cort'.³²

The magistrates sitting on the bench of the Kent County Court took Sarah's allegations against the Bradnoxes seriously. Indeed, her continual accusations against the Bradnoxes, and the evidence she produced against them for abuse, finally resulted in the court's decision to release her from service 'in regard of the eminent danger likely to insew by the invetterat mallice of hur master & mistress toward hure'. Bolstering her testimony before the court by revealing the bruises on her body to the magistrates, Sarah succeeded in gaining her freedom from her master and mistress and was allowed to leave their service.[33]

Though the magistrates had released her from her service contract, the legal battles between Sarah and her mistress continued. Thomas Bradnox, who by this point was on his deathbed, gave his wife, Mary, power of attorney in September 1661 to continue the suits against Sarah. Mary Bradnox sued Sarah Taylor for slander in the Kent County Court. That Bradnox would undergo the time and expense of initiating a legal suit against Sarah demonstrates that she took the allegations of her servant seriously, and that Sarah's testimonies against her had damaged her standing in the community. Bradnox alleged that Sarah 'did take a falce oath in Court to theire great indamagmt'. Sarah, in a show of legal manoeuvring, requested a nonsuit for lack of evidence. The court consented, 'finding noe caus of seut', and ordered Bradnox to pay costs.[34]

However, in a show of persistence, in November 1661 Bradnox filed another petition against Sarah for slander and breaking her indenture by leaving her household before her contract had expired. Bradnox's petition stated that Sarah was 'unjustly freed' and that she 'craves such sattisfaccon of Sarah Taylor for such her conspiracy and running away from her service to accomplish her unchristean designe'.[35] An almost identical petition, presented to the court three months later, confirms that Bradnox's first petition was unsuccessful in forcing Sarah to pay damages for not fulfilling her service contract.[36] Perhaps in an admission of defeat, in June 1662 Mary Bradnox sued each of the four magistrates that had set Sarah Taylor free for 220 lb of 'good casked tobacco' as compensation for the loss of her servant.[37]

A testimony given by Joyce Northall, servant to Richard Deadman, a coffeeman of the City of London, reveals that female servants in England endured sexual abuse by their masters and also sought redress in court against them. In February 1674 Northall gave her deposition before a city alderman, accusing Deadman of making continuous advances towards her and raping her one night while her mistress was away. In her testimony before the magistrates, she related that 'severall tymes dureing the tyme shee was his servant hee would have forced her to have laine with him which shee refused & often putt him by'. Northall's testimony reveals the vulnerability that female servants faced from persistent masters who took advantage of their wives' absence. Northall related that only about a week before she gave her testimony, her master had raped her 'when her Mistresses was abroad & noe person in the house but her master & herselfe'. In her detailed deposition before the court, Northall related that Deadman had

> forced her to goe upstaires and shee asking the reason or cause why hee answered that hee would speake with her above staires & then hee tooke her & threw her on the bed: but then some person knocking at the doore her master lett her goe down & when shee came to the doore noe person being there thereuppon she sate herselfe down to her work that shee was about below and then her master came down & tooke her uppin his armes & carryed her to the staire foote & then thrust her upp before him & threw her on the bed & tooke upp her coates & had the carnall knowledge of her bodye this informant cryeing out for help and desired & begged on him to be quiett & lett her alone which hee refused to doe. But with his weight and greater strength almost stifled and overcame her.[38]

Northall left her master's service the day before she gave her testimony, no doubt fearing the punishments he might inflict on her for making his crime known before the court and community. Given the nature of Deadman's abuse, Northall might have expected little help from her mistress. The *ménages à trois* that sometimes emerged between masters, mistresses and their young female servants could strain household relationships.[39] Mistresses also had an incentive to keep such incidents quiet; a public allegation of rape would expose the entire family to humiliation. As a result, maidservants who had been sexually abused might find themselves isolated. In these situations, testifying before the legal authorities might have been the only hope for a maidservant who endured sexual abuse during her time of service.

Some masters and mistresses bribed or threatened their maidservants to keep them from making a public accusation of sexual abuse in court. In March 1692 Hannah Harvey, a 17-year-old servant from Wenham, Massachusetts, caused a scandal when she publicly accused her married master, Mordica Larcum, of raping her in his barn near his house. When she was questioned before the court she related that her master had often threatened to kill her if she told of his wrongdoings towards her, and that after the rape had taken place her master and mistress had bullied her into clearing Larcum of the charges. According to her deposition, she had been pressured into maintaining her master's innocence before the court in Salem a few months before 'because he and his wife that evening before perswaded her soe to doe and she being under their charge and he having before threatened her she dare doe noe other and also promised her cloth or stuff to make her a mantle if she would so do'.[40] However, she must have retracted her former statement before the court and formally charged him again with rape. The magistrates took her accusation seriously: at the time Hannah made her deposition Mordica Larcum was already in jail. Larcum, who pleaded his innocence in a petition before the court, maintained that 'he niver did lye with her nither with nor without her consent I did never forc her nor had carnall knolidg of her body'. However, the allegations against him must have been serious enough for him to genuinely fear for his life. Larcum alleged that Harvey had only accused him of rape in a plot to kill him, saying in his petition 'she did it to take away my life'.[41]

Two female witnesses who spoke on Harvey's behalf corroborated her testimony and bolstered her case against Larcum. Sarah Edwards, whose relation to Hannah is not specified, reported that she was in the company of her friend Bethiah Herrick who 'tould mee ... that thay had putt Mordica Larcum in prison without the said Bethiah's testimony and ... that if shee should bee brought to courte shee was afraid that if she should say what shee could say against him the said Larcum her evidence would hang him'.[42] Hannah Wooding, aged 21, also testified that Mordica Larcum had made inappropriate advances towards her one night as he walked her home to her father's house. In her deposition, she related that 'he tould mee hee must have a kiss' and that he would 'have my maden head'.[43] Though Larcum's interaction with Hannah Wooding apparently did not go beyond these verbal threats, Wooding's testimony reveals it might have taken a few women to step forward with allegations of abuse to bring Larcum to justice.[44]

Servants in colonial Massachusetts submitted petitions to the court complaining of maltreatment. Joan Suiflan, 'a poore Irish servant woman' who lived in the household of Thomas Mawle and his wife Naomi, complained in a petition to the Salem Quarterly Court in 1681 that Thomas was a 'cruell master' to her, and that she had been 'brought from another country & here destitute of any friend to keep me'. She explained that Thomas had 'many tymes unreasonably beate me with an unlawful weapon ... which by the English is called a maunatee, or hors whip ... which my master Mawle hath some tymes stroke me at least 30 or 40 blowes at a tyme'. Joan feared for her life, saying that after these beatings she had 'spitt blood for a fortnights tyme ... and that I should have died by his violent beating of me'. She asked the court that she be released from her indenture 'and putt to some other where she may be more Christian like dealt with all'. Seven witnesses – four women and three men – came forward to speak on Joan's behalf. Frances Croad, a neighbour, reported that she saw Mawle beat his maid cruelly. She said that Mawle was 'knowne to be a greate lyar & a contentious person amongst his neighbors reviling & backbiting of them'. Another neighbour, Lucretia Derby, took pity on Joan, calling her 'a stranger & my fellow creature, seeing her soe much wronged'.[45]

Slaves might be compelled by the courts to provide evidence of a crime committed by their masters, although since slaves had no hope of being released from their bondage, doing so would put them in an impossible position with their masters. Such may have been the case with Sarah, a mixed race slave, who was compelled by the York County Court in Virginia to give evidence against her master and mistress in a case against them for theft and disorderly conduct in 1683. Her evidence was necessary to the case because Sarah had been the only other person present at the time that her mistress apparently made off with a horse and saddle belonging to one of her neighbours. Sarah argued that she had only consented to go with her mistress because her mistress had 'commanded' her to do so, and that she was afraid of being beaten if she refused. Sarah's version of the event was recorded as a 'declaration' rather than a sworn deposition, belying the fact that she was a slave and therefore her capability to swear an oath was questionable. Since there was no question of her being released from her bondage after giving her evidence against her master and mistress, the order for her to testify was probably not something she wished to do.[46]

Conclusion

Female servants and slaves were bound under the patriarchal authority of their masters and mistresses. But the ability of these women to seek legal redress if their masters violated their patriarchal responsibilities could vary drastically. Women who worked under contract, a group which included apprentices, indentured servants and domestic servants, could seek legal action against their masters and mistresses if they felt that the terms of their service had been violated or if their masters had abused them. Servants of colour possessed the ability to seek legal restitution in court just as their white counterparts did. The pivotal issue was not race but whether the woman was a contracted servant rather than a slave.

Slavery, however, depended not on a contractual agreement between masters and servants, but on master's ownership of the persons of his slaves. While masters of contracted servants owned the labour of those servants, they never had absolute or unconditional control of their bodies or persons. Masters of slaves, however, owned the bodies of their slaves, not just their labour.

The legal identity of slaves was more ambiguous in England, where some found the institution itself to be antithetical to the spirit of liberty and freedom that characterised the constitution. Though the precise status of slaves in England was not definitively decided until the early nineteenth century, in practice English magistrates provided slaves with a modicum of protection under the law. Slaves who had been purchased elsewhere and subsequently brought to England were not treated as mere chattels; magistrates upheld the right of slaves to be given adequate maintenance, food and shelter by their masters. Masters who did not fulfil this responsibility could not claim a legal right over their slaves, although English magistrates stopped short of granting slaves manumission. Colonial authorities, on the other hand, increasingly restricted the legal identities of slaves, and tightened their control over when and how a slave might appear before the law. In the Chesapeake, slaves' exclusion from the courtroom at first rested on their status as non-Christians. Yet as more and more slaves came to be baptised, their exclusion from legal rights came to be more starkly based on race. Slaves could not legally testify against their masters or any other white person unless specifically given permission to do so by a magistrate. Slaves could testify only in cases concerning others of African descent, whether free or bonded.

The female servants who presented petitions before the courts, and who acted as witnesses in cases of abuse and sexual violence, show that the law provided justice and redress when the ideal of the patriarchal family broke down. While female servants were bound by both law and household hierarchy to submit to their masters and mistresses, these women could and did present petitions to the courts when they felt they had been treated unjustly. Magistrates supported female servants' petitions not only when masters had violated the terms of the service contract but also when masters had neglected to fulfil their patriarchal responsibility to provide for their servants.

The extraordinary legal capabilities of female servants in the Chesapeake were unique. Chesapeake authorities' support of the petitions of female servants reflected the necessity of providing an outlet for grievances that had few other mechanisms of resolution outside of the law. Unlike the Dissenting communities of New England, the Chesapeake never possessed the stable patriarchal structures and religious homogeneity that underpinned the societies of the northern colonies.

Notes

1 Terri Snyder, in *Brabbling Women: Disorderly Speech and the Law in Early Virginia* (Ithaca: Cornell University Press, 2003), pp. 90–1, argues that female servants and slaves in Virginia skilfully petitioned the courts with words that were 'deliberately chosen to reflect badly on the masters who were supposed to head their households'. Similarly, Christine Daniel's study of petitions in colonial Maryland argues that masters were expected, 'by courts and society' to treat their servants fairly. If a master failed in his duty, 'he violated the terms of responsibility on which his control was based and gave the lie to his position as an independent man'. See Christine Daniels, '"Liberty to complain": servant petitions in Maryland, 1652–1797', in Christopher Tomlins and Bruce Mann (eds), *The Many Legalities of Early America* (Chapel Hill: University of Norton Carolina Press, 2001), p. 225. Marcia Schmidt Blaine, 'The power of petitions: women and the New Hampshire provincial government, 1695–1770', *International Review of Social History*, 46 (2001), pp. 57–77.
2 Sara Mendelson and Patricia Crawford, *Women in Early Modern England* (Oxford: Clarendon Press, 1998), pp. 92–108; Tim Meldrum, *Domestic Service and Gender, 1660–1750: Life and Work in the London Household* (Harlow: Pearson, 2000), pp. 15–17.
3 Eleanor Hubbard, *City Women: Money, Sex, and the Social Order in Early Modern London* (Oxford: Oxford University Press, 2012), pp. 23–5.
4 William Blackstone, *Commentaries on the Laws of England*, 4 vols (Oxford: Clarendon Press, 1765–69), vol. 1, pp. 411–17. See also Meldrum, *Domestic Service and Gender*, pp. 25–6.
5 Laura Gowing, 'Girls on forms: apprenticing young women in seventeenth-century London', *Journal of British Studies*, 55 (July 2016), pp. 447–54.
6 5 Eliz, c. 4 (1563).
7 5 Eliz, c. 4 (1563).
8 Mendelson and Crawford, *Women in Early Modern England*, pp. 102–3, 106; Meldrum, *Domestic Service and Gender*, p. 23; Hubbard, *City Women*, pp. 31–5.
9 Alan Taylor, *American Colonies: The Settling of North America* (London: Penguin, 2002), p. 142; Lois Green Carr and Lorena S. Walsh, 'The planter's wife: the experience of white women in seventeenth-century Maryland', *William and Mary Quarterly*, 3rd series, 34:4 (1977), pp. 545–6.
10 Daniels, '"Liberty to Complain"', pp. 221–3; Snyder, *Brabbling Women*, p. 97; Thomas D. Morris, *Southern Slavery and the Law: 1619–1860* (Chapel Hill: University of North Carolina Press, 1996).
11 William Waller Hening (ed.), *Statutes at Large: Being a Collection of all the Laws of Virginia from the First Session of the Legislature, in the Year 1619* (New York: R. W. G. Bartow, 1808), vol. 3, p. 298; vol. 4, p. 327; Morris, *Southern Slavery and the Law*, pp. 231–2.

12 Hening (ed.), *Statutes at Large*, vol. 4, pp. 128, 327.
13 On the origins of the practice of petitioning, see William Searle Holdsworth, *A History of English Law*, 18 vols (London: Methuen, 1903–1972), vol. 1, pp. 446–7; vol. 10, p. 696; Gwilym Dodd, 'The hidden presence: Parliament and the private petition in the fourteenth century', in Anthony Musson (ed.), *Expectations of the Law in the Middle Ages* (Woodbridge: Boydell Press, 2001), p. 135; Gwilym Dodd, 'Reason, conscience, and equity: bishops as the king's judges in later medieval England', *History*, 99 (2014), pp. 215–16.
14 Gwilym Dodd and Sophie Petit-Renaud, 'Grace and favour: the petition and its mechanisms', in Christopher Fletcher et al. (eds), *Political Life in England and France, c. 1300–c. 1500* (Cambridge: Cambridge University Press, 2015) p. 242. See also James Daybell, 'Scripting a female voice: women's epistolary rhetoric in sixteenth-century letters of petition', *Women's Writing*, 13:1 (2006), pp. 3–22.
15 London Metropolitan Archives (hereafter LMA), MJ/SP/1692/01/012, Petition of Gertrude Kirby (1692).
16 W. J. Hardy (ed.), *Middlesex County Records: Calendar of the Sessions Books, 1689–1709* (London: R. Nicholson, 1905), p. 63
17 LMA, MJ/SP/1696/09/004, Petition of Grace Hearle (1696).
18 LMA, MJ/SP/1690/09/001, Petition of Hannah Brandon (1690).
19 LMA, MJ/SBB 472, Middlesex Sessions Bundles, February 1690, p. 41. Also transcribed in Sara Mendelson and Laura Gowing (eds), *Women's Worlds in Seventeenth-Century England: A Sourcebook* (London: Routledge, 2000), pp. 76–7.
20 Carr and Walsh, 'The planter's wife'; Snyder, *Brabbling Women*, p. 40.
21 Daniels, '"Liberty to Complaine"', pp. 233–4.
22 Elizabeth Merritt (ed.), *Proceedings of the Provincial Court, 1679–1680/1*, vol. 69 (Baltimore: Maryland Historical Society, 1961), pp. 123–4, accessed 11 October 2018 through https://msa.maryland.gov/megafile/msa/speccol/sc2900/sc2908/000001/000069/html/am69-123.html.
23 Merritt (ed.), *Proceedings of the Provincial Court*, vol. 69, pp. 207–8, accessed 11 October 2018 through https://msa.maryland.gov/megafile/msa/speccol/sc2900/sc2908/000001/000069/html/am69-207.html.
24 This ruling was established in a case brought before the Maryland Provincial Court by a former servant named Francis Gumby. See J. Hall Pleasants (ed.), *Proceedings of the Provincial Court, 1663–1666*, vol. 49 (Baltimore: Maryland Historical Society, 1932), pp. 140–1, accessed 11 October 2018 through https://msa.maryland.gov/megafile/msa/speccol/sc2900/sc2908/000001/000049/html/am49-141.html. See also Daniels, '"Liberty to Complaine"', p. 246.
25 Merritt (ed.), *Proceedings of the Provincial Court*, vol. 69, p. 197, accessed 11 October 2018 through https://msa.maryland.gov/megafile/msa/speccol/sc2900/sc2908/000001/000069/html/am69-197.html.
26 Holdsworth, *A History of English Law*, vol. 9, pp. 185–90; Barbara Shapiro, *A Culture of Fact, 1550–1720* (Ithaca: Cornell University Press, 2000), pp. 12–13; James Brundage, 'Juridical space: female witnesses in canon law', *Dumbarton Oaks Papers*, 52 (1998), pp. 147–8; Charles Donahue, 'Proof by witnesses in the church courts of medieval

England: an imperfect reception of the learned law', in Morris Arnold *et al.* (eds), *On the Laws and Customs of England: Essays in Honor of Samuel E. Thorne* (Chapel Hill: North Carolina University Press, 1981), pp. 130–3.

27 Alexandra Shepherd, *Accounting for Oneself: Worthy, Status, and the Social Order in Early Modern England* (Oxford: Oxford University Press, 2015), pp. 180–3.

28 Edward Papenfuse (ed.), *A Biographical Dictionary of the Maryland Legislature, 1635–1789* (Baltimore: Johns Hopkins University Press, 2010), p. 319.

29 J. Hall Pleasants (ed.), *Proceedings of the County Courts of Kent (1658–1676), Talbot (1662–1674), and Somerset (1665–1668) Counties*, vol. 54 (Baltimore: Maryland Historical Society, 1937), pp. 167–8, accessed 11 October 2018 through https://msa.maryland.gov/megafile/msa/speccol/sc2900/sc2908/000001/000054/html/am54-167.html.

30 Pleasants (ed.), *Proceedings of the County Courts*, vol. 54, pp. 178–9, accessed 11 October 2018 through https://msa.maryland.gov/megafile/msa/speccol/sc2900/sc2908/000001/000054/html/am54-178.html.

31 Pleasants (ed.), *Proceedings of the County Courts*, vol. 54, pp. 179–81, accessed 11 October 2018 through https://msa.maryland.gov/megafile/msa/speccol/sc2900/sc2908/000001/000054/html/am54-179.html.

32 Bernard Christian Steiner (ed.), *Proceedings of the Provincial Court, 1658–1662* (Baltimore: Maryland Historical Society, 1922), vol. 41, pp. 500–6, accessed 11 October 2018 through https://msa.maryland.gov/megafile/msa/speccol/sc2900/sc2908/000001/000041/html/am41-500.html.

33 Pleasants (ed.), *Proceedings of the County Courts*, vol. 54, pp. 213, 225–6, accessed 11 October 2018 through https://msa.maryland.gov/megafile/msa/speccol/sc2900/sc2908/000001/000054/html/am54-213.html.

34 Pleasants (ed.), *Proceedings of the County Courts*, vol. 54, pp. 225–6, 228, accessed 11 October 2018 through https://msa.maryland.gov/megafile/msa/speccol/sc2900/sc2908/000001/000054/html/am54-225.html.

35 Steiner (ed.), *Proceedings of the Provincial Court, 1658–1662*, vol. 41, p. 506, accessed 11 October 2018 through https://msa.maryland.gov/megafile/msa/speccol/sc2900/sc2908/000001/000041/html/am41-506.html.

36 Steiner (ed.), *Proceedings of the Provincial Court, 1658–1662*, vol. 41, p. 525, accessed 11 October 2018 through https://msa.maryland.gov/megafile/msa/speccol/sc2900/sc2908/000001/000041/html/am41-525.html.

37 Pleasants (ed.), *Proceedings of the County Courts*, vol. 54, p. 234, accessed 11 October 2018 through https://msa.maryland.gov/megafile/msa/speccol/sc2900/sc2908/000001/000054/html/am54-234.html.

38 LMA, CLA/047/LJ/13, February 1675.

39 Laura Gowing, 'The haunting of Susan Lay: servants and mistresses in seventeenth-century England', *Gender and History*, 14:2 (2002), p. 188.

40 Phillips Library (hereafter PL), Essex County Court File Papers, 52-92-2.

41 PL, Essex County Court File Papers, 52-97-1.

42 PL, Essex County Court File Papers, 52-97-3.

43 PL, Essex County Court File Papers, 52-97-3.

44 See Rebecca Black's successful case against a fellow servant for rape in 1656/57 before the court in Ipswich. PL, Essex County Court File Papers, 3-60-4.
45 George Francis Dow (ed.), *Records and Files of the Quarterly Courts of Essex County, 1636–1686*, 9 vols (Salem: Essex Institute, 1911), vol. 8, pp. 224–6, accessed 11 October 2018 through http://salem.lib.virginia.edu/Essex/vol8/images/essex224.html.
46 Snyder, *Brabbling Women*, pp. 109–12.

4

Wives and (unwed) mothers: women's claims for financial support

The responsibilities incurred by men upon marriage and fatherhood were legally enforced by local authorities and the women who had a stake in seeing that these obligations were upheld. Wives who had been deserted or neglected by their husbands appealed to local magistrates to compel their husbands to provide financial maintenance, while unwed mothers and midwives often worked with local legal authorities to hold fathers accountable for child support. When male heads of household shirked their responsibilities to provide for their wives and the mothers of their children, the law provided a mechanism that could require men to fulfil these obligations. Women certainly stood to benefit from the support of magistrates in these cases: wives were sometimes abandoned by their husbands, leaving them without sufficient means to maintain their households and children, and with few economic opportunities that would allow them to maintain themselves. In these cases, magistrates could order that a husband pay his wife an allotted sum for her support, or risk being jailed or fined. Women who had children out of wedlock, supported by the testimonies of the midwives who attended their delivery, could also legally compel the father of the child to pay for the child's maintenance. At the same time, local legal authorities clearly had an interest in these cases. They sought to ensure that men fulfilled their financial responsibilities to their children; to abandon this responsibility undermined the social order, and increased the risk of women and children becoming a burden to the system of poor relief, which provided monetary assistance to the most vulnerable members of society.

The breakdown of marriages and breakup of families were of concern to religious and legal authorities in all areas of the Anglo-American world. Stable and harmonious marriages were considered the foundation of the household and the social order, and continued to be viewed as the ideal situation for the creation of families. However, concerns over the disintegration of the patriarchal family took on different tones in different places. In England authorities became more concerned with the breakdown of the patriarchal household as the population grew and as more and more people fell into poverty. The issue for them was economic: women and children who were not financially supported within a patriarchal household structure risked becoming dependent on poor relief and a burden on the taxpayers.[1] Women's petitions for financial support therefore aligned with the interests of local authorities in compelling men to uphold their responsibilities to their families. In New England the issue that was most pressing in cases of wives' maintenance and child support was the desire to uphold marital fidelity and protect the successful functioning of patriarchy as the foundation for families and communities. While economic issues were certainly part of the picture, New England magistrates were just as focused on prosecuting moral offences and creating godly societies as they were on the desire to not overburden the system of poor relief.[2]

Petitions for wives' maintenance, marital separation and child support took on yet a different tone in the Chesapeake Bay region colonies. The religious diversity of seventeenth-century Maryland meant that, unlike New England, there was very little social cohesion provided by religion. Catholics and Anglicans in the colony had different interpretations of marriage and family relationships from Dissenters, and there was a lack of a commonly agreed-upon ecclesiastical structure.[3] Consequently, the law became the only common denominator that all could rely upon to ensure that society functioned and the social order was maintained. Chesapeake authorities and communities did not have the desire or mechanisms to prosecute moral offences like fornication and adultery, and most cases for wives' maintenance and child support were only of concern insofar as they compelled fathers to financially support his wife and children.[4]

Marital breakdown and wives' requests for maintenance

While the doctrine of coverture barred married women from initiating a legal suit against another party in courts of common law, Anglo-American magistrates considered petitioning a viable form of legal action for wives. In an effort to provide justice and fairness to those seeking legal redress, magistrates who received wives' petitions largely overlooked the restrictions barring them from seeking legal action at common law. Petitioning was a popular legal mechanism for wives because the process focused on finding equitable solutions to problems rather than strict adherence to the letter of the law. Often, wives gave some sort of justification for why their husbands did not appear as a co-party in the petition: wives commonly related that their husbands were away at sea, were too sick to appear before the court or had simply deserted them. Magistrates recognised that wives who were left in such positions still had recourse to the law, even if their husbands were unable to act as a co-party in the action.

Wives could also submit petitions *against* their husbands. Often alleging physical abuse and financial neglect, wives petitioned the court to ask magistrates to legally force their husbands to uphold their patriarchal responsibility to provide for their families. Magistrates supported a wife's right to seek legal action against her husband if he shirked these obligations, and could compel a wayward husband to fulfil the duties expected of him. Wives' petitions against their husbands are important because they strike right at the heart of the system of patriarchy itself: wives and other dependents owed obedience and submission to the male head of household but masters were bound to provide protection and household necessities appropriate to his family's social rank in return. It was a system based on reciprocity and mutual obligations; if one party failed to uphold their end of the bargain, the law intervened.

Wives' petitions for maintenance were often accompanied by requests for a marital separation. As long as a husband and wife cohabited together, authorities assumed that the husband provided for his wife's financial needs. But it sometimes happened that marriages failed, and husbands and wives agreed to live separately. Wives submitting petitions for marital separation and financial maintenance took different avenues depending on their location. In England wives could petition the common law courts for maintenance, as well as for permission for a separation of bed and board (*divortium a mensa et thoro*). In this type of separation, although the couple did not cohabit together, the partners were still legally married and the husband was therefore still responsible for financially supporting his wife. An English wife who sought a full divorce (*divortium a vinculo matrimonii*), however, had to seek it in the ecclesiastical courts, which alone had the power to dissolve a marriage. The Anglican church considered marriage a sacrament, and the dissolution of a marriage was, therefore, within the purview of the church courts. Full divorces were almost never allowed by the English church courts unless the marriage was never valid to begin with on the grounds of consanguinity, bigamy or sexual incapacity. Marital separation, or separation of bed and board, was allowed in cases of adultery, desertion or cruelty, but did not relieve either partner from the legal obligations of marriage.[5]

In the New England Dissenter colonies, however, the view of marriage as a civil contract rather than a sacrament meant that married women could petition the secular magistrates for financial maintenance and a full divorce. The Puritan philosophy of marriage reasoned that if one partner broke the terms of the marriage contract, whether through neglect, cruelty or infidelity, the other partner should be freed from the contract and allowed to remarry. This would allow women whose husbands had abandoned them to have the opportunity to reengage with the patriarchal household rather than live alone and risk falling into the temptation of adultery. Allowing the full dissolution of marriage was, for Puritans, a way of upholding the sanctity of the marriage relationship. As the Puritan writer William Secker wrote in 1690, 'marriage is like water to quench the sparkes of lusts fire … it is better to be lawfully coupled than to be lustfully scorched'.[6] The more liberal divorce policies of the New England colonies were also designed to prevent bigamy, which had become a widespread practice in England and in colonies in which divorces were difficult to obtain. Full divorce in Connecticut, New Hampshire and Massachusetts could be sought on the grounds of adultery, desertion, cruelty or neglect, though it was often the case that successful women petitioners had to claim all of these.[7]

Settlers in the Chesapeake, however, showed no desire to reform English laws or attitudes about marriage. As in England, only very rarely did magistrates in colonies such as Maryland grant a full divorce. Maryland followed Anglican and Catholic traditions that viewed marriage as a sacrament and could therefore only be dissolved in cases of consanguinity, pre-contract or sexual incapacity. Maryland law did, however, permit separation of bed and board. The major difference between marital separation cases in England and the Chesapeake was that the secular magistrates could grant permission for separation and financial maintenance. Like women in New England, women in the southern colonies could ask for separation and maintenance at the same time. Since colonists never established an ecclesiastical jurisdiction in America, secular authorities who received wives' petitions borrowed from common law and canon law, and granted separation of bed and board in cases of neglect, abuse and desertion.[8]

While the liberality of the divorce laws in New England, which allowed divorced women to remarry, has been touted as a remarkable example of women's greater freedom in the Dissenter colonies, the advantages of a full divorce were not that clear cut.[9] On the one hand, marital separation of only bed and board meant that a husband still had the legal obligation to provide for his wife and children, even if the family no longer lived together. This could certainly work to a woman's advantage, since she would have the law on her side in any cases compelling her husband to provide her with necessaries. In the New England colonies, when a woman obtained a full divorce from her husband, however, he was no longer obliged to give her any maintenance at all. Meanwhile, women who lived separately from their husbands were still bound by the rules of coverture. Even if they lived in their own households, they could not contract a debt in their own name and could not pursue a case in common law without their husband also appearing with them. This could seriously hinder a woman's economic agency since she could not buy anything on credit.

Physical abuse, combined with poverty, often compelled wives to submit petitions for marital separation and financial maintenance to the courts. Wives' petitions to the court reflect what was too often the grim reality of women's marital subordination. It was perfectly legal for a husband to corporally 'correct' his wife and other household dependents, although it was contrary to law, religion and custom for a man to be too immoderate in his use of physical force. A wife's petition to the magistrate was often a last resort aimed at survival rather than a woman's self-conscious effort to flex her legal muscles and undermine the authority of her husband.

To take one example, Mary Gregory of St. Paul's parish in Shadwell, London, petitioned the Middlesex Quarter Sessions in 1699, relating that she had been the wife of Edward Gregory for twenty-four years and had two living children by him. However, for the last year she had been 'deprived of a maintainance & all necesaries and turned out of doors' by her husband, who now kept 'company with one Isabell Barbour an idle person whos husbands at sea'. In addition to her husband's neglect of Mary and her children's financial needs, Mary also alleged that she had suffered greatly by her husband's 'hard usage' and because of his abuse had been unable to work. Since she was not financially able to 'fee councell to plead for her' she 'most humbly committs her case' to the justices, since she was

> in a great dread & feare of her life by his illusage towards her, and if your worps doe not take pittey upon her she must enevitably parish for he will not allow your petr anything towards her maintenance and should have parished before now had she not been receved by her neighbors.[10]

Mary Gregory's petition is just one example of a married woman in desperate circumstances who turned to the law to secure maintenance and find legal redress. The language of her petition appeals to commonly accepted norms of patriarchy, in which a husband was obliged to care for and protect his wife and children. Mary Gregory and other married women like her made arguments that the justices found hard to ignore: if Mary's husband would not uphold his obligation to her of his own volition, the magistrates would be obliged to ensure that he did. The Middlesex magistrates ordered that Edward Gregory pay the parish 2s weekly to care for Mary, and ordered that he stop his abuse of her.

Sarah Graves petitioned the Middlesex justices on more than one occasion to gain maintenance from her husband, Anthony. She stated in her petition of February 1690 that in the last court session the magistrates had referred her issue to parish officials to 'determine differences between your petr and her husband and his father and mother' concerning a sum of money they owed her. What had happened to Anthony Graves is not explained – it is possible that he could have been a sailor and been at sea, or that he had simply deserted his wife, leaving Sarah to negotiate with her in-laws for her financial maintenance. What is clear, however, is that at the time of her petition, everyone involved, including the justice of the peace, considered Sarah Graves a married woman, and she is identified as such in the petition. She explained that after her initial complaint, her husband's father, John Graves, gave her half the money she was due but flatly refused to give her the remainder. When she appeared before the court in February, Sarah explained that she would like the court to draw up a warrant for the arrest of her father-in-law to force him to appear before the magistrates and 'show cause why he will not abide the order'.[11] The magistrates ordered that John Graves pay Sarah 2s weekly for her maintenance until Anthony returned to his wife.

Colonial wives often included many of the same complaints against their husbands that women in England did: they recounted stories of abuse and maltreatment, and asked for financial maintenance from husbands who had disappeared or had deserted them. Wives in New England could also petition for divorce. Many of these women made the argument that since their husbands had disappeared or deserted them, their marriages were no longer valid. Mary Madox, for example, petitioned the Massachusetts General Court in 1678, stating that her husband had deserted her and that she wished to be free of the marriage. The magistrates granted her petition, stating that her husband, Henry Madox, had 'binn absent for thirteen yeares, & never wrote or sent to hir in that time'. They therefore decided that she was 'at liberty from the conjugall bond' and was able 'to dispose of herself as she shall see meete'.[12] In a similar petition, Mary Lyndon, the wife of Augustin Lyndon, petitioned the General Court in October 1679 for the court to 'set hir free' from her marriage, and for a two-thirds portion of the land that had belonged to she and her husband. The petition states that Augustin Lyndon had been absent from the colony for an extended period of time, and Mary argued that she should have sole control of the 'smale estate which she hath earned & got together during the time of hir late husbands absence'. The court granted Mary a divorce as well as the land and money.[13]

New England magistrates who heard petitions concerning desertion, maintenance and divorce nearly always sided with the wife who had been mistreated. If a husband shirked his patriarchal responsibilities to care for and protect his wife, Puritan magistrates saw fit to also release the wife from her responsibilities to her husband. Elizabeth Manning, wife of Captain Nicholas Manning of Salem, petitioned first the local courts and then the General Court in 1680/81 to be divorced from her husband. In her original petition to the Quarterly Court at Salem in September 1680, Elizabeth stated that her husband and his sisters had mistreated her so badly that she was afraid for her life, and that her husband had not allowed her any maintenance. Nicholas Manning and his sisters Anstis and Margaret had been indicted on charges of incest at the same court session in which Elizabeth presented her petition, and were sentenced to be whipped and to stand before the meeting house with a sign outlining their crime. The punishment for Anstis and Margaret was remitted by the payment of a £5 fine instead, and Nicholas fled the town before his punishment could be meted out. In her petition, Elizabeth stated that her husband had never provided her maintenance, and now had 'gone and cannott be found'. She asked for maintenance from his estate so that she might not be a charge to the town. Since the situation Elizabeth outlined was unusual, the local magistrates referred Elizabeth's petition to the General Court. In May 1681 the magistrates at the General Court ordered that Nicholas Manning's estate be 'secured by the County Court at Salem, & by them disposed of for the peticoners maintenance and support'. The local authorities in Salem looked into the matter and ordered that all of the moveable property, as well as Elizabeth's thirds of all the houses and lands, be awarded to her as Nicholas's wife.[14]

While magistrates in New England might have granted divorces routinely in cases of desertion, marital separation was harder for a wife to attain when her husband's whereabouts were well known and there was no specific allegation of physical abuse. A wife's accusations of verbal threats or brutish behaviour were not enough to convince a magistrate to grant maintenance or a full divorce. Beatrice Berry, for example, submitted a petition to the Salem Quarterly Court in 1676, asking that the magistrates grant her a divorce from her husband, Edmund Berry. In the initial petition, Beatrice made no specific claims of abuse or desertion, but did allege that her husband's rancour about their prenuptial agreement had made him intolerable to live with. Beatrice had been married twice before and possessed a large estate in her own right; prior to her marriage to Edmund, she had drawn up a marriage settlement barring her husband from gaining possession of her property. The petition from Beatrice Berry, who was in her seventies at the time she submitted it to the court, is worth transcribing in full because it is written in the first person and seems to have been drawn up in her own hand. She wrote:

> I can prove by testimony verbally & also by writing under his hand the conditionall covenant made between us before our marriage, the which Covenant at the Tyme of our marriage was acknowledged before the honored Major Hathorne, & likewise I can make proofe by John Gover [sic] whom he employed to come to me as a Friend to speake in his behalf; that Edmund Berry desired nothing of my estate he desire nothing but my person. But alas how he carried it to me afterwards I know the Towne & Country hath rung of it, & it cannot otherwise be but your worships must of necessity have heard of his base, brutish & Inhumane carriage to me being truly such as was impossible for any poore woman specially a woman of my Age to live with such a person & this I can bring proof of to the honored court that he did tell John Glover that if I would not give up the writings that were made between us he would make me weary of my life & so indeed I found it; & so at Length with his consent we parted; & now I have declared myself as briefly as I could; & doe desire to ly at the mercy of the court, for what ever I suffer I am not able to live with such a Tyrant.[15]

In spite of her plea and the testimony of witnesses who attested to her good character, the justices ordered her to return to her husband or pay a £5 fine. Given that she had the resources, it is not surprising that she paid the fine.

A year later a grand jury indicted Edmund Berry on charges of drunkenness and verbally abusing his wife. Beatrice submitted another petition to the court, explaining that her husband had told her 'that he will have my estate or elce he will make me weary of my life'. The rest of her petition outlined her woeful situation and she asked the justices to allow her to leave her husband permanently.

> It is but rationall that I should speake something before your worships for the clearing up of myne owne innocency, & also since the thing is brought forth to lay open my grievances before you although god knows my mind was rather to have borne my affection & have waited upon him who is the persuader of the heart. God direct you what to doe with me in this my wofull case, for I am not onely continually abused by my husband ... but also his son who lives in howse with him hath in his father's presence threatened me to throw me downd head long downe the staires.[16]

After her second petition, the Salem magistrates allowed Beatrice to live separately from her husband. She died in 1683 with an inventory of goods worth £181.[17]

While obtaining a full divorce was rarely an option in colonial Maryland, wives did seek to live separately from their husbands and to secure financial maintenance from them. In one such case Elizabeth Tennyson, wife of John Tennyson, petitioned the Council of Maryland on 25 October 1680. Elizabeth appeared in person before the members of the council, explaining that she could not live with her husband and asking that he give her maintenance so she could live separately. In making her statement before the council, Elizabeth said that she 'could not live peaceably and quietly with him, but with a great deal of danger and hazard to her person', and asked the council to allow her 'competence maintenance'. The council summoned John Tennyson to appear and answer Elizabeth's complaints. Though he denied Elizabeth's allegations of severe abuse, he did admit that he could 'never entertain that love and respect of his said wife or neither afford her that countenance in his house as is property due from a man to his wife'. The justices therefore ordered that separate maintenance be awarded to Elizabeth to live apart from her husband. The household goods included Elizabeth's 'owne bed' with its furniture, all of her clothes and a yearly maintenance of three barrels of corn, 300 lb of meat and 1,000 lb of tobacco for the remainder of her life.[18]

Unlike Massachusetts, which had tight-knit communities that acted as a surveillance system for misbehaviour, the population of colonial Maryland was spread over a wide area, making it easy for a husband to disappear without any common knowledge of his whereabouts. Sarah Harris petitioned the Council of Maryland in 1683, complaining that her husband had abandoned her and her five children 'for the most part of the yeare except the dead of the winter'. She alleged that her husband contributed nothing to the maintenance of the household, so that she feared that she and her children would starve or fall on the poor rates unless some action was taken. When the weather turned colder, her husband stayed in the household and 'hath eaten up all ... the childrens maintenance, which she all the yeare provides for the keeping of them'. The authorities who heard Sarah's petition referred it to be decided by the Lord Proprietary and the General Assembly, which was advised to provide relief for the defendant with 'all convenient speed'.[19]

The willingness of magistrates to support wives' petitions for separation and maintenance is a remarkable example of the law's power within the patriarchal family. When relationships between husbands and wives collapsed, the law provided the only assurance of equity and justice that women could expect to receive.

The legal power of midwives and unwed mothers' claims for maintenance

Marriage was not required for a woman to be entitled to financial maintenance: a woman who had a child out of wedlock could legally claim child support from the man she named as the father. For local authorities, marriage was the preferable option for these couples; marriage would establish a patriarchal household with a clear responsibility by the father to maintain and support his family. But some couples could not, or would not, marry – a situation that left the mother and child outside of the support and protection of a household. In the eyes of local magistrates, women and children living outside of the realm of family had the potential to lead to a variety of social problems: the mother and the baby could become the financial responsibility of the taxpayers, the mother might commit infanticide if she perceived her situation to be hopeless, or she could fall into prostitution in her desperation to eke out a living independently of a husband. It was therefore a high priority of local legal officials to ensure that fathers recognised and fulfilled their responsibilities to provide for their families, whether they were married or not.

Midwives were on the front lines of this social problem. As the experts on women's bodies and childbirth, they were often the ones responsible for questioning the mother about the identity of the father during the birth of the child and they worked closely with local legal officials to compel these men to financially support their families.[20] In an age when many women died in childbirth, contemporaries believed that no woman would risk making a false allegation about the paternity of her child while she was giving birth. Unwed mothers and midwives were often allies in the legal process to prove the paternity of an illegitimate child, although their motivations could be different. Unwed mothers clearly stood to gain financial support from the father that could be essential in helping her to maintain her child. Midwives, on the other hand, had a clear responsibility to help maintain the stability of the patriarchal household that was the foundation of the social order.

In many cases, the relationship between the mother and midwife was cooperative; each had an interest in finding the father of the child and compelling him to provide support. However, other situations arose in which the mother and midwife could be set at odds with one another. Midwives might have a vested interest in seeing that a certain man, and not another, was named as the father of the child; mothers might wish to keep the identity of the father a secret for fear of bringing shame upon him. The relationships between unwed mothers and midwives were caught up in the vagaries and contexts of local communities, and could vary widely according to the specifics of the situation.

Local authorities considered the mother's childbirth testimony, reported to the court by herself or through the deposition of the midwife, as sufficient proof of paternity. In other words, magistrates took women at their word. Legal writer Michael Dalton, whose *Countrey Justice* was the definitive legal handbook for both English and colonial justices throughout the seventeenth century, considered it critically important that women accused of bastardy be able to speak on their own behalves. He wrote that local authorities should always record the sworn depositions of women charged with illegitimacy, for 'the matter and the trial thereof depends chiefly upon the examination and testimony of the mother'.[21]

While illegitimacy was a social and economic problem in all areas of the Anglo-American world, different areas had their own particular concerns when it came to how to address the issue. In England a growing population meant that authorities were concerned about the possibility of the mother and child becoming a financial burden on the poor rates.[22] An Elizabethan statute of 1576 stated that a mother who could not prove the paternity of her child or maintain it with her own resources might possibly be jailed until she could give the authorities some assurance that she could care for the child.[23] This injunction was repeated in a statute of 1609, which stated that any woman who had a 'bastard that may be chargeable to the parish' could be committed to a workhouse to earn her living.[24] The important issue in England was the expense of maintaining the mother and child, and the desire to keep them from becoming a further drain on an already overburdened system of poor relief. One study found that 80 per cent of couples presented to the courts for illegitimacy in Warwickshire, Hertfordshire and the North Riding of Yorkshire received no punishment, only the injunction to care for and maintain the child that was born.[25] As long as the child was maintained, the mother and father generally avoided any further punishment.

The colonial perspective on the issue of illegitimacy was different depending on the colony. In Massachusetts illegitimacy was a moral problem and an obstacle to the proper functioning of the patriarchal family. Even illicit and unsanctioned sex that did not produce a child could be punished by the authorities with a fine, and authorities were insistent on holding the mother and father accountable for their actions.[26] Despite the accusation of one Massachusetts woman that 'the court did not regard the sin so they could get the mony', Massachusetts magistrates viewed fornication and bastardy as a violation of the laws of God.[27] Since there was no real division between secular and religious authorities in Massachusetts Bay, local authorities prosecuted both offences in the county courts. As in England, New England magistrates relied on the testimonies of the mother and the midwife in court to identify the putative father of a child. However, Massachusetts law went beyond English practice by upholding these women's testimonies even if a man flatly denied the accusation. A statute of the Massachusetts General Court in October 1668 stated that

> the man charged by the woman to be the father, she continuing constant in it (especially being put upon the reall discovery of the trueth of it in the time of her travaile) shall be the reputed father & accordingly be liable to the charge of maintenance … notwithstanding his deniall.[28]

This law meant that the testimony of the midwife and the mother was enough to convict the father, even if he vehemently denied it in his own testimony. Perhaps in an effort to get more men to confess, the law also stated that a man who claimed paternity and agreed to maintain the child would be free from prosecution and punishment by the court. A father thus accused would be compelled by the magistrates to fulfil his patriarchal responsibility to care for his child, even if he and the mother did not marry.[29]

Authorities in the Chesapeake were alarmed at the sharp rise in illegitimacy rates in the colony and the threat that illegitimacy posed to the productivity of the female workforce. Female indentured servants were young and single, and since men vastly outnumbered women in the region, they were perhaps seen as sexual outlets for the many men who lived in the colony.[30] Even if they became pregnant, by the terms of these women's service contracts marriage was not an option until they had gained their freedom. Further, if they did not identify the fathers of their children, either in childbed or in court, they risked having extra time added to their contracts in recompense for their master's expense in caring for their children. Local authorities, midwives and unwed mothers therefore had a significant interest in rooting out the fathers of illegitimate children, and Chesapeake law vigorously supported their efforts.

The Maryland General Assembly addressed the problem in a statute of 1658, descriptively titled 'An Act Concearning Servants that have Bastards'. As in England, the statute stated that the testimonies of the mother herself, combined with the testimony of the midwife and other women present at the birth, were pivotal in proving paternity. If the woman could prove the father of her child in court, 'either by sufficient testimony of witnesses or confession', then the man she named as the father would be held legally responsible for financially supporting the child. If he was a servant, he would be bound to provide half of the child's maintenance, with his master providing the other half. If he was a freeman, he would be bound to the full charge of maintaining the child, and if the mother could prove that he had promised her marriage then he would be compelled to perform his promise 'or to recompense her abuse'. If she was not able to 'sufficiently' prove that 'the party charged to be the better of such child' then the mother risked having time added to her indenture contract to repay her master for the maintenance of the child. This proviso to the statute certainly must have compelled some unwed mothers to come forth and name the father of their children. The 1658 statute was affirmed by additional statutes in 1662 and 1669 which emphasised the centrality of the testimony of the mother 'in the extremity of her paynes and throwes of travaile' as a legally valid proof of the father's identity.[31]

Chesapeake servants charged with illegitimacy were in a more vulnerable position than their counterparts in England and New England, where maidservants were generally bound to their service contracts for a year or less and could leave their master's household with a quarter's notice. However, indenture contracts in colonies such as Maryland could stipulate seven to ten years of service before the woman would be freed and allowed to marry.[32] This situation became more complicated if it was widely suspected that the young woman's master was also the father of her child. In one case in 1659, when Ann Doob, Ann Hill, Katherine Gammer and midwife Anne Blunt attended the delivery of servant Elizabeth Lockett in Kent county, Maryland, they repeatedly questioned her about her relationship with her master, Matthew Read. Midwife Blunt and the matrons suspected that Read was the real father of Elizabeth's child and that Elizabeth had been coerced into silence to protect him. Matthew Read would have certainly had an incentive to keep Elizabeth quiet: if found to be the father he would be liable to bring the child up at his own expense, and he was a married man to boot. Elizabeth also had an incentive to name another man as the father of the child. Doing so would incur her master's good graces and would place the responsibility for the child on another man's shoulders. Elizabeth maintained that her master was not the father of her child, but the midwife and matrons remained suspicious. According to their depositions, the midwife and matrons asked Elizabeth what 'hur master dide to hure in the husks in the tobaco house'. Elizabeth responded that 'hur master did but tickell hur' and that 'she never knew hur Master but by his face and hands'. Perhaps still doubting Elizabeth's statement of the paternity of her child, Blunt made Elizabeth swear on the Bible 'when the childs heed wase in the birth' that her master was not the father. Elizabeth instead named Thomas Bright as the father, and that he 'promised hur mariege before the child wase gott'. The testimonies of the midwife and Elizabeth herself was enough to 'plainly convict' Bright as the father, and the magistrates ordered that he pay for Elizabeth's delivery and for the maintenance of the child.[33]

Female indentured servants in Maryland were under pressure from all sides to name the fathers of their illegitimate children. A master might pressure a servant to name another man as the father of the child, since he would incur any costs associated with the birth of the child and its upbringing if he was found to be the father. In 1673 Denise Holland, an indentured servant of Captain William Coleborn, appeared before the court to charge Henry Smith, another prominent landowner, with fathering her three-month-old child.[34] Though Coleborn was the legal master of Holland and held her indenture contract, she had become pregnant while 'on loan' to Smith as a temporary servant during the winter of 1672. In her petition before the magistrates, Holland recounted in detail how Henry Smith had coerced and seduced her while she lived with him, stating that she had not been in Smith's service a fortnight before he began to make advances towards her. 'Seeing he would not take my denyall and could not be quiet and being overperswaded by his sweete oratory', she stated, 'I yielded to his unjust request'. Despite Denise's protestations, Smith's advances continued over the next few weeks. When she discovered she was pregnant, Smith told her that 'it could be no worse then it is', and that she was 'his servant and he would doe what he pleased with me'.[35]

Whether Holland appeared before the court of her own volition or at the behest of her master is not clear. However, it is certain that Captain Coleborn, as Holland's legal master, would have been responsible for bearing the charges of her delivery and the maintenance of her child unless the true father could be ascertained, and he likely had a vested interest in seeing that Smith was prosecuted for the offence. It is also clear that Henry Smith did everything he could to avoid bearing responsibility for the child. Holland related to the court that Smith had first implored and then ordered her not to name him before the court, and that he would ensure that 'the midwife would not put me to my oath'. Further, he encouraged her to name Coleborn as the father, saying that 'if my master Captain Coleborn had but once occupied me that I should be sure not to spare him but to lay the child to him, forasmuch as he was best able to maintain it'.

Illegitimacy cases in England reflected the desire of the authorities to keep the mother and child from becoming a burden on the ratepayers. Midwives and local legal authorities worked together to root out the fathers of illegitimate children and compel them to pay for the child's upbringing. The testimony of Margarett Wainswright, a midwife practising in Colchester, was essential in two bastardy cases heard before the Quarter Sessions in the 1630s and 1640s. Margarett appeared before the court in 1638 to testify on behalf of unwed mother Joane Mumford. Margarett was clearly the leading witness in the case, with the other women present at the birth only confirming what she reported. Margarett testified that she was at Joane Mumford's delivery

> at the howse of Edmond Preston in Beerechurch the 23th daie of Februarie last 1637 when Joane Mumford was delivered of one male child & shee the said Margarett with the other women abovesaid did before at & after the tyme of that the said Joane Mumford was delivered of the said child, charge the said Joane to tell them whoe was the true father of the said child, shee the said Joane did saie that John Garland was the true father of that child, & that hee the said John Garland onlie did knowe her carnallie & none other.

The justices of the peace confirmed John Garland as the 'reputed father' of the child and ordered that he pay weekly to help maintain the child 'with meate drinke apparell and all other necessaries until the said child shall be of the age of seaven yeeres'.[36] In this case, the testimony of the midwife was sufficient for the justices to identify the father of the child and order him to pay maintenance.

In a similar case heard before the Colchester Quarter Sessions in 1641, Margarett Wainswright testified on behalf of Grace Thropley, another young woman charged with bastardy. Margarett stated that she was with Grace Thropley when she delivered a male baby, and 'shee charging the said Grace when she was in her greatest extremitie' to name the father of the child, Grace confessed it was Peter Clark and 'wished that if shee charged the said Peter Clarke wrongfully that shee might continue in that paine seaven yeeres that shee & that child might never parte if hee the said Peter Clarke were not the father of that child'. Margaret's testimony was again confirmed by other women who attended Grace during her delivery. Based on Margarett's testimony, the justices ordered that Clarke pay 2s 6d weekly to the churchwardens and overseers of the poor of St Giles in Colchester, who would then deliver the maintenance to Grace. Clarke was responsible for paying this early modern form of child support until the child reached the age of 14.[37]

Midwives would have been just as familiar with the courtroom as they would the birthing chamber, and their roles in securing financial support for unwed mothers and their children was pivotal. Anne Jeys, the 50-year-old midwife who attended the delivery of Mary Lee in April 1673, reported to the Borough Court in Colchester that Lee had charged William Pryor to be the father of her child. Jeys stated that when Lee was

> in the extremity of her paines uppon her delivery this deponent and the other women then there present charging her truely to discoverr & make knowned hoe was the father of the said child she did declare and affirm that the said William Prayor [sic] was the father of it and that none other ever had any carnall knowledg of her body but he.[38]

Elizabeth Drake and Elizabeth Hammond, the matrons present at Lee's delivery, corroborated Jeys's testimony, deposing that Lee 'did uppon her life and death declare and affirm that William Pryor was the father and that noe man but he had had any carnall knowledg of her'. The justices of the Quarter Sessions considered these testimonies sufficient proof of the paternity of the child and two weeks later they issued an order confirming Pryor as the father and outlining his responsibilities. Pryor was ordered to pay 20s to the churchwardens within six days of the order, 2s a week until the child was 12 years old, and £5 when the child came of age. Mary Lee, for her part, was given no punishment, but only ordered to maintain the child.[39]

In New England the problem of illegitimacy was dampened by the tendency of pregnant couples to marry once the woman's body started to show. Couples who married prior to the birth of the child might still receive a fine for fornication but the problem of the mother and child's maintenance was solved by the marriage. Shorter service contracts also allowed women who wanted to marry to do so more easily than the indentured servants in the Chesapeake. In a remarkably well-documented illegitimacy case from Massachusetts in 1674, maidservant Mary Talbut charged her fellow servant Obadiah Wood before the court in Ipswich with fathering her child, stating that he had often 'assured her & promised her marriage'. By claiming that she had been the victim of a broken marriage contract, Mary argued that she was not a whore but a virtuous woman who had simply been taken advantage of. At the time of her appearance before the court, Mary was about six months pregnant. She related that she had told Wood that she was carrying his child, 'and he did not disowne it'. Despite Mary's claim that she lived a chaste lifestyle and that 'no man but Obadiah Wood ever had to doe with her', Obadiah himself appeared in court to deny Mary's accusation. He deposed that she 'hath beene knowne to be much given to the company of young men, and did affect the company of some others more then my selfe'. He further testified that before Mary's pregnancy he had even offered marriage but she had refused him. It was not until she discovered she was pregnant that, according to Obadiah, Mary found herself 'put her into a necessity to seeke that as a cover to her folly'.[40]

Mary Talbut called no fewer than nine witnesses, seven of whom were women, to vouch for her virtuous lifestyle and to prove that she and Wood were betrothed before they began their sexual relationship. The witnesses who spoke on Mary's behalf testified that Mary and Obadiah had a verbal contract for marriage and that they were frequently in company together. The deposition of Mary Talbut, combined with the witnesses who spoke on her behalf, convinced the magistrates that Obadiah Wood was indeed the father of the child. Soon after Mary's delivery in early November 1674, the magistrates of the Ipswich court ordered Wood to pay Mary 3s per week every week, or at least 12s per month for the care of the child.[41]

In illegitimacy cases the man considered to be the rightful father of the child could sometimes be not a matter of biological paternity but a question of which man could best maintain the child.[42] The amount of evidence and testimonies a woman could marshal in her defence was key. Sara Stickney, a 35-year-old widow from Ipswich, Massachusetts, accused of bastardy in March 1681, first charged Samuel Lowell to be the father of her child. However, when Stickney's accusation against Lowell was found to be dubious, a year later she shifted her focus to another man, charging John Atkinson to be the father. Atkinson, a 49-year-old married man with nine children of his own, might have seemed an unlikely target. Nevertheless, Stickney maintained that Atkinson was the father of her child, and she had only concealed this fact at her last court appearance because Atkinson had promised to secretly maintain the child if she kept his identity from the authorities. Stickney related that

> a littell before Ipswich court which was in March last John Atkinson came to my house called mee out of my house & tould mee that the court was neer & that he was goeing to Boston & he said he was willing to speake with me before he went on which John Atkinson gave me thirty shillings in money & bid mee to be true to him.[43]

In addition to speaking on her own behalf, Stickney called over a dozen witnesses to buttress her case against Atkinson. John Stickney, Sarah's 16-year-old son, testified that Atkinson had sent him to fetch a quart of wine, which Atkinson and Sarah drank together at her house. On a different occasion, Atkinson had asked him to keep his horse out of sight while he stayed at the Stickney household.[44]

Atkinson, who denied Stickney's charge and felt himself much aggrieved by the accusation, asked for a jury to be impanelled to come to verdict in the case. The jury decided that Atkinson was 'the reputed father of Sarah Stickney's child [and] that the said Atkinson to pay from the brining upp of the child for the time past unto this time eight pounds in money & for the future to pay her 2s 6d. per week until September court'. Further, he had to pay court fees of £5.[45] Atkinson petitioned the court two months after his sentencing, alleging that his payments were too burdensome, and the court ordered that half his payments should be in money and the other half in provisions or clothing for the child.[46] Sarah Stickney's legal victories did not stop there. When Atkinson's wife called Sarah an 'impudent baud', Sarah even sued Atkinson for slander that same month and won.[47]

Midwives' testimonies in cases of infidelity

In legal cases involving an extra-marital relationship that produced a child, midwives played a pivotal role in questioning the woman during childbirth and estimating when the child might have been conceived. If a woman's husband was known to be away when the child was believed to be conceived, midwives could use that evidence before the court to argue that the child did not belong to him. The issue at stake in these cases was that husbands did not want to be financially responsible for a child that was not theirs, and the law upheld the responsibility of the true father to support the child. As one midwife put it, care was taken to 'put the saddle on the right horse'.[48] Since the mothers in these cases were married, their financial maintenance was not at issue: though they had apparently committed adultery, their husbands were still bound to provide for them unless the couple obtained a full divorce that dissolved the marriage.

In cases of paternity and marital infidelity, midwives acted as expert witnesses and as liaisons between the birthing chamber and the courtroom. Such was the case when Massachusetts midwife Waiborough Getchell testified in a paternity case concerning Ruth Williams in 1682.[49] Ruth's husband, Gregory Williams, was a sailor and was away at sea, and it was well known that he could not be the father of Ruth's newborn baby. Waiborough acted as the midwife in Ruth's delivery, and was subpoenaed in April by the constable of Marblehead along with two other female witnesses, Elizabeth Smith and Rebecca Sweet, to testify in the case. The court records note that Waiborough was so busy in her profession that she did not have time to appear in person before the court; Moses Maverick, a court examiner, was therefore sent to her home to take her testimony. In her deposition Waiborough reported that she had witnessed the birth of Ruth's child and that during her delivery Ruth had named Peter Goite the father. Elizabeth Smith and Rebecca Sweet testified that they had seen Goite go into Ruth's house late at night. Although according to the midwife's testimony Ruth had named Goite as the father of her child during her delivery, when Ruth came before the court to make her own testimony she disavowed this statement and maintained that her husband was the father of her child. However, in the end the magistrates sided with Waiborough's account of the situation. Goite was charged as the father of the child and was ordered to pay 4s per week for the first four weeks, and 3s per week after, for food and clothing for the child.[50]

Midwives in colonial Maryland could play a similar role in cases of marital infidelity and paternity, and they were often essential in pressing the woman to name the true father of the child. In April 1653 midwife Ann Johnson gave a lengthy testimony in an adultery and paternity case concerning Mary Taylor, the wife of Robert Taylor. Mary's child had been born full-term the previous December; however, according to the court records, Mary had taken a long trip to Virginia without her husband the previous spring, about the time the child would have been conceived. She had stayed in the house of George Ketchmey during her visit. Midwife Johnson related in her testimony that she, along with several other women, were present at Mary's delivery but had not pressed her at that time to speak about the child's father, 'for she had sorrow enough at that instant'. Johnson told the court that a few days after Mary's delivery she came back to the Taylor house to check on Mary and her child, at which time she confronted Mary about the child's paternity. Mary maintained that her husband was the true father of the child; however, Johnson pressed her, saying that 'it could not be so, for there was a writing in Mr Preston's hand would testifye the time of her going away'. Johnson related that when Mary asked her how she could believe she would do such a thing, she replied that 'had not the thing proved it self, I should never have believed it'.

The other women who testified in Mary's case confirmed Johnson's account and also added details of their own to support the argument that the baby could not be Robert Taylor's. According to Margaret Broome's testimony, the 'black headed boy' was 'like Ketchmey', and she urged Mary to 'not let your husband worke to maintain another man's child'. Johnson testified that she agreed with Margaret, and urged Mary Taylor to tell the truth about the child's paternity. Mary finally broke down and affirmed that George Ketchmey of Virginia was the father of the child. Midwife Johnson wanted to send word to Ketchmey in Virginia to make him own the child but her husband had talked her out of it, saying that she should 'have noe hand about it to bring him thither for fear of disturbance'.[51] Ann Johnson's detailed testimony before the court was enough to convict George Ketchmey as the father of Mary Taylor's child and the court ordered that Ketchmey pay Ann Johnson for the delivery of the child.[52]

Conclusion

For women seeking financial maintenance from husbands and from the fathers of their children, the law was an essential mechanism of support. It was often the case that the reality of human relationships did not match the patriarchal ideals set forth by religious authorities and social commentators: husbands abandoned wives and left them penniless, promises of marriage went unfulfilled and children were born outside of the economic and moral framework of the family. When marriages and the patriarchal family structure broke down, women could and did seek justice and restitution in the courts. By taking legal action, women had the opportunity to gain vital financial resources to maintain themselves and their children. Local legal authorities reinforced women's claims for financial support; authorities in all areas of the Anglo-American world had an interest in seeing that the moral and social order was upheld, and sought whenever possible to hold men accountable to their responsibilities.

The circumstances in which women argued for financial support varied according to the different economic and religious climates of England and America. In England the growing population and the increasing stress on the system of parish poor relief led local authorities to become more vigilant in holding husbands and fathers to their obligations to financially support their families. English legal authorities compelled husbands to provide for their wives, and ordered fathers charged with illegitimacy to support the child that was considered theirs. In the colonial Chesapeake the issue of a wife's right to maintenance and the problem of illegitimacy was also primarily an economic concern. Magistrates in Maryland upheld women's requests to live separately from their husbands and to be provided with maintenance sufficient to their social standings; the ultimate goal was to keep women from asking the local government officials for poor relief.

Illegitimacy in the Chesapeake, which primarily affected female servants, was of concern to authorities insofar as it restricted the productivity of the female workforce. Women who bore children during their years of service could not undertake the often-gruelling tasks required on tobacco plantations, for example. It was also possible that the woman might die during pregnancy or childbirth, leaving a master with no way to recoup the expense of her indenture. Women could certainly benefit from naming the fathers of their children before the court, since doing so would mean that the expense of caring for the child would become his responsibility and she would not have years added to her contract to repay her master.

While economic considerations were the most pivotal issues in England and the Chesapeake, in New England the strength of patriarchal ideals and the centrality of the Puritan theological outlook meant that questions concerning marriage and marriage breakdown were viewed within the larger context of achieving a godly society. Husbands who abandoned their wives and left them without sufficient maintenance were compelled to provide financial support because failure to do so would undermine the authority of patriarchy itself. Illegitimacy and the subsistence of women and children outside the protection of the patriarchal household also destabilised the centrality of male-led households.

Notes

1 Martin Ingram, *Church Courts, Sex, and Marriage in England, 1570–1640* (Cambridge: Cambridge University Press, 1987), pp. 234–6; Keith Wrightson, 'The nadir of English illegitimacy in the seventeenth century', in Peter Laslett, Karla Oosterveen and Richard M. Smith (eds), *Bastardy and Its Comparative History* (Cambridge, MA: Harvard University Press, 1980), p. 176.
2 Cornelia Hughes Dayton, 'Was there a Calvinist type of patriarchy? New Haven colony reconsidered in the early modern context', in Christopher Tomlins and Bruce Mann (eds), *The Many Legalities of Early America* (Chapel Hill: Omohundro Institute of Early American History and Culture, 2001), p. 344–5; Roger Thompson, *Sex in Middlesex: Popular Mores in a Massachusetts County, 1649–1699* (Amherst: University of Massachusetts Press, 1986), pp. 94–6, 104.
3 Debra Meyers, *Common Whores, Vertuous Women, and Loveing Wives: Free Will Christian Women in Colonial Maryland* (Bloomington: Indiana University Press, 2003).
4 Lois Green Carr and Lorena S. Walsh, 'The planter's wife: the experience of white women in seventeenth-century Maryland', *William and Mary Quarterly*, 3rd series, 34:4 (1977), p. 551.
5 Sara Butler, *Divorce in Medieval England: From One to Two Persons in Law* (New York: Routledge, 2013).
6 William Secker, *A Wedding Ring for the Finger* (Boston: Samuel Green, 1690), pp. 23–4, 26–7, 53–4.
7 Cornelia Hughes Dayton, *Women Before the Bar: Gender, Law, and Society in Connecticut, 1639–1789* (Chapel Hill: University of North Carolina Press, 1995), p. 110–11, 117;

Nancy Cott, 'Divorce and the changing status of women in eighteenth-century Massachusetts', *William and Mary Quarterly*, 3rd series, 33:4 (1976), pp. 586–614; Sheldon Cohen, 'What man hath put asunder: divorce in New Hampshire, 1681–1784', *Historical New Hampshire*, 41:3 (1986), pp. 118–41.

8 Lorena Walsh, '"Til death us do part": marriage and family in seventeenth-century Maryland', in Thad W. Tate and David L. Ammerman (eds), *The Chesapeake in the Seventeenth Century: Essays on Anglo-American Society* (New York: Norton, 1979), pp. 137–8.

9 Richard Morris, *Studies in the History of American Law: With Special Reference to the Seventeenth and Eighteenth Centuries* (New York: Octagon, 1930), pp. 126–8, 200; Cott, 'Divorce and the changing status of women', pp. 586–614; Cohen, 'What man hath put asunder', pp. 118–41.

10 London Metropolitan Archives (hereafter LMA), Middlesex Quarter Sessions Petitions, MJ/SP/1699/05/004, MJ/SP/1699/07/007, MJ/SP/1699/12/006, Petitions of Mary Gregory.

11 LMA, MJ/SP/02/005, Petition of Sarah Graves (1690).

12 Nathaniel B. Shurtleff (ed.), *Records of the Governor and Company of Massachusetts Bay in New England*, 6 vols (Boston: W. White, 1853–54), vol. 5, p. 188.

13 Shurtleff (ed.), *Records of the Governor and Company*, vol. 5, p. 248–9. See also Elizabeth Stevens' petition for divorce: Shurtleff (ed.), *Records of the Governor and Company*, vol. 4, pt. 2, p. 465.

14 George Francis Dow (ed.), *Records and Files of the Quarterly Courts of Essex County, 1636–1686*, 9 vols (Salem: Essex Institute, 1911), vol. 8, p. 87, accessed 11 October 2018 through http://salem.lib.virginia.edu/Essex/vol8/images/essex087.html; Shurtleff (ed.), *Records of the Governor and Company*, vol. 5, p. 317. For more petitions for maintenance from wives, see Rachel Clinton's petition, Dow (ed.), *Records and Files of the Quarterly Courts*, vol. 7, p. 100, accessed 11 October 2018 through http://salem.lib.virginia.edu/Essex/vol7/images/essex100.html; Mary Russell's petition, Dow (ed.), *Records and Files of the Quarterly Courts*, vol. 8, p. 344, accessed 11 October 2018 through http://salem.lib.virginia.edu/Essex/vol8/images/essex344.html.

15 Dow (ed.), *Records and Files of the Quarterly Courts*, vol. 6, p. 194, accessed 11 October 2018 through http://salem.lib.virginia.edu/Essex/vol6/images/essex194.html.

16 Dow (ed.), *Records and Files of the Quarterly Courts*, vol. 6, p. 297, accessed 11 October 2018 through http://salem.lib.virginia.edu/Essex/vol6/images/essex297.html.

17 Sidney Perley, *The Essex Antiquarian*, vol. 9 (Salem: The Essex Antiquarian, 1905), p. 88.

18 William Hand Browne (ed.), *Proceedings of the Council of Maryland, 1671–1681*, vol. 15 (Baltimore: Maryland Historical Society, 1896), pp. 321–2, accessed 11 October 2018 through https://msa.maryland.gov/megafile/msa/speccol/sc2900/sc2908/000001/000015/html/am15-321.html.

19 William Hand Browne (ed.), *Proceedings and Acts of the General Assembly, October 1678 – November 1683*, vol. 7 (Baltimore: Maryland Historical Society, 1889), p. 504, accessed 11 October 2018 through http://aomol.msa.maryland.gov/000001/000007/html/am7-504.html; Browne (ed.), *Proceedings of the Council of Maryland, 1671–1681*,

vol. 17, p. 192, accessed 11 October 2018 https://msa.maryland.gov/megafile/msa/speccol/sc2900/sc2908/000001/000017/html/am17-192.html.

20 Laura Gowing, 'Ordering the body: illegitimacy and female authority in seventeenth-century England', in Michael Braddick and John Walter (eds), *Negotiating Power in Early Modern Society: Order, Hierarchy, and Subordination in Britain and Ireland* (Cambridge: Cambridge University Press, 2000), pp. 45–9; Rebecca Jo Tannenbaum, *The Healer's Calling: Women and Medicine in Early New England* (Ithaca: Cornell University Press, 2002), p. 93–4; Mary Beth Norton, *Founding Mothers and Fathers: Gendered Power and the Forming of American Society* (New York: Knopf, 1996), pp. 222–39; Mary Beth Norton, '"The ablest midwife that wee knowe in the land": Mistress Alice Tilly and the women of Boston and Dorchester, 1649–1650', *William and Mary Quarterly*, 3rd series, 55:1 (1995), pp. 106–7; Else Hambleton, *Daughters of Eve: Pregnant Brides and Unwed Mothers in Seventeenth-Century Massachusetts* (New York: Routledge, 2004).

21 Michael Dalton, *Countrey Justice* (London: The Company of Stationers, 1655 [1618]), pp. 39–42.

22 Wrightson, 'The nadir of English illegitimacy in the seventeenth century', p. 178.

23 18 Eliz, c. 3 (1576).

24 7 Jac, c. 4 (1609).

25 Walter King, 'Punishment for bastardy in early seventeenth-century England', *Albion*, 10:2 (1978), pp. 136–7.

26 Dayton, *Women Before the Bar*, pp. 159–61.

27 From the deposition of Sarah Haines, a witness in the bastardy case against Sarah Stickney. Phillips Library (hereafter PL), Essex County Quarterly Courts, File Papers, 46-9-3. Salem, Massachusetts.

28 Shurtleff (ed.), *Records of the Governor and Company*, vol. 4, pt. 2, p. 394.

29 Hambleton, *Daughters of Eve*, p. xiv.

30 Carr and Walsh, 'The planter's wife', pp. 542, 545, 548; James Horn, *Adapting to a New World English Society in the Seventeenth-century Chesapeake* (Chapel Hill: University of North Carolina Press, 1994), p. 31.

31 William Hand Browne (ed.), *Proceedings and Acts of the General Assembly, January 1637/8 – September 1664*, vol. 1 (Baltimore: Maryland Historical Society, 1883), pp. 373–4, 441, accessed 11 October 2018 through https://msa.maryland.gov/megafile/msa/speccol/sc2900/sc2908/000001/000001/html/am1-373.html; Browne (ed.), *Proceedings and Acts of the General Assembly, 1666–1676*, vol. 2 (Baltimore: Maryland Historical Society, 1883), p. 216, accessed 11 October 2018 through https://msa.maryland.gov/megafile/msa/speccol/sc2900/sc2908/000001/000002/html/am2-216.html.

32 Norton, *Founding Mothers and Fathers*, p. 336.

33 J. Hall Pleasants (ed.), *Proceedings of the County Courts of Kent (1648–1676), Talbot (1662–1674), and Somerset (1665–1668) Counties*, vol. 54 (Baltimore: Maryland Historical Society, 1937), pp. 211–12, accessed 11 October 2018 through https://msa.maryland.gov/megafile/msa/speccol/sc2900/sc2908/000001/000054/html/am54-211.html.

34 Henry Smith had a long history of being in trouble with the law. See Irmina Wawrzyczek, 'The women of Accomack versus Henry Smith: gender, legal recourse, and the social

order in seventeenth-century Virginia', *Virginia Magazine of History and Biography*, 105:1 (1997).
35 Atwood S. Barwick (transcriber), *Somerset County Judicial Records, 1671–1675*, vol. 87 (Annapolis: Maryland State Archives, 1999), pp. 302–7, accessed 11 October 2018 through https://msa.maryland.gov/megafile/msa/speccol/sc2900/sc2908/000001/000087/html/am87-302.html.
36 Essex Record Office (hereafter ERO), Colchester Quarter Sessions, D/B 5 Sb 2/7, 9 April 1638.
37 ERO, Colchester Quarter Sessions, D/B 5 Sb 2/7, 1 June 1641.
38 ERO, D/B 5 Sb 2/7, 1 April 1673.
39 ERO, D/B 5 Sb 2/7, 14 April 1673.
40 PL, 22-67-1, 2, Essex County Quarterly Courts, File Papers.
41 PL, 22-67-2, 3, Essex County Quarterly Courts, File Papers; Dow (ed.), *Records and Files of the Quarterly Courts*, vol. 5, pp. 411–13, accessed 12 October 2018 through http://salem.lib.virginia.edu/Essex/vol5/images/essex411.html.
42 Gowing, 'Ordering the body', pp. 52–3.
43 PL, 46-11-1, Essex County Quarterly Courts, File Papers. This case is also examined in Hambleton, *Daughters of Eve*, chapter 5.
44 Dow (ed.), *Records and Files of the Quarterly Courts*, vol. 8, pp. 260–3, accessed 11 October 2018 through http://salem.lib.virginia.edu/Essex/vol8/images/essex260.html.
45 PL, 46-5-3, Essex County Quarterly Courts, File Papers.
46 Dow (ed.), *Records and Files of the Quarterly Courts*, vol. 8, p. 296, accessed 11 October 2018 through http://salem.lib.virginia.edu/Essex/vol8/images/essex296.html.
47 Dow (ed.), *Records and Files of the Quarterly Courts*, vol. 8, pp. 259–63, accessed 11 October 2018 through http://salem.lib.virginia.edu/Essex/vol8/images/essex259.html.
48 From the testimony of midwife Ann Johnson of Maryland, April 1653. William Hand Browne (ed.), *Judicial and Testamentary Business of the Provincial Court, 1649/50–1657*, vol. 10 (Baltimore: Maryland Historical Society, 1891), pp. 280–2, accessed 11 October 2018 through https://msa.maryland.gov/megafile/msa/speccol/sc2900/sc2908/000001/000010/html/am10-280.html.
49 Waiborough Getchell was the wife of John Getchell, and her unique name suggests that she may have been of Native American descent, although there is no conclusive evidence on this. The spelling of her name in the court documents is given variously Wibera, Waiboro, Wiburrough, Waiboroe.
50 Dow (ed.), *Records and Files of the Quarterly Court*, vol. 8, p. 345–6, accessed 11 October 2018 through http://salem.lib.virginia.edu/Essex/vol8/images/essex345.html; Tannenbaum, *The Healer's Calling*, p. 105.
51 Browne (ed.), *Judicial and Testamentary Business of the Provincial Court, 1649/50–1657*, vol. 10, pp. 280–2, accessed 11 October 2018 through https://msa.maryland.gov/megafile/msa/speccol/sc2900/sc2908/000001/000010/html/am10-280.html.
52 Browne (ed.), *Judicial and Testamentary Business of the Provincial Court, 1649/50–1657*, vol. 10, p. 442, accessed 11 October 2018 through https://msa.maryland.gov/megafile/msa/speccol/sc2900/sc2908/000001/000010/html/am10-442.html.

5

Inheritance and family feuds: the legal power of elite women

Elite women in England and the colonies were actively involved in litigation throughout their lives as they helped to manage large estates and ensure the inheritances of their children. With so much wealth and property at stake, these women could not afford to be uninformed about their legal rights and their claims to property. Women found it in their interests not only to be knowledgeable about the law but also to be actively involved in the maintenance and protection of that property. Armed with education, connections and resources, these women could often be formidable legal opponents. Women of the elite across the Anglo-American world had much in common: as members of the governing class, these women were often the mothers, wives, daughters and sisters of the men who served in positions of local authority, and as such had front-row seats to the practical workings of the law and personal connections to the powerful and influential.

The English women examined in this chapter ranked as members of the aristocracy, while elite women in the colonies often had close ties with aristocratic families in England. They possessed large amounts of land, often more than one estate, and a substantial amount of moveable property such as household furnishings, livestock, farm equipment and, in the colonies, slaves. Many of them kept legal books and treatises for reference in their own libraries, while others meticulously guarded the deeds, wills and marriage agreements that outlined their claims to property. Nearly all of them worked with family lawyers and legal advisors to ensure the protection of their property claims.

Yet pivotal differences in demographics and family composition, the availability of legal jurisdictions and distinctive religious outlooks shaped how and why elite women interacted with the law. In England family members vied with each other for control of wealth and property; widows who claimed their portions of the estate often got into protracted legal battles with their sons or step-sons who were eager to come into their inheritance. This was especially the case when widows lived into old age and retained control of a portion of the family estate for decades.[1]

In the Chesapeake Bay region, however, elite families were not marked by these bitter legal disputes between aging widows and heirs: widows often died before their children and step-children reached middle age, lessening the tensions between generations for control of family resources. Additionally, the traditional family in the Chesapeake had a shorter life-span than families in England and New England; spouses often died and remarried, creating blended families of step-parents and step-children. Men therefore provided generously for their widows and gave them a great deal of control over property even if they chose to remarry. By trusting widows with more control over property, men ensured that the resources left after their deaths would be used for the benefit of their children and not a greedy step-father.[2]

Colonies such as Maryland also embraced the example of English canon law, which gave women the right to act as executors to the estates of their late husbands. The Dissenter colonies in New England, however, eschewed this connection with the English ecclesiastical jurisdiction and instead embraced the patriarchal rights of fathers, husbands and sons upheld by the common law. For Puritans, giving women the ability to control property made them independent of the patriarchal family and undermined the authority of male heads of households, which was the foundation of the social and moral order.[3]

Marriage, inheritance and women's property

The patriarchal family and the restrictions surrounding married women's relationship to property applied to women of the elite just as they did to women further down the social hierarchy. Women of the elite surrendered their rights to property upon their marriages, and husbands had the right to manage and reap the benefits of the property his wife brought into the marriage. A wife had to gain her husband's consent before making a will bequeathing property to heirs of her choice. English inheritance practices reflected and reinforced this patriarchal worldview. Under the common-law rules of primogeniture, which had been established in England since the mid-thirteenth century, real property held by a father at his death descended to his eldest son, with daughters and younger sons inheriting moveable property jointly. In the absence of a son, daughters inherited real estate and moveable property jointly. The increasing use of entails in the seventeenth and eighteenth centuries added an additional barrier to daughters' inheritance: entails could stipulate that the estate would pass to the nearest male descendant of the settlor, which might favour a collateral male relative over a nearer female descendant.[4]

Common law did, however, entitle widows to the use of one-third of the real and moveable property left by their husbands. This was a widow's dower right, which extended over any land a widow's husband had held at any time during their marriage, not just the land he owned at his death. A husband who wished to sell part of the estate had to have his wife's consent; if he did not have it, his widow could claim a dower right against the purchaser. Widows could collect dower rights even if the estate was entailed to an heir, and she could not make a contract that sold or gave away dower lands. If a husband left a will, he could choose to leave his widow more property, but not less. Dower rights ensured that a widow would not be left destitute and turned out of the house by an heir eager to take hold of the estate.[5]

Over the course of the seventeenth century, dower rights became more difficult to claim, and wealthy families devised a variety of different legal mechanisms to ensure that a once-wealthy woman would not be impoverished by a spendthrift husband. Prenuptial marriage settlements went some way towards circumventing these common law practices and making their access to property more secure. Often these marriage settlements took the form of a jointure, a legal mechanism enforceable in equity courts that stipulated that if one of the partners should die, the other would inherit a lifetime interest in a portion of land exclusively set aside for their benefit.[6] Jointure agreements had two advantages over dower rights: claiming dower rights might take years if the heir to the estate contested the widow's right to it. In contrast, jointure lands descended to the widow on the day her husband died. Additionally, jointures were more flexible: unlike dower rights, which excluded any land held by copyhold, leasehold or land that had been entailed, jointures guaranteed the use of any lands stipulated in the agreement.[7] There were drawbacks to jointure agreements, however. By the terms of the Statute of Uses (1536), a woman who agreed to a jointure settlement prior to her marriage nullified her ability to collect her dower rights under common law. In other words, a widow could not collect both her dower rights and her jointure rights. This law worked to a widow's advantage so long as the jointure provided her with an estate equal to or greater than that which she could have claimed as her dower right.[8]

While jointure benefits could fall to a husband or to a wife, jointure agreements were particularly important for women. Men were, of course, never bound by the doctrine of coverture; their relationship to property did not change when they married, and the land they owned prior to marriage was still theirs once they entered wedlock. With women, this was not the case. Women of the elite were well aware of the dangers that could befall them if they failed to ensure and protect the property that would sustain them if they became widows. Even the most well-meaning husbands sometimes fell into debt, and unless there was some legal contract barring it, the wealth or property that a wife had brought into the marriage could be sold in a way that did not benefit her in the slightest.[9]

The Chesapeake colonies followed English precedent in establishing the practice of primogeniture from the earliest days of settlement. The growth of large tobacco plantations also made entails an attractive option for families of the colonial elite, and both Maryland and Virginia passed successive laws that made it more difficult to reverse the terms of an entail.[10] However, as in England, a widow's rights to property were upheld by the practice of dower rights as well as marriage settlements and jointures.[11] A Maryland law of 1642 guaranteed a widow the use of at least one-third of her husband's real estate after his death; if the marriage had been childless, she was entitled by law to receive the estate in its entirety.[12] The relative liberality of the laws regarding widow's portions reflects the unique demography of the Chesapeake as well as the diversity of religious outlooks. In Maryland and Virginia the life-span of the traditional family was short: parents succumbed to a variety of diseases rampant in the region, including malaria, and it often happened that one partner would die and remarry before the children came of age.[13] Chesapeake men took care to provide well for their widows and trusted them to use the resources left to them for the benefit of their children and protect them from profligate step-fathers.

The relatively privileged status of widows under Chesapeake law stood in stark contrast to women in New England, where a widow's right to collect dower was more uncertain and ambiguous. *The Book of the General Lawes and Libertyes Concerning the Inhabitants of Massachusetts* of 1648 gave widows the use of a 'competent portion' of their husbands' estates, but left the exact portion of land and moveable property to the discretion of the magistrates. Reflecting the Puritan focus on harmony and reciprocity within the household, the law stated that widows who had separated from their husbands were not eligible to receive dower rights; however, this did not include cases in which a wife had been deserted, or in case of a divorce 'where she is the innocent partie'. Further, it stipulated that only widows who 'shall not commit or foster any strip or wast' to the property would be judged worthy of its possession.[14]

In addition to leaving the status of widows' inheritance up to the discretion of the magistrates, the New England colonies also departed significantly from English common law tradition in inheritance practices. The earliest inheritance laws in Massachusetts, Rhode Island and Connecticut left the distribution of property among heirs to the decision of local authorities. At the beginning of the eighteenth century, the New England colonies began practicing multigeniture, which granted the eldest male heir a double share of his father's real estate, with younger sons and daughters inheriting one share each.[15] This more egalitarian view of descendant's inheritance benefitted daughters before their marriages, and may have been crucial in attracting a good marriage partner. However, upon the marriage of these daughters, control of the property passed to their husbands.

Elite women in England: marriage settlements and family feuds

Marriage settlements were quite effective in providing wives with some financial protection and the guarantee of an income should they become widows. However, marriage settlements were the subject of endless legal battles between family members. The central conflict in these legal cases was that while a widow secured a lifetime income from the property named in her marriage contract, at the same time she barred the next heir from his full inheritance. Wealthy widows with lifetime interests in portions of the estate could be perceived by male heirs as obstacles that had to be overcome. The protracted and bitter legal disputes that resulted from this situation pitted aging mothers against adult sons and step-sons, and undermined patriarchal ideas of mutual obligations and reciprocity. To maintain control of the property that would provide their income during their widowhood, women had to seek protection from outside of the patriarchal family. The law alone had the power to enforce the legal agreements that guaranteed women financial security as widows.

While married women were barred from prosecuting or defending legal cases in common law courts without their husbands, wives went to great lengths to legally protect jointure lands that would be their maintenance if their husbands died. The official court documents often name these women as co-parties with their husbands and other relatives; however, it is clear from their letters, accounts and inventories that they were integrally involved in the prosecution and direction of their cases. This was especially true in cases in which a wife had an interest in the property by right of her marriage settlement or inheritance. This should not be surprising: it was clearly in a wife's interest to seek legal protection of jointure lands, since the lands would guarantee her an income during her widowhood.

As the mothers, wives and sisters of men who had been extensively trained in the law, women possessed a detailed understanding of English law that may have been cultivated by close contact with kinsmen who acted as legal officials. Aristocratic women in England were often related to the most prominent legal officials in the land. The skill with which Lady Hester Sandys Temple prosecuted her many legal cases reflected her family's many connections to the English legal regime. In 1595 Lady Hester married Sir Thomas Temple, who had trained in the law at Lincoln's Inn and served as High Sheriff for Oxfordshire in 1606/7, for Buckinghamshire in 1616/17 and for Warwickshire in 1620/21.[16] Through the marriage of her daughter Bridget Temple, Hester was also related to John Lenthall, one of the Six Clerks of the Court of Chancery.[17]

An inventory of the library of Lady Hester Temple drawn up in the 1650s shows that she purchased a copy of William Leonard's *Reports and Cases of Law Argued and Adjudged in the Courts of Law at Westminster*, a digest of cases heard in King's Bench, Common Pleas and the Court of Exchequer compiled in the late sixteenth century, and Sir Edward Coke's *Reports*, a compendium of famous cases and an essential reference book for seventeenth-century lawyers.[18] Lady Hester's inventory also included legal tracts that probably circulated in manuscript form: the list included titles such as the 'Layman's Lawyer' and 'The Exact Lawgiver'.[19] Given her extensive involvement in litigation throughout her life, and the fact that the inventory was drawn up in her own hand, it is likely that she was the one who purchased these books and consulted them as she pursued her legal affairs.

The letters and correspondence of Lady Hester Temple show that she was often actively involved in administering and managing any lawsuits that arose concerning her jointure lands. After she married Sir Thomas Temple in 1595, the couple held land in Warwickshire jointly as husband and wife, with Hester having a lifetime interest in the land should her husband die before her. Though she was under coverture during her forty-two-year marriage, and was always named as a co-party with her husband in any legal suit in which she was involved, she nevertheless was centrally involved protecting the lands that would be hers should she become a widow. Between 1613 and 1655 she was party to no fewer than fourteen legal cases, most of which involved the protection of land in Warwickshire.

The issue that caused decades of strife within the Temple family was that both Lady Hester and Sir Thomas Temple lived long and active lives, a fact that kept their son and heir Peter Temple from gaining his full inheritance until he was well into adulthood. Peter Temple was, by Hester and Thomas' account, a profligate and excessive spender who lived well beyond his means and was in constant need of cash. In an effort to help him financially, Lady Hester and Sir Thomas borrowed £10,000 against the value of their Warwickshire jointures lands to provide Peter with a short-term loan.[20] In 1629, after years of waiting for the loan to be repaid, Hester and Thomas brought a suit against Peter in the Court of Chancery in an attempt to force him to repay the debt. If he did not, they would be forced to forfeit the lands, a situation that would leave Lady Hester with very little income should she become a widow.[21]

Lady Hester understandably viewed the protection of the jointure lands as critically important, and spent a good deal of time writing to legal advisors and personally travelling to London to help manage the case against her son. The frequent letters she received from the family attorney, Robert Payton, reflect that Lady Hester followed the case with the utmost care and was well acquainted with its details. In the spring of 1629 Hester sent Payton to London to obtain copies of the depositions of witnesses involved in the case. He wrote to her of his dealings with the clerks of the court in detail on 16 March 1629. He suspected that one of the court officers 'did not deale clerely with you when you tooke out your copies' of the interrogatories of witnesses in the case. He continued that 'when you had your copies out there were 35 interrogatories in courte but you had copies ... only of 12'. According to Payton, 'this was not fayrely done ... for by this meanes our informacion will fall shorte'.[22] Two days later, Payton wrote to Hester that he had convinced the clerk to give him copies of the missing interrogatories and had also obtained copies of 'Sir Peters 2 severall affidavittes which are all that he hath made and filed'. After receiving Payton's letters, Hester decided to travel to London herself to help manage the case, asking one of her younger sons, a lawyer in training at Lincoln's Inn, to arrange lodging for her near the Court of Chancery.[23] Her son Thomas wrote to her from Lincoln's Inn in anticipation of her arrival, saying that he had finally secured the depositions in the case but that he would do nothing until she arrived.[24]

After the death of Sir Thomas Temple in 1637, Lady Hester continued to be actively involved in her family's legal affairs. As a widow, Lady Hester was party to nine cases in the Court of Wards and the Court of Chancery.[25] In December 1639, then aged 70, she petitioned the Commissioners of Chancery when her son, now Sir Peter Temple, lodged a complaint against her. According to Sir Peter's account, his mother had failed to pay a debt owed to the vicarage at the family seat at Burton

Dasset, Warwickshire. Sir Peter alleged that the debt was his mother's responsibility, since she claimed a portion of the land at Burton Dasset as part of her jointure.[26] In her petition to the Commissioners of Chancery, she explained that 'each partie should pay his proportionable parte, which I am readye to do', but that she knew that 'my sonne will stand hard against me, indeavouring to lay the whole arreare upon me'. She asked that she not be bound to 'paying beyond my proportion'.[27] The Commissioners granted her request that she only pay a portion of the arrears with the remainder falling to her son Sir John.

The discord between Lady Hester and her son Sir Peter Temple show that the patriarchal ideals of reciprocal obligations and family harmony could break down. Family relationships did indeed become strained and complicated when an adult son was expected to defer to the wishes of his aging mother: when a male heir inherited his father's titles and estates, he became the new head of the family and expected deference from subordinates, even his mother. Widows who lived into their eighties, as Lady Hester did, were not only dependent upon their marriage settlements for their maintenance in their old age, they were also vilified for standing in the way of the male heir inheriting the full estate. As Lady Hester Temple's cases showed, property that was guaranteed to a wife under the terms of a marriage settlement gave her an interest in protecting that property, even during her marriage. While Lady Hester could not bring a suit in a common law court independently of her husband, her letters and correspondence show that she was clearly involved in ensuring that the land that would become hers if she became a widow was protected. In Lady Hester's case, she outlived her husband by nearly twenty years and her hard work in protecting this property throughout her marriage paid off.

Patriarchal family relationships and women's relationship to property was further complicated by early deaths, remarriages and the creation of blended families of step-parents and step-children. A widow who possessed jointure rights from a previous marriage and chose to marry again would often negotiate another prenuptial contract with her new husband, ensuring her financial security should she become a widow yet again. Such was the case with Lady Judith Smith Barrington. Under the terms of her marriage settlement with her first husband, Sir George Smith, Lady Judith would receive jointure lands in Flamstead, Hertfordshire, should she become a widow. Sir George died in 1620 fighting in the Palatinate in the Thirty Years' War, and Lady Judith, who was still a young woman in her twenties, married Sir Thomas Barrington in 1624. Upon their marriage, Lady Judith became a step-mother to Sir Thomas's four young children by his first wife. The terms of her marriage contract with Sir Thomas entitled her to a house in London on Great Queen's Street, properties in Essex and the manor of Swanston on the Isle of Wight as her jointure lands. While Sir Thomas and Lady Judith held all of these properties jointly during their twenty-year marriage, Lady Judith was integrally involved in protecting and maintaining her interest in the lands, even while she was under coverture. She clearly had an incentive to protect the land since it would become part of her maintenance should she become a widow. She was also careful keep copies of her marriage contracts, deeds and wills that would ensure her claims to land. She maintained what she called her 'evidence trunk', which included deeds, inventories, bills and other documents relating to her jointure lands in Hertfordshire and Swanston. She had a clear organisation for these documents that she laid out for the family steward, John Kendall: she wrote to him that she had a 'black box that is titled my purchase lands' and that 'my boxe of my jointure deeds is by ittselfe'.[28]

It was essential that women kept track of these documents: they were absolutely necessary to prove their claims to land if any legal dispute arose. Lady Judith seemed well aware of the value of being organised and prepared. When Sir John Bingley, who owned land next to Swanston, brought a suit against the Barringtons in the Court of Chancery in 1632, Lady Judith gave her steward detailed instructions concerning the documents and advice he would need to pursue the case in London. Unlike Hester Temple, Lady Judith did not go to London herself to oversee the case, although her letters show that she was integrally involved in managing the lawsuit through detailed instructions to her agents from the family estate in Essex. Her letters reflect that she possessed a detailed knowledge of the particulars of the case and also had a keen sense of strategy in dealing with her opponents and legal counsel. She wrote to Kendall that to 'consider whether its not better for us to entertaine an atturney in London if the suite must be followed at London'. She added that the property in question 'is soe certainly ours that its a cleer case', but that 'we must be watchefull & diligent; and not delaye witnesses and proofes soe late as our counsell will have noe convenient time to consider thorowly of them'. She enclosed the documents Kendall would need to prove the Barrington's ownership of the land: 'Heer is all the papers concerning that busines. Loose not them … if you must leave them with counsell then be sure you take a coppy least it be lost.'[29]

The relationship between Sir Thomas and Lady Judith seems to have been one of mutual respect, but conflicts about property and its management could arise between even the most affectionate of husbands and wives. Lady Judith had long been of the opinion that her husband was not as careful with his money or his estates as he should have been, and her letters show that she was continually frustrated with her husband's ill-management of their jointure properties. She therefore had been careful to ensure the protection of her land and estate should he predecease her. She wrote to John Kendall in 1632 that she was glad he had encouraged Sir Thomas to initiate a legal suit to protect the timber on the Swanston estate. She wrote: 'I think it wear very fitt you gott your master to begin a suite with John Smyth aboute his spoyling Cottingham Woods.'[30] She also charged Kendall with reminding Sir Thomas, who was in London, of the specifics of the case, writing that the Chancery case was a matter of 'great consequence', and Sir Thomas would need to be continually 'put in mind of it'.[31]

Another potential conflict arose when Sir Thomas sold Lady Judith's jointure property from her first marriage to pay one of his outstanding debts. Since Lady Judith was under coverture, and therefore all of her property was her husband's, this was a perfectly legal action for him to take. While Lady Judith apparently gave her consent to the sale of the Flamstead property, she was careful that such an event would not happen again. In 1638 Lady Judith authorised Kendall to repurchase the manor of Flamstead for £300, and place the property in trust for her during her marriage to Sir Thomas. Sir Thomas would therefore have no claim to ownership of the property and could not sell it under any circumstances. While Kendall acted as the trustee for the property, Lady Judith retained control of the any profits arising from the land.[32]

When Thomas Barrington died in 1644 Lady Judith almost immediately came into conflict with Sir Thomas's son and heir, Sir John Barrington, who clearly resented the fact that his step-mother had such a generous claim to the family property.[33] Sir Thomas had died intestate, meaning he left no will and therefore no specific instructions for Lady Judith's portion for her widowhood outside of the jointure lands stipulated in her marriage contract. As a widow and thus no longer under coverture, Lady Judith reclaimed her jointure land from her first marriage that had been put in trust with Kendall and also now claimed the jointure estates in London, Essex and the manor of Swanston on the Isle of Wight that had been part of her contract with Sir Thomas. As a widow with a lifetime interest in the land, Lady Judith had complete control over the management of the land and its natural resources. However, Sir John also had an interest in seeing that the land and its resources were not spoiled or squandered since they would revert to him as part of his estate upon Lady Judith's death.

For years, step-mother and step-son attempted to settle their differences out of court, but their correspondence reflects that the two were coming into increasing conflict with one another. Sir John's correspondence with his step-mother reflects that he felt some resentment towards her holding of land that he felt was his. One of the issues at play in the dispute was Lady Judith's right to fell timber on the Swanston lands. Sir John wrote to Lady Judith in May 1647 that she would 'be as carefull to preserve my right as you are desirous of a little profit, and as willing to allowe mee my due as you looke to have what is yours'.[34] According to Sir John, Lady Judith did have a rightful claim to the land itself, but had no right to profit from the sale of the timber on the land. Sir John wrote that Lady Judith attempted to 'deface my inheretance by destroying my timber upon your joyntur. I beg nothing but what is fitting, the inheritance being mine'.[35] Lady Judith fired back, writing to Sir John that she had to fell the trees on 'her' land to make repairs to her tenant's houses. This was one of the obligations she had as lady of the manor, and her failure to make sufficient repairs to the property would decrease its value. She explained, 'I must fell for suffitient suplyes for repaires and such like that I am to provide my tenants (theire houseing being left to me too much out of repaires) else you would another day more blame me for ruins.'[36]

The conflict between Lady Judith and Sir John erupted into litigation in the late 1640s when Lady Judith began to determinedly pursue legal action against him in Chancery. Lady Judith was clearly a well-known and well-respected member of the gentry and she had many connections with the Cromwellian government in London, including Bulstrode Whitelocke, one of the justices of the Court of Chancery. It seems that she used all of the connections she had to pursue legal action against her step-son. Sir John was incensed by his step-mother's legal actions and claimed in a petition to Parliament that Lady Judith had insinuated herself into the good graces of the justices of Chancery, and 'with all violence' proceeded against him, and had obtained an 'injurious decree' against him for contempt of court.[37]

In 1652 Sir John entered two cases in Chancery against Lady Judith, one claiming an interest in her jointure lands in Essex and one for her lands in the Isle of Wight. Sir John's case hinged on his assertion that Lady Judith's right to the jointure land such as Swanston was contingent upon her having children by Sir Thomas. Since the marriage had been childless, Sir John claimed the jointure lands reverted to him as the eldest male heir of his father. Beleaguered by the constant litigation with her step-son, Lady Judith's tactic was to stall: she successfully delayed the case from progressing by procuring an order to have Sir John's cases dismissed because he had failed to file his pleadings in the time allowed.³⁸ Chancery finally ruled against her in 1657, the year before her death. However, that Lady Judith continued to control the lands for the majority of her widowhood reflects her adept management of litigation concerning her property.³⁹

As Lady Hester Temple's and Lady Judith Barrington's cases reflect, women of the English elite could not afford to be ignorant or neglectful of their rights under the law and found it in their interest to be centrally involved in any legal action involving their property. Widows who lived for decades after the deaths of their spouses came into conflict with their husband's heirs, who might resent the fact that their mothers and step-mothers possessed a fairly generous portion of what he considered his estate. In these cases, women had recourse to the law when patriarchal family relationships broke down, and when sons and step-sons could not be relied upon to promote the interests of their mothers.⁴⁰

Elite women in the colonial Chesapeake Bay region: marriage, death and remarriage

While some wealthy families in the Chesapeake used jointures and marriage settlements to protect a widow's financial security, Maryland and Virginia had robust practices in place for securing dower rights. Jointures were therefore not frequently used in the seventeenth century. In Maryland and Virginia, common law granted widows a life interest in one-third of the land and moveable property that the couple had held during their marriage; if a husband left his wife less than dower thirds, she had the option to disregard the will and claim her dower rights. However, men in Maryland very often bequeathed more to their wives than the one-third share stipulated by law; in St. Mary's and Charles counties, more than 75 per cent of men left their wives more than law of dower required and often gave them outright ownership of the moveable property to the estate. One-fifth of husbands gave their wives the whole estate even if there were children; this indicated the husband trusted his wife to make equitable bequests to the children in her own will. If there were no children, a man nearly always left his widow the entire estate.⁴¹

The more generous laws regarding widow's property in the Chesapeake was a product of the frequency of death and remarriage. Diseases were rampant in the marshy and damp climate of Chesapeake Bay, and death, widowhood and remarriage was the norm. The tendency for men to leave their wives in possession of most of their estates meant that there was a lively marriage market for wealthy widows, who, considering the dearth of women in the colony, often had their choice of marriage partners. High-status Maryland widows might act as the executors of two or three husbands' estates over the course of their lifetimes, each time gaining more experience with the law and amassing more property to their own use.

The three successive marriages of Jane Fenwick Smith Taylor Eltonhead allowed her to accumulate a substantial amount of property. She was the executor of each of her husbands' estates, and at her death in 1659 left a substantial property to her four children. To Gertrude and Jane Smith, her daughters from her marriage to Thomas Smith, she left some household goods, half of her livestock, a mare and three servants.[42] To her two children by Philip Taylor, she left an estate of 2,000 acres at Cedar Point to her son Thomas Taylor and all her moveable goods to her daughter Sarah Taylor.[43] She married her third husband, William Eltonhead, in 1650. After he was captured and executed by parliamentary forces at the Battle of the Severn in 1655, Jane was a party to at least fifteen different legal cases as she settled his estate.[44] In September 1657 she sued the estate of Edmond Scarborough for 'satisfaction for six oxen' owing to the Eltonhead estate, and the following year she brought suit against Josias Fendall for 2,000 lb of tobacco.[45] In October 1658 Jane also petitioned the Provincial Court to have Eltonhead's assets, which had been sequestered by the court after his conviction for treason, returned to her as his widow. Eltonhead's estate, while not vast, was still substantial: at his death he possessed 1,130 acres of land, over 14,000 lb of tobacco and the indentures of two servants.[46]

In her petition, Jane lamented that her husband had made an oral will while he was imprisoned after his capture, in which he had left 'all his lands with all his other goods & cattles to her disposing, for the good of her & her children & desyred her to allow unto Robert Fenwick & Richard Fenwick [Jane's nephews] some part of the lands, according to her discretion'. The court ordered that, considering the unavailability of pen, ink and paper in prison, William Eltonhead could not have been able to make his will in writing 'as in law is requyred for the passing of lands by testament', and that 'Jane Eltonhead shall possesse the said land in as full, free, & large estate as if the said William had conceaved his will in writing'.

Jane Eltonhead was certainly central in the process of securing her possession of William's estates, yet her male family members, many of whom were among the leaders of the colony, also clearly had an interest in seeing that their kinswoman retained control of the Eltonhead property. Jane's brother Cuthbert Fenwick, for instance, sat as a Justice of the Peace for St. Mary's County. Jane's male relatives who sat on the bench of the Provincial Court ensured that Jane retained legal ownership of the Eltonhead estate, even against the claims of William's younger brother Richard Eltonhead. William had no living descendants at the time of his death and his brother was therefore the heir to William's estates in both England and possibly America. However, Maryland law stipulated that the deceased nearest kin in the colony would be privileged over next of kin elsewhere. Since Richard Eltonhead lived in England, this law gave Jane a strong claim to the Eltonhead estate in Maryland. She asked the court to debar any of William's kinsmen from claiming the estate from her, stating that 'all the heyres att laww of the said William are for ever barred all claime to the said lands'.[47] At times, women retained control of property both because they were willing to fight for it, and also because it was in the interest of their male relatives to keep property in the family.

Unlike families of the English elite, wealthy planters in the Chesapeake were not plagued by intergenerational conflict. Jane Eltonhead had four children who lived to adulthood from two different marriages, yet there is no trace that any of them pursued legal conflicts with their mother after the deaths of their respective fathers. With land and opportunity in ready supply, heirs often had enough land at their disposal even if their parents or step-parents lived to old age. However, it was rare for anyone in the Chesapeake to live past the age of 60, and in fact most died much younger. Jane Eltonhead was only 44 when she died in 1659, with her children still in their teens and early twenties at the time. The shorter life-spans of people in the Chesapeake acted as a release valve for conflict between successive generations; it was likely that the older generation would pass on before the younger generation had a chance to become overly eager for their inheritance.

Jane Eltonhead was successful in securing access to her late husband's estate against the claims of his creditors and his kinsmen. Jane managed the properties she collected from her successive marriages in such a way that she was able to leave a substantial inheritance to her children. Yet things did not always go so smoothly for widows in the Chesapeake: estates in Maryland were often heavily encumbered with debt, and the payment of creditors from an estate had the potential to encroach on the payment of the widow's portion. In theory, a Maryland widow should collect at least one-third of her husband's property; however, estate creditors were often eager to be repaid and became frustrated when they felt a widow had collected what they considered more than her fair share. Such situations could plague a widow for years as she attempted to protect what was due to her from the estate of her husband against his many would-be creditors.

One particularly shrewd marriage settlement negotiated between Mary Perry and John Bateman anticipated this eventuality. Mary Perry and John Bateman married in London in August 1649 and ten years later set sail for Maryland after John received a patent to farm a parcel of land along the Susquehanna River. John Bateman had been a wealthy London haberdasher and had made a fortune in trade prior to his move to Maryland. Upon his arrival in the colony, John sat as a member of the Maryland governor's council and as a justice on the Provincial Court. He also owned substantial properties in Maryland and Virginia, amounting to 7,000 acres.[48] When he died in 1663 he left behind not only a sizeable estate in real and personal property but also an astute widow who managed to secure access to the large estate against the claims of John's many creditors.

Soon after John's death, Mary's mother, Margaret Perry of London, sent a copy of Mary's marriage settlement to the Maryland Provincial Court. Under the terms of the marriage settlement, signed in London in August 1649, John had contracted a £2,000 bond with Margaret Perry, ensuring that he would leave Mary at least £1,000 in lands or personal property as her maintenance should she become a widow. If John failed to leave Mary the £1,000 of property in his will, the initial bond of £2,000 could then be redeemed against his estate. The problem was that John Bateman's estate was heavily encumbered with debt: according to an inventory Mary filed in the Provincial Court, the Bateman estate was worth only about £870 after the debts were paid, a sum which fell short of the £1,000 mark stipulated in the marriage agreement. Mary's mother, Margaret Perry, therefore entered a suit to claim the £2,000 owed to her daughter. The strategy here was that Mary now became the preferred creditor and would thus be paid out of the estate first before any of the other creditors. Ensuring that Mary would receive some financial security should she become a widow, even if Bateman's estate was encumbered with debt, was certainly the intent of the original marriage settlement. In December 1664 the Provincial Court ruled that Mary would be the sole recipient of the remainder of John Bateman's estate under the terms of the marriage settlement and the bond guaranteed by her mother.[49]

Marriage settlements of the kind drawn up between John Bateman and Mary Perry, which stipulated that a husband must leave his widow a certain sum or be penalised, were certainly unusual. At the time the settlement was drawn up, John and Mary, both from trading families, were both rich in cash and business connections rather than in land, so it would make sense that the marriage contract would concern cash rather than a landed estate. Mary only became the beneficiary of real property after they moved to Maryland and established a plantation.

After securing the £2,000 sum due to her from her marriage settlement, a sum that was now solely hers and could not be used to pay John's debts, Mary went about settling the estate. Mary used petitions to the court as well as litigation to ensure that debtors to the Bateman estate paid their just dues. Between 1664 and 1666 she submitted twelve petitions to the Maryland Provincial Court, brought fourteen different suits as a plaintiff against debtors to the Bateman estate and acted as a defendant in five suits brought by creditors of the estate.[50] This combination of petitions and litigation was Mary's method for the next two years as she collected debts due to the estate. She appointed Thomas Manning to be her attorney as she settled the estate; Manning was one of the most educated men in the colony, acting as Attorney General for the province from 1660 to 1663, as sheriff in 1665 and as a burgess for Calvert County from 1661 to 1669. However, the court records show that Mary was integrally involved in the progression of her suits and that she often appeared before the court herself to submit her petitions or to call witnesses on her behalf.[51]

On 13 February 1663 Mary entered suits against Augustine Herman and the estate of Richard Wright for the collection of debts due to the Bateman estate.[52] Only a few days later, on 17 February, she entered petitions to the Provincial Court asking that the court grant her 'speedy payment' for these debts and demanded that the court administer the estate of Richard Wright, which stood indebted to the Bateman estate for 1,445 lb of tobacco and £9 10s. She explained that there was as yet 'no executor or administrator to represent [Wright's] estate or answere for it: by reason of which shee can commence noe suite att law for recovery of her right'. In a separate petition, she complained against Augustine Herman, who owed the Bateman estate 5,000 lb of tobacco and £5 sterling, which Herman was refusing to pay. At the court session on 26 March 1664 she put in a writ against James Jolly and also petitioned the court that Jolly pay her the 1,200 lb of tobacco he owed to the estate.[53]

Though the court's decision to uphold Mary's position as a privileged creditor of the Bateman estate certainly benefitted her, the other creditors of the estate were not as happy with the court's ruling. John Bateman had acted as a trustee for a London merchant named Henry Scarborough, who had authorised John to invest his resources in the colony. Under the terms of the trust, Scarborough had placed £1,000 in a trust to John Bateman, who was supposed to use it to invest in land and trade. The problem for Scarborough was that Bateman had indeed used the money to purchase lands, but the lands were purchased in Bateman's name. When Bateman died, Mary claimed the money in the trust as part of the Bateman estate that could be used to fulfil the £2,000 penalty imposed by her marriage settlement. Scarborough petitioned Cecil Calvert, Lord Baltimore, stating that the Bateman estate was heavily indebted to him and that Mary had deliberately undervalued the inventory of the estate in order 'to defraud the creditors'. In his petition, submitted through a representative, he demanded that the Bateman estate be reappraised, which the court granted. A new inventory was returned in April 1666. It showed that the Bateman estate was indeed extensive: it had a large holding of livestock, four black slaves, five indentured servants and a variety of household furniture and utensils. Yet the new inventory increased the value of the estate only slightly, from the original amount of £870 to about £900. This meant that Mary retained her status as the privileged creditor to the estate and that legally the other creditors, including Henry Scarborough, would not be paid.

After two years of nearly constant litigation, Mary now sought to protect herself from any further disputes concerning the estate of John Bateman. In 1666 she entered an order of *quietus est* to the Provincial Court. This phrase, meaning literally 'he is quit', was a legal mechanism used in common law courts to recognise that a debt had been paid or terminated. In Mary's case, she used this order to debar any further proceedings against Bateman's estate, an order that was confirmed by Cecil Calvert, Lord Baltimore, on 6 April 1666.[54] Mary's connections with the justices on the Provincial Court, a bench on which her husband had served prior to his death, contributed to her success. The men of the colony wanted to ensure that residents of the colony retained their land and wealth, and had an interest in seeing that this wealth did not flow back to London merchants. At the same time, the entire situation was shrewdly handled by Mary, who was tenacious in defending what she viewed as her right to the land.

Remarkably, inheritance patterns and the liberality of women's control of property in Maryland changed according to the different religious populations across the colony. Women were most likely to inherit larger portions of land in areas dominated by Anglicans and Roman Catholics, such as St. Mary's County. Both Jane Eltonhead's cases and Mary Perry's cases were heard before the Provincial Court at St. Mary's. Significantly, in counties with larger populations of Protestant Dissenters, such as

Somerset County, Maryland, women were less likely to inherit property. Dissenters in colonial Maryland followed similar practices as patriarchs in New England in limiting their wives' control of property.[55]

Elite women in New England: the patriarchal family idealised

In the Puritan colonies in New England, the belief in the patriarchal family as an institution, and the mutual obligations this entailed for each member of the family, was as strong as anywhere in Anglo-America. There was a belief that legal mechanisms like marriage settlements were not necessary: since husbands would fulfil their patriarchal obligation to care for and provide for their wives and children, sons who inherited their father's estates would not evict their mothers or step-mothers from their households. Additionally, marriage settlements were seen as a sign of 'unnatural' mistrust between husbands and wives, and gave wives too much power within the family. Widows who inherited large estates through marriage settlements and became independently wealthy challenged the very basis of the patriarchal worldview. They not only became independent from male authority by establishing households of their own but also had fewer incentives to remarry. This was at least part of the reason why colonies like Massachusetts and Connecticut never established Courts of Chancery, which enforced the terms of marriage settlements and protected property held in trust for married women.[56]

Since marriage settlements of the kind used in England were infrequently used in colonial New England, widows depended upon the collection of common law dower rights for their maintenance. Inheritance laws in seventeenth-century Connecticut, Rhode Island and Massachusetts mandated that widows receive a one-third share of their husbands' real estate for their lifetimes. If a husband had made a will that left his wife less than this amount, she had the option to disregard the will and claim her dower rights. However, before a widow actually came into possession of her dower rights, she had to receive the permission of a magistrate or local authority. These men had the power to limit or delay what the widow received according to their discretion. Additionally, by the end of the seventeenth century a husband who left a will could choose to leave his widow whatever amount of moveable property he saw fit. New England widows could choose to disregard the wills of their husbands, but they could not claim moveable property as part of their dower right.[57] While New England widows could therefore claim a one-third share of her husband's real estate, she could not inherit his moveable property unless he specifically willed it to her.

Unlike the leaders of the southern colonies in the Chesapeake, who seemed to have frequently sided with widows pursuing their claims to property, the leaders of Massachusetts nearly always sided with a male relative of a widow should her claim be contested in court. This was in spite of the fact that these women were connected to the highest men in the colony. Elizabeth Endicott of Salem, the widow of Massachusetts Bay Governor John Endicott, came into conflict with her two sons, John Endicott Jr. and Zerobabel Endicott, over her right to collect a portion of her husband's estate after his death in 1665. Elizabeth and John had married in 1630 and, in addition to serving as the governor of Massachusetts Bay, John sat on the bench of the General Court and the Court of Assistants.[58] John's position as a governor and as a justice in the highest court in the colony would have brought Elizabeth into contact with the legal elite. Under the terms of Governor Endicott's will, drawn up six years prior to his death in 1659, his wife Elizabeth was to receive an estate valued at nearly £600. Elizabeth's portion comprised a farm in Salem called Orchard, the moveable goods at his house in Boston, all his linens and plate, all the cattle and sheep, and land at Catta Island, which Elizabeth had use of 'during her natruall liefe & after her decease to my twoe sonnes, John and Zerobabel'. He also made Elizabeth his 'sole & onelie executrix of this my last will and testament'.[59]

Like the intergenerational conflicts that marked the relationships of elite families in England, widows in Massachusetts fought with their children and in-laws for the property left by a dead patriarch. Though the terms of Endicott's will seemed clear, almost immediately after his death in March 1665 legal disputes arose between Elizabeth and her sons over the division of Endicott's land and moveable property. John Jr. disputed the will on the grounds that there were no witnesses to it and that it was therefore not valid. John Jr.'s contestation of the validity of his father's will suggests that he was suspicious that his mother had somehow altered the document in order to receive a more generous share of the family estate. John Jr. also had a prior claim to the Orchard farm as part of the property settled to him upon his marriage in 1653.[60] Elizabeth responded by petitioning the General Court of the colony, reiterating her desire to have the estate settled according to the terms of her late husband's will. However, in August 1665 the General Court ruled that the will was indeed invalid and declared that the real estate belonged to John Jr. as the male heir. Elizabeth was left with a lifetime interest in a small portion of the family's land and moveable property, which amounted to only £80.[61] This sum fell far short of the £700 estate that had been left to Elizabeth under the terms of her husband's will.

Elizabeth Endicott's case reflects the precarious position of Massachusetts widows. While widows in Massachusetts were certainly able to appear in litigation in defence of property they claimed as their own, even the claims of the most high-status women were not upheld by justices in the courts. Since the validity of the will of her husband was contested and found to be inadmissible in court, Elizabeth had to claim her dower rights at common law instead. This meant that while she was entitled to one-third of her late husband's land, she did not have a claim on the moveable property of the estate, including livestock, farming utensils, household furnishings and cash. It also reflects the propensity of Massachusetts courts to rule in favour of a male heir over the claims of a widow. In May 1671 Elizabeth Endicott had been reduced to such a 'low condition' that the General Court ordered that she receive £30 per year to sustain herself.[62]

In addition to feuding with sons who were intent on gaining their due inheritance, Massachusetts widows who were the beneficiaries of large estates were required to petition the General Court to gain legal title to the land and to confirm any sales they wished to make of the property. This practice was meant to ensure that wealthy female property owners acted responsibly with the land and did not use it to deleterious ends. Margery Flynt, widow of Henry Flynt, rector of the church at Braintree and one of the original settlers of Massachusetts Bay, acted as co-executor with her son Josiah of the estate of her husband in 1668. She was obviously a trustworthy and well-regarded member of her family and her community: her husband gave her wide discretion to settle his estate after his death, and she also acted as executrix to the estates of other family members and as a witness to the wills of her neighbours.

Henry Flynt left a large estate with lands valued at £770 and named Margery as having a life investment in the estate as long as she remained unmarried.[63] Between 1668 and 1680 Margery and her son Josiah seemed to have worked harmoniously together on the administration of the estate, making joint decisions about the use of the land and acting as co-parties in any litigation that arose. When Josiah died in the summer of 1680, Margery intended to sell some of the land in order to meet her expenses. Since she was now sole executrix of the estate and still a widow, this would seem to have been not only entirely within her prerogative but also routine. However, in order to sell the land she had to seek the approval of the General Court before taking any action.[64] Even as feme soles, Massachusetts widows were bound by strict statutes limiting their widow's portions and by the custom that bade them to be subject to male authorities, even with land they controlled outright.

Conclusion

Elite women in England and the colonies who wanted to maintain their interests in property had to be knowledgeable of the law and proactive in pursuing their claims to property. The common law practices of coverture and primogeniture, which governed the descent and control of property in lieu of other legal agreements, meant that it was a very real possibility that a once-wealthy woman could fall into poverty unless some other provision was drawn up. This reality compelled elite women to be informed of their legal affairs and actively involved in pursuing litigation that protected their financial security. The detailed sources we have about the legal activities of elite women suggests that even while under coverture, wives were central in the direction and prosecution of their cases. Married women actively sought to protect property that they had brought into the marriage and frequently wrote to lawyers and legal advisors in how to manage cases in which these interests were at stake.

The breakdown of patriarchal ideals and mutual obligation between family members necessitated the use of the law as mediator in family conflicts. The disunity and feuds of elite families overflowed into the courts, where families looked to the law to resolve disputes that they could not work out themselves. Widows in England often had to resort to the law to claim the property owed to them under the terms of their marriage contracts. Women who lived decades longer than their husbands might come into conflict with the heirs to the estate, who were often keen to take possession of the entirety of their inheritance. In the Chesapeake the reality of death and remarriage meant that women's access to and control of property was as robust as anywhere in the Anglo-American world. The vast majority of men left their widows more property than the common law required and trusted them to use the resources to provide for the children. In colonial New England the ability of elite women to control and benefit from property was the most circumscribed in the Anglo-American world. While widows were entitled to dower rights under common law, in reality magistrates mediated when a widow would receive her property and how much she would get. New England courts very rarely used marriage settlements and jointure agreements, eliminating the other avenues by which wealthy women could protect their property and secure financial security in their widowhood. In New England the strength of patriarchal ideals and the belief in the value of wives' submission and reliance upon their husbands meant that men retained control of property.

Notes

1. Barbara Harris, *English Aristocratic Women, 1450–1550: Marriage and Family, Property and Careers* (Oxford: Oxford University Press, 2002), pp. 114–15; Eileen Spring, *Law, Land, and Family: Aristocratic Inheritance in England, 1300–1800* (Chapel Hill: University of North Carolina Press, 1993), pp. 40, 55–6.
2. Lorena Walsh, '"Til death us do part": marriage and family in seventeenth-century Maryland', in Thad W. Tate and David L. Ammerman (eds), *The Chesapeake in the Seventeenth Century: Essays on Anglo-American Society* (New York: Norton, 1979), pp. 136–7; Lois Green Carr and Lorena S. Walsh, 'The planter's wife: the experience of white women in seventeenth-century Maryland', *William and Mary Quarterly*, 3rd series, 34:4 (1977), pp. 555–6.
3. Debra Meyers, *Common Whores, Vertuous Women, and Loveing Wives: Free Will Christian Women in Colonial Maryland* (Bloomington: Indiana University Press, 2003), pp. 128–31, 170–1; Cornelia Hughes Dayton, *Women Before the Bar: Gender, Law, and Society in Connecticut, 1639–1789* (Chapel Hill: University of North Carolina Press, 1995), pp. 27–8, 40–4.
4. Spring, *Law, Land, and Family*, pp. 27–8, 66–7; Amy Erickson, *Women and Property in Early Modern England* (London: Routledge, 1993), pp. 26–7.
5. Erickson, *Women and Property*, pp. 26–7; Carole Shammas, 'English inheritance law and its transfer to the colonies', *American Journal of Legal History*, 31:2 (1987), p. 152.
6. Maria Cioni, *Women and Law in Elizabethan England with Particular Reference to the Court of Chancery* (New York: Garland, 1985), p. 84; Tim Stretton, *Women Waging Law in Elizabethan England* (Cambridge: Cambridge University Press, 1998), pp. 58–9; Marylynn Salmon, *Women and the Law of Property in Early America* (Chapel Hill: University of North Carolina Press, 1986).
7. Stretton, *Women Waging Law*, pp. 26–7, 109–10; Amy Erickson, 'Common law versus common practice: the use of marriage settlements in early modern England', *Economic History Review*, 43:1 (1990), pp. 24–5.
8. 27 Henry VIII, c. 10; William Searle Holdsworth, *A History of English Law*, 18 vols (London: Methuen, 1903–72), vol. 9, p. 196; Spring, *Law, Land, and Family*, pp. 42–65; Harris, *English Aristocratic Women*, pp. 19–23; Rosemary O'Day, *Women's Agency in Early Modern Britain and the American Colonies: Patriarchy, Partnership and Patronage* (London: Pearson, 2007), p. 478.
9. Erickson, 'Common law versus common practice', p. 22.
10. Shammas, 'English inheritance law and its transfer to the colonies', p. 157.
11. Mary Beth Norton, *Founding Mothers and Fathers: Gendered Power and the Forming of American Society* (New York: Knopf, 1996), pp. 111–12; Shammas, 'English inheritance law and its transfer to the colonies', pp. 158–9.
12. William Hand Browne (ed.), *Proceedings and Acts of the General Assembly, January 1637/8 – September 1664*, vol. 1 (Baltimore: Maryland Historical Society, 1883), pp. 156–7.
13. Darrett and Anita Rutman, '"Now wives and sons-in-law": parental death in a seventeenth-century Virginia county', in Tate and Ammerman (eds), *The Chesapeake*

in the Seventeenth Century, pp. 153–4; Carr and Walsh, 'The planter's wife', p. 554; Walsh, '"Til death us do part"', pp. 136–7.
14 The Book of the General Lawes and Libertyes Concerning the Inhabitants of Massachusetts (Cambridge, MA: Matthew Day, 1648), pp. 17–18.
15 Norton, Founding Mothers and Fathers, pp. 111–12; Shammas, 'English inheritance law and its transfer to the colonies', Table 1.
16 E. F. Gay, 'The Temples of Stowe and their debts: Sir Thomas Temple and Sir Peter Temple, 1603–1653', Huntington Library Quarterly, 2:4 (1939), pp. 401–2.
17 Charles Mosley (ed.), Burke's Peerage and Baronetage, vol. 2, 106th edn (London: Routledge, 1999).
18 Henry E. Huntington Library (hereafter HEH), Temple Family Addenda, Box 1, HM 46533. Rosemary O'Day also cites this list in Women's Agency in Early Modern Britain, p. 266. William Leonard, Reports and Cases of Law Argued and Adjudged in the Courts of Law at Westminster (London: Thomas Roycroft, 1658); Edward Coke, Reports (London: W. Lee, M. Walbanck, D. Pakeman and G. Bedell, 1600–58). See also Allen D. Boyer, 'Coke, Sir Edward (1552–1634)', Dictionary of National Biography Online (Oxford: Oxford University Press, 2009), accessed 4 October 2018 through www.oxforddnb.com/view/10.1093/ref:odnb/9780198614128.001.0001/odnb-9780198614128-e-5826.
19 The lack of an author or publication date for these works make it difficult to ascertain whether they were published or circulated in manuscript form. Since they are not in the Short Title Catalogue, it is possible that they may have been works that only circulated in manuscript form.
20 Gay, 'The Temples of Stowe and their debts', p. 414.
21 HEH, Temple Legal Case No. 178, Sir Thomas Temple and Lady Hester Temple v. Peter Temple, Chancery, 1629.
22 HEH, Hastings Manuscripts, 46443, Payton to Hester Temple, 16 March 1629.
23 HEH, Hastings Manuscripts, 46444, Payton to Hester Temple, 18 March 1629.
24 HEH, Temple Correspondence, Thomas Temple to Lady Hester Temple, STT 2209, 30 April 1630.
25 HEH, Temple Legal Cases, Lady Hester Sandys Temple.
26 The legal case between Sir Peter Temple and Lady Hester was the result of an earlier ruling in Chancery in favour of Robert Kenwicke, Vicar of Burton Dasset. See HEH, Temple Legal Case No. 70, Chancery, 1636–40.
27 HEH, Temple Correspondence, HM 46550, Hester Temple to the Commissioners of Chancery, 18 December 1639
28 British Library (hereafter BL), Egerton Manuscripts, 2650/176, Judith Barrington to John Kendall [undated, probably from the 1630s].
29 BL, Egerton Manuscripts, 2646/44, 'Memorandums for London: Michelmas Term, 1632', Lady Judith Barrington to John Kendall. See also BL, Egerton Manuscripts, 2646/46, Lady Judith Barrington to John Kendall, 25 October 1632. Lady Judith also wrote to her husband with advice and instructions. See BL, Egerton Manuscripts, 2647/175, Judith Barrington to Thomas Barrington, 1643.
30 BL, Egerton Manuscripts, 2646/44, 'Memorandums for London: Michelmas Term, 1632', Lady Judith Barrington to John Kendall.

31 BL, Egerton Manuscripts, 2646/46, Lady Judith Barrington to John Kendall, 25 October 1632.
32 The National Archives, UK, C 5/7/21, 20 April 1648. The repurchase of the Flamstead property was the subject of a later legal dispute in Chancery between Lady Judith and Kendall. Lady Judith alleged that Kendall had, 'in a sublte, deceitfull way', used part of the money to purchase a portion of the land for his exclusive use.
33 Essex Record Office (hereafter ERO), D/DBa L26, 'The Coppy of the first Agreement betwixt the Lady Judith Barrington & Sir John Barrington, 1644' and 'The coppy of Sir John Barringtons demands of his mother, 1645'.
34 BL, Egerton Manuscripts, 2648/136, Sir John Barrington to Lady Judith Barrington, 4 May 1647.
35 BL, Egerton Manuscripts, 2648/139, Sir John Barrington to Lady Judith Barrington, 20 May 1647.
36 BL, Egerton Manuscripts, 2648/137, Lady Judith Barrington to Sir John Barrington, 20 May 1647.
37 BL, Egerton Manuscripts, 2651/183, Sir John Barrington's petition against Lady Judith Barrington, 1650.
38 ERO, D/DBa L51, Depositions in Lady Judith Barrington v. Sir John Barrington, 1656.
39 ERO, D/DBa F26, Sir John Barrington to Lady Judith Barrington, 1657.
40 The cases of Lady Hester Temple and Lady Judith Barrington are only two examples – there are many more cases of aristocratic women pursuing legal action against men in their families. See the many cases between Lady Eleanor Davies Douglas and her son-in-law Ferdinando Hastings, Earl of Huntingdon. HEH, Hastings Legal Papers, and the letters of Eleanor Davies Douglas in HEH, Hastings Correspondence. Eleanor's daughter Lucy, Countess of Huntingdon, also prosecuted several cases against the family of her daughter-in-law over the payment of her dowry. See HEH, Hastings Legal Papers and Lucy's letters in HEH, Hastings Correspondence. Lady Anne Temple Roper, who was Lady Hester Temple's granddaughter, pursued litigation against her father Peter Temple and her brother Sir Richard Temple. See HEH, STT Temple Correspondence, Temple Family Catalogues, Temple Legal Cases, Temple Legal Papers. Jane Paulet Egerton pursued legal action against her brother Charles, Second Duke of Bolton. See HEH, Ellesmere Manuscripts, Bolton Papers.
41 Shammas, 'English inheritance law and its transfer to the colonies', pp. 158–9; Carr and Walsh, 'The planter's wife', pp. 555–6; Meyers, *Common Whores, Vertuous Women, and Loving Wives*, pp. 128–30.
42 Louis Green Carr (ed.), Women's Career Files, 'Gartrud Smith Anderton', *Maryland State Archives Online*, accessed 11 October 2018 through https://msa.maryland.gov/megafile/msa/speccol/sc4000/sc4040/000001/000026/html/sc4040-0026-1.html.
43 Louis Green Carr (ed.), Women's Career Files, 'Jane Eltonhead', *Maryland State Archives Online*, accessed 11 October 2018 through https://msa.maryland.gov/megafile/msa/speccol/sc4000/sc4040/000001/000493/html/sc4040-0493-01.html.
44 Edward Papenfuse (ed.), *A Biographical Dictionary of the Maryland Legislature, 1635–1789* (Baltimore: Johns Hopkins University Press, 2010), p. 304; Bernard Christian Steiner

(ed.), *Proceedings of the Provincial Court, 1658-1662*, vol. 41 (Baltimore: Maryland Historical Society, 1922), accessed 11 October 2018 through http://aomol.msa.maryland.gov/000001/000041/html/index.html.

45 For the case against Scarborough's estate, see William Hand Browne (ed.), *Judicial and Testamentary Business of the Provincial Court, 1649/50-1657*, vol. 10 (Baltimore: Maryland Historical Society, 1891), p. 523, accessed 11 October 2018 through https://msa.maryland.gov/megafile/msa/speccol/sc2900/sc2908/000001/000010/html/am10-523.html. For the case against Fendall, see Steiner (ed.), *Proceedings of the Provincial Court, 1658-1662*, vol. 41, p. 78, accessed 11 October 2018 through https://msa.maryland.gov/megafile/msa/speccol/sc2900/sc2908/000001/000041/html/am41-78.html.

46 Papenfuse (ed.), *A Biographical Dictionary of the Maryland Legislature*, p. 304.

47 Steiner (ed.), *Proceedings of the Provincial Court, 1658-1662*, vol. 41, pp. 178-9, accessed 11 October 2018 through https://msa.maryland.gov/megafile/msa/speccol/sc2900/sc2908/000001/000041/html/am41-178.html.

48 Lois Green Carr (ed.), St. Mary's City Men's Career Files, 'John Bateman', *Maryland State Archives Online*, accessed 11 October 2018 through https://msa.maryland.gov/megafile/msa/speccol/sc5000/sc5094/000001/000275/html/sc5094-0275-01.html.

49 J. Hall Pleasants (ed.), *Proceedings of the Provincial Court, 1663-1666*, vol. 49 (Baltimore: Maryland Historical Society, 1932), pp. 291-4, 321, 366-7, accessed 11 October 2018 through https://msa.maryland.gov/megafile/msa/speccol/sc2900/sc2908/000001/000049/html/am49-291.html.

50 J. Hall Pleasants (ed.), *Proceedings of the Provincial Court, 1666-1670*, vol. 57 (Baltimore: Maryland Historical Society, 1940), p. xxxvi, accessed 11 October 2018 through https://msa.maryland.gov/megafile/msa/speccol/sc2900/sc2908/000001/000057/html/am57p-36.html.

51 Pleasants (ed.), *Proceedings of the Provincial Court, 1663-1666*, vol. 49, p. 144, accessed 11 October 2018 through https://msa.maryland.gov/megafile/msa/speccol/sc2900/sc2908/000001/000049/html/am49-144.html.

52 Pleasants (ed.), *Proceedings of the Provincial Court, 1663-1666*, vol. 49, p. 160, accessed 11 October 2018 through https://msa.maryland.gov/megafile/msa/speccol/sc2900/sc2908/000001/000049/html/am49-160.html.

53 Pleasants (ed.), *Proceedings of the Provincial Court, 1663-1666*, vol. 49, pp. 162-3, accessed 11 October 2018 through https://msa.maryland.gov/megafile/msa/speccol/sc2900/sc2908/000001/000049/html/am49-162.html.

54 Pleasants (ed.), *Proceedings of the Provincial Court, 1666-1670*, vol. 57, pp. 19, 46-50, 54, 106, accessed 11 October 2018 through https://msa.maryland.gov/megafile/msa/speccol/sc2900/sc2908/000001/000057/html/am57-19.html.

55 Meyers, *Common Whores, Vertuous Women, and Loveing Wives*, pp. 128-30.

56 Kim Rogers, 'Relicts of the New World: conditions of widowhood in seventeenth-century New England', in Mary Kelley (ed.), *Woman's Being, Woman's Place: Female Identity and Vocation in American History* (Boston: G. K. Hall, 1979); Salmon, *Women and the Law of Property*, p. 123.

57 Shammas, 'English inheritance law and its transfer to the colonies', pp. 158, 162.

58 Lawrence Mayo, *John Endecott: A Biography* (Cambridge, MA: Harvard University Press, 1936), pp. 2–5.
59 John Endicott's will and inventory is reprinted in *Essex Institute Historical Collections*, vol. 25 (Salem: Essex Institute, 1885), pp. 137–45.
60 Jonathan Chu, 'Nursing a poisonous tree: litigation and property law in seventeenth-century Essex County, Massachusetts, the case of Bishop's Farm', *American Journal of Legal History*, 31:3 (1987), pp. 222–3.
61 Nathaniel B. Shurtleff (ed.), *Records of the Governor and Company of Massachusetts Bay in New England*, vol. 4, part 2 (Boston: W. White, 1853), pp. 279, 311–12.
62 Shurtleff (ed.), *Records of the Governor and Company*, vol. 4, part 2, pp. 487–8.
63 *Suffolk County Wills: Abstracts of the Earliest Wills Upon Record in the County of Suffolk, Massachusetts* (Boston: New England Historical and Genealogical Society, 1984), p. 326.
64 Shurtleff (ed.), *Records of the Governor and Company*, vol. 5, pp. 274, 277, 297.

Part III

The economy and equity

6

Economic expansion and the erosion of patriarchy

During the eighteenth century, Anglo-American law and jurisprudence changed as legal personnel became more professionalised, common law courts adopted more systematic and rationalised court procedures and women participated in the expansion of the commercial economy. The increasing formalism of Anglo-American law has led some scholars to conclude that these changes marginalised everyone but elite men from the legal process. As the power of the centralised imperial state grew, the courts increasingly excluded ordinary men and women from seeking legal redress. As a result, these scholars would argue, the poorer classes were disempowered relative to their social superiors. This process took place not only within English common law courts but also increasingly in the colonies.

Scholars have argued that during the eighteenth century the colonies underwent a process of anglicisation in which the legal system came more and more to resemble that of the mother country. These changes limited the accessibility of the courts for women: common law litigation increasingly concerned commerce, credit and the exchange of goods, features of the economy from which women were purportedly excluded. In New York, for example, the legal system became more formalised and focused on the enforcement of contracts; since women had only a marginal role in this new market economy, they tended to be less involved in litigation than they had been in the seventeenth century. Similarly, the legal system in Connecticut shifted from a more inclusive platform for community grievances to one that exclusively served the interests of men of business.[1]

The argument set forth here, however, is that women continued to appear in litigation during the eighteenth century at levels consistent with the seventeenth century, in spite of significant changes in common law jurisprudence, procedure and the increasing use of lawyers. Far from being marginalised from the new commercial economy, women played a central role as traders, lenders, borrowers, rentiers and investors. These roles drew them into the courts as they prosecuted and defended cases concerning their business transactions and properties. The common law courts extended the practice of allowing married women to trade as feme soles, a status that gave them the ability to make contracts independently of their husbands. At the same time, new legal devices developed by the equity jurisdiction supported women's separate property and made women accountable for their own financial decisions. While in the seventeenth century the equity courts had defended property held in trust for married women as well as marriage settlements, in the eighteenth century the variety and scope of legal devices that protected women's separate property allowed them more direct control over their financial decisions than ever before. The increasing flexibility of the common law, and the expansion of the equity jurisdiction on women's property, underpinned their participation in a thriving and rapidly growing economy.

The legal regimes in some colonies, such as Maryland and South Carolina, closely emulated the expansion of women's economic and legal opportunities taking place in England. These colonies enacted policies that allowed married women to trade as feme soles, and chancery courts in Maryland and South Carolina adopted English procedures and precedents that gradually expanded the rights of married women to own property separately from their husbands.[2] The economic and legal capabilities of women in the New England colonies, however, were more marginal. While magistrates in New England and other areas that did not establish separate equity jurisdictions could dispense equitable justice, the lack of official chancery courts in these colonies meant that they never developed the sophisticated legal instruments that protected wives' separate estates. Patriarchy remained strong in Puritan New England, where women did not have the benefit of a robust jurisdiction in equity and in which patriarchal obligations between family members was still the foundation of relationships.

While patriarchal ideals and structures remained in place in New England during the eighteenth century, the growing financial independence of women in England and the southern colonies contributed to the increasing erosion of patriarchy as the basis for familial relationships. Common law and equity law increasingly recognised that the patriarchal ideals of wifely dependence and submission, embodied in the doctrine of coverture, constricted the purchasing power of women and placed women's property into the hands of squandering or neglectful husbands. Women who were financially capable of maintaining their own households might choose not to marry, and could more easily seek to separate from their spouses. In cases of marital separation, equity courts could compel husbands to abide by the terms of separation agreements that gave wives the right to financial support.

As more and more women participated in the economy, and as more legal provisions for control of money and property came to be at their disposal, the idea of coverture, and the system of patriarchy on which it was based, began to erode. The relationships between members of the household thus became centred on ideas of contract rather notions of patriarchal obligations. This was most apparent in the changing legal relationship between husbands and wives. While wives in the seventeenth century pleaded with the courts to compel husbands to remember their patriarchal responsibilities to provide for them, in the eighteenth century wives sought the support of equity law in compelling husbands to uphold the terms of their marriage contracts. The quickly expanding commercialised economy could not function on the basis of mutual obligation and reciprocity; as a result, the law provided a more secure mechanism for the performance of obligations between individuals.

Women, common law and the commercial economy

Women in England and some colonies played a central role in the quickly expanding commercial economy of the eighteenth century. Far from dropping out or being excluded from the world of commerce, women acted as traders, investors, creditors and financiers in urban economies in areas such as London and Manchester, as well as in major colonial cities. This was not only true of wealthy women but also of middle-class women who ran smaller businesses catering to the increasing taste for luxury items like china and glass, as well as millinery and mantua-making.[3] Widows held a prominent position in the expanding economy of the eighteenth century, since many of them had independent resources that allowed them to act as investors and rentiers.[4] Yet the economic and legal activities of widows were an extension of their undertakings as wives. Married women were active participants in the economy in a variety of capacities, and their ability to assume these economic roles rested upon the law's recognition of them as independent economic agents.[5] Married women's legal status and their ability to control property independently of their husbands changed substantially over the course of the eighteenth century in ways that allowed them greater economic power.

Women's participation in the economy took place within changing legal contexts. In the late seventeenth and early eighteenth centuries, common law jurists adopted many of the ideas of natural law that were rooted in the equity tradition, and sought to systematise and rationalise its more arcane features.[6] In the 1720s and 1730s Parliament passed a number of statutes for reform of the common law which ended the use of Latin and Law French in the courts, required the registration of attorneys and solicitors, created a royal commission to make fees and standards for office-holding consistent in all courts of justice and formed parliamentary committees to oversee gaols and provide relief for debtors.[7] In the early eighteenth century both common law and equity courts began publishing reports of important cases decided by the justices in order to establish firm precedents for judicial decisions. By the 1760s William Blackstone noted that that the common law had adopted a 'liberality of sentiment' drawn from equity law, and that equity and common law were by this point working in harmony with one another rather than in competition.[8]

By the early eighteenth century the free flow of goods and the availability of credit that defined the commercial economy were increasingly incompatible with the restrictions imposed by coverture. If the doctrine were applied strictly, wives would not be able to start lines of credit independently of their husbands; this was highly inconvenient in an age when coinage was scarce and most transactions were carried out on credit rather than in cash. As the eighteenth century progressed, the need to find workarounds to the doctrine of coverture led to the development of new legal instruments that allowed married women more economic agency.[9] The increasing use of the law of necessaries and the expansion of feme sole trading status in England and in the colonies gave married women more economic power under common law. Neither the law of necessaries nor feme sole traders were new in the eighteenth century; both had been around in some form since the Middle Ages. However, with the expansion of the economy in the eighteenth century, these mechanisms became more common and widely practiced.

The law of necessaries, sometimes also called the law of agency, gave wives the ability to purchase household goods on their husband's line of credit, and allowed them to make contracts with vendors to procure household goods that were appropriate to their status and wealth. A wife could draw on her husband's line of credit even if he had not given his express consent: legal authorities and vendors alike considered husbands' permission implicit in wives' requests for purchases. Husbands who wished to bar their wives from using their credit line had to give written notice to local vendors. Only in cases in which a wife ran away from her husband without cause, or if the husband and wife had mutually agreed to separate, would a husband be released from his obligation to provide for his wife.

The increasing use of the law of necessaries by wives to uphold their claims to their husbands' credit lines allowed them more purchasing power as well as a legal defence in case that power was contested.[10]

American courts generally followed the English example in holding husbands legally responsible for purchases made on credit by their wives. The ability to claim their husbands' credit was especially important for colonial wives, since men were often away from home for long periods of time as they transacted business throughout the Atlantic world. Without some flexibility and independence in married women's purchasing power, trade would have slowed to a halt and the courts would have been tied up with needless litigation. As in England, wives who had been deserted or neglected by their husbands, or those who were forced to flee their households because of abuse, could claim their line of credit.[11]

Like the law of necessaries, the practice of granting married women feme sole trading status expanded to keep pace with the growing economy. Feme sole status, used in major urban areas in England and the colonies, allowed wives who worked in a trade separately from their husbands to make legal contracts in their own names, and be held legally responsible for their own debts.[12] As *The Laws Respecting Women* put it in 1777:

> If a feme covert trades by herself, in any trade with which her husband doth not intermeddle, and buys and sells in that trade, there the feme shall be sued, and the husband named for conformity only. If judgement be given against him, execution shall be only against the feme.[13]

In other words, in order for a woman to be considered a feme sole merchant, a husband must have nothing at all to do with his wife's business and operate in a different trade entirely.

Local city courts held feme sole traders responsible for any debts contracted in their pursuit of their business, and heard any litigation arising concerning their debts. The benefit of trading as a feme sole was that it gave a wife more independence and flexibility: feme sole traders had exclusive ownership of their business assets and any profits arising from the trade. Another reason a woman might take on feme sole status was to shield her property from her husband's creditors. Wives' property that had not been specifically protected or held in trust could be seized as the property of the husband, and could legally be confiscated by creditors who wished to be paid. The business assets and property of a feme sole trader, however, could not be claimed by her husband or his creditors. There were some drawbacks: feme sole traders could not claim protection under the law of coverture, and could not make their husbands responsible for paying their debts. If given the status of feme sole trader, a woman was personally accountable to pay her own bills and to appear in court to answer any charges concerning debts.

The laws of South Carolina closely followed English practice in allowing married women to practice a trade as feme soles. A statute of 1712 made any feme sole merchant in South Carolina liable for the payment of her own debts. The purpose of the statute was to prevent married female traders from defrauding their creditors by 'sheltering and defending themselves from any suit brought against them by reason of their coverture'. Wives trading under feme sole status could thus not hold their husbands responsible for any debts they contracted for the businesses. Instead, the statute ensured that any feme sole trader should 'be liable to any suit or action to be brought against her for any debt contracted as a sole trader ... as if such woman was sole and not under coverture'.[14]

While the 1712 statute protected the creditors of feme sole traders, a statute in 1744 ensured that feme sole traders could recover a debt from defaulting customers. The statute stated that 'sole traders are often under difficulties in recovering payments of debts contracted with them by reason of the absence of their husbands ... sometimes not being able to produce any power or authority from their husbands'. Thereafter, feme sole traders in South Carolina were able to sue in their own names, with the name of the husband being mentioned 'out of conformity'.[15] Feme sole traders in South Carolina carried out their business in cities such as Charleston; local authorities did not require women to officially register as feme sole traders, although many women petitioned the courts to officially declare their legal and economic independence.

While Pennsylvania also enacted a statute allowing for married women to trade as feme soles, the purpose of the law was much different to that practised in English cities or in South Carolina. The Pennsylvania law titled the 'Act Concerning feme sole traders' of 1718 stipulated that only wives whose husbands were away at sea, or who had deserted them, could act as feme sole traders. Women who cohabited with their husbands did not qualify. The purpose of the act was to give women some means to maintain themselves in their husbands' absences, and prevent any wealth the woman had generated from her own labour from being squandered by her husband upon his return. The statute noted that it often happened that some husbands who, having 'lost sight of their duty to their wives and tender children ... not only waste what they may get abroad, but misapply such effects as they leave in this province'. Therefore, the purpose of the statute was to ensure that the estate of the husband was 'secured for the maintenance of their wives and children, and that the goods and effects which such wives acquire ... may be preserved for satisfying of those who so entrust them'.¹⁶ The statute provided wives with a means of subsistence while their husbands were absent and kept them from needing poor relief from their communities. The expanded use of the law of necessaries and feme sole trading status, enforceable in common law courts, gave married women more latitude to operate in the new commercial economy. Without the greater flexibility of the doctrine of coverture, the economy would not have been able to operate smoothly or efficiently.

Massachusetts followed Pennsylvania's precedent in allowing only those wives who had been abandoned, and who therefore needed a means by which to support themselves, to have feme sole trader status. However, the Massachusetts legislature did not enact this law until 1787. Prior to that time, wives who wished to support themselves through trade did not have the support of the law. Even after 1787, wives had to formally apply to gain feme sole status and had to demonstrate that their husbands were gone and that they had no other way to support themselves. When women could successfully demonstrate these facts before the court, Massachusetts justices often supported their cases. However, the law stipulated that wives' status as feme soles only applied while their husbands were away; if their husbands returned, the courts considered wives' status as independent traders void.¹⁷

Women, equity law and economic expansion

In the eighteenth century, women's participation in the commercial economy was reflected in their increasing appearance in equity litigation concerning mortgages, annuities, bonds and trusts. As active players in the expanding credit market, women appeared in court in the roles of borrowers and lenders, prosecuting and defending cases concerning mortgage foreclosure and the payment of bonds. Equity courts in England and the southern colonies widely adopted these new legal devices as a way to keep pace with the expansion of an economy increasingly based on trade, credit and markets. The equity jurisdiction provided the legal security for the expansion of international and domestic markets in the eighteenth century through the use of sophisticated legal instruments that supported investment and trade.¹⁸

Women's participation in the courts of equity took place against a backdrop of change within the system of equity courts that stretched from England to the colonies. From the late seventeenth century onwards, the equity jurisdiction expanded both in terms of the number of courts and in jurisdictional scope. Successive Lord Chancellors in England streamlined equity procedures and systematised precedents to make the outcome of litigation more predictable and less arbitrary. The English Court of Chancery, based in London, continued to be the preeminent court of equity in the Anglo-American world into the eighteenth century. It handled the largest caseload, and established procedures and precedents for the smaller equity courts in provincial England and in the colonies. In England, however, there were a variety of other equity courts that exercised jurisdictions concurrent with Chancery, and acted as 'courts of conscience' that addressed legal issues concerning mortgages, trusts and estate administration. The Court of Exchequer, an equity court also based in London, arose in the early eighteenth century specialising in cases concerning mortgages.[19]

While Chancery had been the enclave of the aristocracy and the upper gentry in the sixteenth and seventeenth centuries, by the eighteenth century the various courts of equity in England had become accessible for middle- and lower-class litigants. Filing a bill to commence suit in the English Exchequer or Chancery cost between £3 and £6, and litigants could be relieved from any costs of litigation by petitioning for their cases to be heard *in forma pauperis*.[20] Maryland, South Carolina and Virginia established chancery courts modelled on the English example, and closely followed English procedures and precedents. Maryland was the first colony to establish a separate equity jurisdiction on the English model in 1669, followed by South Carolina in 1720.[21] Virginia established a separate equity jurisdiction a while later, in 1777; however, since 1645 the Virginia General Court had operated as both a court of common law and colonial court of chancery, and routinely upheld women's separate estates throughout the eighteenth century.[22] These courts followed English precedent in developing legal instruments for mortgages, trusts, bonds and estate inheritance.

Widows and unmarried women appeared to prosecute or defend cases at equity law in their own names. While equity law allowed married women to prosecute cases in their own names, very few women did so; having husbands act as co-parties in their cases strengthened the position of married women before the courts, and avoided any confusion about the husband's whereabouts or his role in the case. Married women most often appeared alongside their husbands as co-parties, although they still tended to be integrally involved in the management of their cases. Litigation in equity courts often concerned property belonging to married women, and cases in which husbands and wives appeared together as joint parties usually concerned property held by the wife. The only type of case in which a married woman appeared as a sole party in equity litigation was if the suit was *between* a husband and wife.

Table 6.1 Women acting as plaintiffs and defendants in litigation in equity courts

	Number of female litigants	Number of male litigants	Number of cases including a female litigant	Number of suits sampled
English Court of Exchequer[a]				
1685	72 (14%)	441	54 (36%)	150
1735	102 (18.5%)	449	52 (35%)	150
1785	84 (14.3%)	502	58 (39%)	150
Maryland Court of Chancery[b]				
1700–01	25 (10.7%)	208	25 (25%)	100
1720–45	67 (22.4%)	232	50 (50%)	100
1745–74	101 (27.5%)	266	63 (63%)	100
South Carolina Court of Chancery[c]				
1721–48	56 (20.9%)	212	46 (46%)	100
1755–71	64 (20.6%)	247	46 (46%)	100

Sources: Figures based on cases abstracted in [a] Henry Horwitz, *Exchequer Equity Records and Proceedings, 1649–1841* (London: Public Record Office, 2001); [b] Debbie Hooper (ed.), *Abstracts of Chancery Court Records of Maryland, 1669–1782* (Westminster, MD: Family Line Publications, 1996); [c] Anne King Gregorie (ed.), *Records of the Chancery of South Carolina, 1671–1779* (Binghampton: Vail-Ballou Press, 1950).

Women's use of equity courts in England and the southern colonies remained stable, or even increased, over the course of the eighteenth century (see Table 6.1). In the English Court of Exchequer, the percentage of cases including at least one female litigant rose slightly over the period, from 36 per cent of cases in 1685 to 39 per cent in 1785. The percentage of women appearing in the English Court of Chancery may have been even higher than in Exchequer. Chancery had jurisdiction over marriage settlements and the use of trusts to protect wives' separate estates. One study estimated that women comprised 18.8 per cent of plaintiffs in Chancery in 1627, a number which had by 1818/19 expanded to 30.6 per cent.[23] Another study put women's engagement in equity litigation at an even higher rate: between 1700 and 1800, women participated in 46.5 per cent of cases heard before the Chancery and Exchequer courts.[24] Women's increasing participation in the economy, especially in the use of legal devices which were upheld by the equity courts like mortgages, trusts, annuities and estate inheritance, meant that women were using these courts more than ever.

The percentages of female litigants in colonial courts of chancery were even higher than in England. In South Carolina, a colony that strongly upheld married women's access to separate property, women comprised about one-fifth of litigants before the court, and at least one woman appeared in nearly half of all cases heard before the court during the eighteenth century. The rising percentage of women in the Maryland Court of Chancery is remarkable: the percentage of female litigants rose from 10.7 per cent in 1700/01, to 22.4 per cent in the period 1720–45, and rose again to 27.5 per cent in 1745–74. The proportion of cases involving at least one female litigant also rose dramatically in the Maryland Court of Chancery over the course of the eighteenth century: in 1700–01, 25 per cent of cases included at least one female litigant, but this rose to 50 per cent in 1721–45 and 62 per cent in 1745–74. The increasing number of women appearing before the Maryland Court of Chancery reflects women's ownership and control of property in the colony.

Women who owned or rented urban property and dwelling houses were frequently involved in cases concerning mortgages and mortgage foreclosure. Many of them used a new principle called 'equity of redemption', which by the eighteenth century had become a common part of equity proceedings. The principle was designed to protect against mortgage foreclosure, and to ensure that borrowers could not be evicted for even the smallest infraction in their payment schedule. The principle stated that if a mortgagor (the borrower) did not make payments in a timely manner and the legal estate of the property passed to the mortgagee (the lender), the mortgagor was entitled to a reconveyance of the property upon timely payment of the principle and 'damages', or interest. If the borrower failed to pay the principle and interest at the time specified, the court would declare a foreclosure and the borrower would lose her right to equity of redemption for the property.[25]

The principle of equity of redemption was used in a case heard before the English Court of Exchequer in 1734 when Mary Aylett, a spinster, brought suit against a husband and wife, John and Alice Shrofield. Alice was drawn into the suit as the executrix of the estate of her sister Jane Everard, who had mortgaged her house in Hornchurch, Essex, to Mary Aylett as security for the payment of a £450 debt. By the terms of this agreement, Mary Aylett would have legal control of the property until Jane Everard repaid the debt. As it happened, Jane died before she repaid the debt to Mary, and the execution of Jane's estate and the responsibility for the payment of Jane's outstanding debts passed to Alice Shrofield.

Mary Aylett's side of the case seemed straightforward: she asked the court to compel Alice, as the executrix of Jane's estate, to pay the £450 debt. If this was not performed, Mary had a legal right to foreclose on the property, a move that would allow her to take full legal ownership. Alice Shrofield, for her part, managed the suit astutely. She acknowledged that the value of Jane's remaining estate was insufficient to pay Mary the £450 debt. However, in lieu of foreclosure that would give Mary full ownership of the property, Alice pleaded before the court that she was entitled to the right of equity of redemption. When Alice claimed the right of equity of redemption, she ensured that she would be able to reclaim the property if she could pay the debt at a future date.[26]

The Maryland Court of Chancery heard cases similar to those heard in the equity courts in England, including cases concerning mortgage payments and foreclosure. Mary Sim, a widow from Prince George's County, initiated a suit in 1746 against her sister-in-law, Lucy Brooke, for mortgage payments. Lucy was the widow of Mary's half-brother Thomas Brooke, who had died in 1744, leaving Lucy in financial difficulty. Though Thomas had owned 1,000 acres and five slaves (who under Maryland law were considered chattels), he had mortgaged the land and the slaves to Mary to raise ready cash to pay his debts. Mary Sim's suit against Lucy was an attempt to compel her to pay the arrears on the mortgage.[27]

Like the English Chancery, the South Carolina Chancery exercised a broad jurisdiction over property held in trust. Husbands in the southern colonies often bequeathed property to their wives in trust in order to keep it from falling into the hands of a greedy or profligate second husband. Such was the case in Elizabeth St. John Beaty's suit against Lambert Lance, heard before the South Carolina Chancery in 1765. Elizabeth sought to gain possession of property left in trust to her by the will of her husband, John St. John. Prior to his death in 1757 John St. John had owned a substantial amount of land in Charleston and the surrounding countryside. He, along with his older brother Miller St. John, was one of the heirs of his wealthy father, James St. John. Under the terms of John St. John's will, Elizabeth was to received 250 acres of land that she would own in fee simple. Under this type of land tenure, Elizabeth would own the land outright and be able to devise it to heirs of her choice. For Elizabeth, the problem was that Lambert Lance, as the executor of the estates of James St. John and Miller St. John, had a competing claim to the property. However, the court sided with Elizabeth, ordering that the terms of John St. John's will be upheld: Elizabeth gained the 250 acres of land held in fee simple. She also received half of the slaves that had belonged to the estate of her father-in-law, James St. John, during his lifetime. The other properties belonging to the estate, both in Charleston and in the country, were to be sold, with Elizabeth receiving the remainder after the payment of court and solicitor's fees.[28]

Equity and married women's separate property

One of the most important developments in women's legal status during the eighteenth century was the expansion of equity principles that upheld married women's separate property. While trusts had been used since the late sixteenth century to protect wives' estates, equity law developed a variety of other types of agreements in the eighteenth century whereby wives could retain independent control of their property.

Beginning in the 1720s the English Chancery law upheld the right of wives to inherit and possess property without the use of a trustee. In Bennet v. Davis, heard before the English Chancery in 1725, Anne Bennet brought suit against her husband, Henry Bennet, and one of his creditors, Thomas Davis. The case concerned property that Anne's father had devised for her sole and separate use by the terms of his will. Since the will had not designated trustees for Anne's property, Henry ostensibly had a legal claim to the land as Anne's husband. Henry was badly in debt and had declared bankruptcy; Anne initiated the suit to keep the property from being seized by Henry's creditors. Davies argued that since no trustees had been designated in the will, the land thereby came under the control of the husband, who had a legal right to it notwithstanding the intentions of Anne's father, the testator. However, the court ultimately sided with Anne. The justices argued that if a testator did not designate trustees for property bequeathed to a feme covert, the court adjudged the husband to act as the nominal trustee for the wife. This arrangement did not give the husband any claim to the property or any profits arising from it. He could not sell the property or bequeath it, nor could his creditors legally seize the property to pay his debts.[29]

The precedent established by Bennet v. Davis, which protected property inherited by a feme covert, extended to the colonies. In a case heard before the South Carolina Court of Chancery in 1762, the court upheld the right of a married woman who was the beneficiary of a will to have her property put in trust for her sole and separate use. In these cases, the court could compel a husband who sued to gain his wife's inheritance to establish a trust for the benefit of his wife. Mary Lloyd, wife of Thomas Lloyd, was one of the beneficiaries of the 'considerable' estate of her father, James Matthews. Since no trust had been devised by the terms of Matthews's will, Thomas Lloyd believed he had a claim to the inheritance in right of his wife. However, the court ordered that the property inherited by Mary Lloyd be put in trust, and that the 'interest arising therefrom be paid yearly and every year to the said Mary Lloyd during the term of her natural life for her own and separate use'. The court's decision to have Mary's substantial inheritance placed in trust for her reflects the desire to protect married women's inheritance from profligate or irresponsible husbands. Thomas Lloyd would never see a penny of Mary's inheritance: after Mary's death, the property held in trust for her would pass on to her son.[30]

These developments in equity law went some way towards protecting property inherited by wives from being squandered or sold by spendthrift husbands. At the same time, there was a possibility of a wife being coerced or pressured into signing over her property to her husband. With the expansion of legal devices supporting married women's property came the concern that this property could be 'kissed or kicked' from her. A wife might, in other words, be compelled by love or violence into giving her husband legal control of her property. English equity law developed the principle of 'restraint upon anticipation' to protect wives from the coercion of their husbands. This principle prevented wives from borrowing against their capital, or simply transferring their capital into their husbands' names. The intention of the law was to ensure that wives could not be compelled by their husbands to sell their property, and thereby deprive themselves of future maintenance. Wives who sold or borrowed against the capital of their property put their future financial security in danger; should they become widows, they would have no means of support for themselves or their children.[31]

The ability of wives to make prenuptial contracts for their separate estates without the use of trustees came into use in the mid-eighteenth century. This type of marriage settlement came to be known as a 'simple agreement', and allowed married women to have direct control over their property. The case of Rippon v. Dawding, heard before the English Chancery in 1767, concerned a prenuptial bond entered into by Dorothy Rippon and her intended husband, John Dawding. The bond enabled her to maintain control over her separate property during their marriage, and bequeath it to heirs of her choice. If her husband failed to uphold his end of the agreement, the bond stipulated that he would incur a penal sum of £1,400. Dorothy wrote her will while a feme covert, devising her estate to her children from her previous marriage. After her death, Dorothy's children initiated a suit in Chancery arguing that the terms of their mother's will should be upheld. The court decided in their favour, judging that the bond made between Dorothy and John prior to their marriage gave Dorothy the ability to devise her property to heirs of her choice, even while she was a feme covert.³²

The Maryland Court of Chancery upheld the practice of simple agreements on the English model. A case heard in 1792 concerned a contract for a simple agreement made between Levin and Ann Woolford. The agreement gave Ann, if she should predecease her husband, the authority to devise property to her three children from a previous marriage to John King. When Ann fell ill and notified her husband that she wanted to write her will, he apparently reneged on their agreement. He believed he had already provided adequately for Ann and her heirs, and that no further inheritance was necessary for their maintenance. Ann, however, clandestinely wrote her will against the wishes of her husband, and Levin contested the validity of the will in court. One of the issues at stake in the case was whether the simple agreement made between Levin and Ann prior to their marriage was still valid once they were husband and wife. As a feme covert, could Ann own property and devise it to heirs of her choice in her will? Levin argued that she could not – since there were no trustees in place for Ann's property, any property she owned became his upon their marriage. However, the justices of the Maryland Court of Chancery disagreed, and ruled in favour of the simple agreement. As a result, Ann's will was declared valid and the property devised in it would go to the heirs she had designated.³³

The expansion of legal devices that supported married women's access to property also supported women seeking financial support and marital separation. Though these cases accounted for less than 5 per cent of the total volume of cases heard before the equity courts, they are a significant indicator of the equity jurisdiction's support of women's property and financial security.³⁴ In England, only the ecclesiastical authorities had the power to grant full divorces and legal separations; however, the equity jurisdiction enforced the terms of agreements made between divorcing or separating couples. In cases of an annulment, the equity jurisdiction could compel a husband to return the property the wife had brought into the marriage. Since the ecclesiastical courts granted annulments on grounds that marriages had never been valid in the first place, the equity courts reasoned that the wives were never truly feme coverts, and husbands therefore did not have a claim to their property. In cases of legal separation, in which couples were still legally married but no longer cohabited, the equity courts compelled husbands to pay damages to their wives, and made them abide by agreements for financial support drawn up during the separation process on penalty of imprisonment. While couples who desired annulments or separation had to appeal to the ecclesiastical authorities, those concerned with the distribution of property after separating would inevitably be drawn into the equity jurisdiction.[35]

A case heard before the English Chancery in 1737 reflects the notion that contractual views of familial relationships were increasingly supplanting older ideas of patriarchy and deference. In this case, the marriage agreement between Sir Richard Moore and his intended wife, drawn up prior to their marriage in 1707, stipulated that Lady Moore was to receive £100 per year for her sole and separate use out of the profits of land held in trust for her. This annuity, commonly called 'pin money', was usually commensurate with the amount of property wives had brought into the marriage. Wives had exclusive discretion over how they used this money: they could bequeath it in their wills and could invest it in any manner they saw fit. Further, a husband who had agreed to the payment of pin money prior to marriage was obliged to pay it, regardless of the conduct of his wife. While older practices of dower and jointure were sometimes dependent on a wife's faithfulness to her husband, the payment of pin money was legally enforceable just as any other contract would be. Even wives who had deserted their husbands for another man could still legally collect pin money from their husbands.[36]

The issue at stake in Moore v. Moore was whether Richard Moore had to pay pin money to Lady Moore even though she lived openly with another man. Although the couple lived together harmoniously for over twenty years, Lady Moore moved to France in 1728 and thereafter lived separately from her husband. According to the court record, the £100 annuity had not been paid to Lady Moore since she left for France, and the payments were now in arrears. Richard Moore initiated suit in Chancery against his wife to be released from the terms of the contract: he and his counsel argued that he was no longer obliged to pay the annuity if his wife chose to live separately from him, and that her desertion was just cause for the forfeiture of the money. Further, they argued that her annuity was intended for her to spend while she was a part of Richard Moore's family. Lady Moore and her counsel countered that she had been subject to cruel usage from her husband, which justified her separation. The most compelling argument, however, was that in terms of her entitlement to the payment of the annuity, Lady Moore should be considered a feme sole, and a 'stranger' to her husband. The contract should, in other words, be considered binding and valid as would a contract between any other individuals. The court decided in favour of Lady Moore, and ordered that the terms of the marriage settlement be upheld.[37]

Since it gave wives financial freedom independently of their husbands, introduction of pin money into marriage contracts reflected the further erosion of the patriarchal relationship between husbands and wives – the financial obligations of a husband to his wife was now fulfilled by his adherence to a contract rather than to a sense of patriarchal duty. And wives were not bound by any rules of conduct to be able to collect the support from their husbands.

Courts of chancery in the colonies had the power to grant marital separations and order the payment of financial support for wives and children. The process of seeking separation as well as maintenance was therefore more streamlined for women in fledgling America.[38] In 1707 in one of the earliest cases of marital separation upheld by the Maryland Court of Chancery, Margaret Macnamara petitioned for separation from bed and board from her husband, Thomas, and for a quarterly allowance to be paid by him for her maintenance. Margaret related how Thomas had been a most 'barbarous', 'inhuman' and 'unnatural husband toward her', and that he had an 'ungovernable temper to frighten a poor helpless woman out of her life'. She therefore pleaded that she may 'be permitted to lye separate from him' and be provided with maintenance that supported her status. She included a list of household goods that she specifically desired. The court decided that Margaret could live separately from Thomas, and that Thomas was to pay his wife £15 sterling each year beginning on the day of the order. Thomas repudiated the decision of the court. Although he was commonly accounted by 'undeniable testimonies' as a violent man, he was not ignorant of the workings of English law. He argued that only the ecclesiastical jurisdiction could grant a legal separation of bed and board, and that therefore the decision of the Lord Chancellor in this case was illegal and contrary to English practice. The justices of the Chancery, however, stated that the 'infancy' of the province and the lack of proper officers prevented them from establishing spiritual courts, and upheld their decision to grant Margaret separation of bed and board.[39]

Jane Pattison of Calvert County, Maryland, entered a bill of complaint in the Maryland Court of Chancery against her husband, Jeremiah Pattison, in 1736. In the case that became Pattison v. Pattison, Jane stated that she was in the possession of a 'considerable estate' left to her by her first husband, Samuel Abbot, who had died in 1723. Since her marriage with Jeremiah the year after Samuel's death, she had 'behaved herself in a virtuous and respectful manner'. However, Jane alleged that Jeremiah had treated her and her children cruelly, and had 'conceived so very great dislike and aversion' to her that he 'used her very cruelly by beating her with tongs' and also 'turned her out of doors … destitute of cloathes and almost naked'. The language Jane used to make her plea before the court was somewhat formulaic: wives often claimed that their husbands had turned them out of their house with only the clothes on their backs, a strategy that was meant to strike right at the heart of the patriarchal obligation of husbands to provide for their wives. Jane Pattison asked the court to compel her husband to give her an annual allowance. Jeremiah Pattison denied these charges: he alleged that after their marriage he had paid the debts owing to her first husband's estate and gave the rest to Jane's children. He also alleged that Jane treated him with the utmost disdain, throwing firebrands and iron candlesticks at him, and shouting the 'most horrid and shocking imprecations' at him. According to Jeremiah's story, he had only used 'moderate' corrective measures to enforce Jane's compliance and argued that she had left their home voluntarily in spite of his entreaties for her to stay. Though Jeremiah vehemently denied Jane's charges, the court decided that Jeremiah should pay Jane £30 per year as a separate maintenance.[40]

In a similar case from the Maryland Court of Chancery, the justices upheld the right of a married woman to sue her husband for marital separation and financial maintenance. Ann Govane, the wife of William Govane, entered a bill of complaint against her husband in October 1750. Like Jane Pattison, Ann explained that she was possessed of a large estate worth £3,000 left to her by her father, Charles Hammond, and her deceased first husband, Thomas Homewood. When she married William Govane in 1740, she greatly increased his fortune. Nevertheless, soon after their marriage he showed himself to be of a 'perverse, turbulent, and violent temper', and 'hath often with a drawn sword' threatened her life, and threatened that he would revenge himself by selling all his estate and her dower interest and moving to Rhode Island, leaving her destitute and without maintenance. She explained that she was obliged to leave the house 'for the preservation of her life which she apprehended to being in great danger from the violence and malice of the said William Govane'. The Lord Chancellor found Mary's story credible, and decreed that William Govane pay her £163 in current money at the conclusion of the suit, and £92 per year on the last day of August unless they mutually agreed to cohabit together again. The court also gave William Govane the option of signing over the title to Ann's dower lands, which would satisfy £50 of the £92 per year. William attempted to appeal the decision, but the court held firm in their original judgement.[41]

The practice of a wife suing her husband for marital separation and financial support was also upheld by the South Carolina Chancery. In 1726 Catherine Taveroon brought suit against her husband, Stephen Taveroon, alleging cruelty and abuse. She asked for the justices of the court 'to have an allowance' made to her so that she might live separately from her husband. Although Stephen claimed that he was willing to welcome his wife back home, and denied 'any illussage as it alledged', the court ruled that Catherine be 'allowed three pounds per week for her maintenance and subsistence'.[42]

The South Carolina Chancery upheld the right of a wife to collect separate maintenance again in 1735, when Ruth Lowndes sued her husband, Charles Lowndes, for separation and financial maintenance. Ruth had inherited a substantial amount of property from her father, Henry Rawlins, a sugar planter from St. Kitts, and had married Charles Lowndes as a wealthy woman in 1717. However, Ruth alleged that Charles had abused her and had squandered her property. In 1731 he was badly in debt, owing one Charleston merchant over £2,000 and mortgaging his property and slaves. By 1735, when Ruth petitioned for separation, his creditors had foreclosed on the mortgages and the family was left nearly destitute. As part of her case before the court, Ruth asked that her husband give her a variety of household goods, including 'fifty pounds in current money' and three slaves. The court granted Ruth's requests. It ordered that Charles remain in the custody of the court until he delivered the goods, money and slaves to his wife. The court also stipulated that Charles provide a security deposit which he would forfeit if he failed to abide by the order.[43]

In colonies outside of Maryland, Virginia and South Carolina, the status of married women's separate estates was tenuous at best. Magistrates in New England showed little interest in expanding married women's control of property and displayed little motivation in upholding the principles of the English Chancery over those of the common law. The Puritan belief in the unity of persons during marriage, and their antagonism to wives' financial independence, shaped New England jurisprudence on married women's legal status well into the eighteenth century. Magistrates in Massachusetts and Connecticut preferred the use of jointures to wives' separate property: jointures provided security for widows, but gave women no opportunity for independence during marriage. Married women in Connecticut had very few rights over their property, and husbands could lay claim not only to the land their wives had brought into the marriage but also to their moveable property.

In addition, there were no legal protections against spousal coercion: while English courts upheld the practice of private interviews for wives prior to agreeing to a land sale, both Connecticut and Massachusetts had no such practice.[44] New England magistrates did have the power to dispense justice in equity when they felt that the cases warranted it; however, without a separate jurisdiction to enforce equity principles, these colonies never developed the legal mechanisms that expanded women's control of property. When equity procedures and principles were practised only informally and sporadically, there was no real legal security for wives' separate property. This had profound and lasting implications for wives in the New England colonies, who had no mechanisms for the protection of their property until the nineteenth century.

As in Massachusetts, Pennsylvania justices were vested with the ability to implement equity principles when they saw fit; however, without a separate equity jurisdiction that embraced the full gamut of chancery rules and precedents, justices often chose more familiar common law principles over equity. Pennsylvania Quakers in the seventeenth century had been divided over the authority of magistrates to dispense equity, with some groups against the equity jurisdiction's ability to overturn judgements from common law courts. This scepticism about chancery courts continued into the eighteenth century. Pennsylvania did not follow English precedent in establishing a wife's equity to a settlement, preferring instead to uphold common law rules concerning a wife's inheritance. Although under common law a wife's inheritance of land could not be taken to pay her husband's debts unless she consented, it was often the practice that land was turned into cash during the process of probate. Since cash was moveable property rather than real estate, it automatically fell within her husband's right to claim it.[45]

New York and North Carolina had chancery courts, but their function and operation was wholly different from those of England, Maryland, South Carolina and Virginia. The New York Chancery was established in 1701, but colonists were bitterly divided through the first half of the eighteenth century over the role equity jurisprudence would play within the colonial legal system. Some argued that a separate equity jurisdiction was not necessary, and that the justices of the Supreme Court of Judicature should act as dispensers of equity. Others argued for the establishment of a separate equity jurisdiction under the leadership of the governor acting as the Lord Chancellor. Though a separate chancery did exist, the deep divisions over the powers of the court and the Lord Chancellor hindered any effective development of equity jurisprudence in New York.

The records of the New York Chancery reflect that the court did not adopt English procedures that upheld married women's separate property, and only rarely alleviated the common law restrictions on women.[46] Though some studies have suggested that the New York Chancery expanded its jurisdiction over married women's property in the nineteenth century, in the eighteenth century the court only rarely took action concerning women's separate estates.[47] North Carolina also established a court of chancery in the late seventeenth century, but like New York its procedures and rules were haphazard and bore little resemblance to the English Chancery or to the chancery courts established in Maryland, South Carolina and Virginia. Any person who felt they had not received justice at common law could appeal to the governor and council sitting as the chancery; for this reason, the court acted more as an appellate jurisdiction rather than an equity court with limited jurisdiction.[48]

Conclusion

The percentages of female litigants appearing before the courts in the eighteenth century were equal to, and sometimes greater than, the rates of female litigants in the seventeenth century. The one exception to this more general trend is the decline of the appearance of women in the ecclesiastical courts. In the seventeenth century the percentage of female litigants in estate administration cases greatly exceeded that of any other legal jurisdiction in Anglo-America. This was because the ecclesiastical courts virtually ignored the doctrine of coverture and allowed married women to prosecute or defend cases in their own names. However, over the course of the eighteenth century the jurisdiction of the ecclesiastical courts in estate litigation drastically declined as more business went to the equity courts. A sample of testamentary cases heard before the diocesan courts in the Archbishopric of York shows that 74 per cent of cases included at least one female litigant between 1640 and 1679, a percentage which dropped only slightly, to 72.6 per cent, for the period between 1680 and 1719 (see Table 6.2). These figures are consistent with the percentages of women who appeared in testamentary litigation in southern England (discussed in chapter 2). However, the percentage of cases in which at least one woman appeared as a plaintiff or a defendant dropped drastically by the middle of the eighteenth century. Between 1720 and 1759, only 37 per cent of cases included at least one female litigant; this percentage dropped again to 27.6 per cent between 1760 and 1799. While women still comprised the vast majority of litigants in slander and defamation cases before the ecclesiastical courts in the eighteenth century, the increasing secularisation of English society meant that the church courts slowly lost ground to the secular courts. The church courts hobbled on until 1857 when they were finally abolished.

The English legal system gave women myriad different legal avenues to seek legal redress; those colonies that followed the English model closest, especially Maryland, Virginia and South Carolina, offered women more robust means of protecting and defending their property. The argument that the process of anglicisation in the colonies led to the increasing

Table 6.2 Testamentary cases heard before the diocesan courts in the Archbishopric of York

Date range	Cases including at least one female litigant	Total cases sampled
1640–79	199 (74%)	269
1680–1719	273 (72.6%)	376
1720–59	115 (37%)	310
1760–99	66 (27.6%)	239

Source: Cause Papers in the Diocesan Courts of the Archbishopric of York, 1300–1858, accessed 5 October 2018 through www.dhi.ac.uk/projects/cause-papers.

marginalisation of women from the courtroom is therefore problematic. English law and jurisprudence became more supportive of women's economic and legal roles over the course of the seventeenth and eighteenth centuries. The decline of women in the courts of colonies like Connecticut and New York are perhaps more the result of dynamics internal to those colonies than a movement that happened across the Anglo-American world.

The trend towards women's increasing participation in the economy and their continued presence in the courtroom seems to have extended into the nineteenth century. In Lincolnshire, England, 30 per cent of defendants appearing before the Boston County Court in 1849 were women, and the vast majority of them were married.[49] Similarly, women accounted for 30.6 per cent of plaintiffs before the English Court of Chancery in 1818.[50] Women's participation in colonial courts may also have accelerated. While women appeared infrequently in the New York Chancery in the eighteenth century, their participation may have increased in the nineteenth century: between 1823 and 1847 at least one female litigant appeared in 21 per cent of cases heard before the court.[51]

Women's legal action in the seventeenth century reflects a shift in how early modern society defined and interpreted the relationships between people within the household. In the seventeenth century the dynamics between husbands and wives, parents and children, and masters and servants, were defined by patriarchal ideals of authority and submission. Within this system, each family member had an expected role to play. Custom and law required male heads of household to provide, care for and instruct their dependents. Household subordinates, on the other hand, were expected to defer to the authority of their masters and obey their commands. When everyone fulfilled their proper roles within the patriarchal family, the household functioned harmoniously and everyone's needs were met. However, as this book has shown, patriarchal ideals often broke down between parents and children, masters and servants, and, at the very heart of patriarchal households, husbands and wives. Over the course of the seventeenth and eighteenth centuries, the law came to increasingly define these household relationships, and progressively intervened to provide redress when patriarchal ideals fractured.

Notes

1 Wilfrid Prest, 'The experience of litigation in eighteenth-century England', in David Lemmings (ed.), *The British and Their Laws in the Eighteenth Century* (Woodbridge: Boydell Press, 2005), p. 134; David Lemmings, *Law and Government in England During the Long Eighteenth Century* (New York: Palgrave and Macmillan, 2011), pp. 11–14, 61–2, 77, 176. On the process of anglicisation, see John Murrin, 'Anglicizing an American colony: the transformation of provincial Massachusetts' (PhD thesis, Yale University, 1966); John Murrin, 'The legal transformation: the bench and bar of eighteenth-century Massachusetts', in Stanley Katz and John Murrin (ed.), *Colonial America: Essays in Politics and Social Development* (Boston: Little, Brown, 1971), p. 563. For the lasting influence of Murrin's thesis, see Ignacio Gallup-Diaz, Andrew Shankman and David Silverman (eds), *Anglicizing America: Empire, Revolution, Republic* (Philadelphia: University of Pennsylvania Press, 2015). For works on colonial women that have drawn from the anglicisation thesis, see Debra Rosen, *Courts and Commerce: Gender, Law, and the Market Economy in Colonial New York* (Columbus: Ohio State University Press, 1997), pp. 59, 95; Cornelia Hughes Dayton, *Women Before the Bar: Gender, Law, and Society in Connecticut, 1639–1789* (Chapel Hill: University of North Carolina Press, 1995), pp. 5, 7, 13.
2 Marylynn Salmon, *Women and the Law of Property in Early America* (Chapel Hill: University of North Carolina Press, 1986), pp. 11–12.
3 See Rosen, *Courts and Commerce*; Dayton, *Women Before the Bar*. However, a growing body of work has revised this view of women in the eighteenth-century economy. See Margaret Hunt, *The Middling Sort: Commerce, Gender, and the Family in England, 1680–1780* (Berkeley: University of California Press, 1996), pp. 126–33; Sheryllynne Haggerty, '"Ports, petticoats, and power?" Women and work in early-national Philadelphia', in Douglas Catterall and Jodi Campbell (eds), *Women in Port: Gendering Communities, Economics, and Social Networks in Atlantic Port Cities, 1500–1800* (Boston: Brill, 2012), pp. 103–5; Sheryllynne Haggerty, *The British-Atlantic Trading Community, 1760–1810: Men, Women, and the Distribution of Goods* (Boston: Brill, 2006), pp. 6–7, 164–7; Patricia Cleary, '"She will be in the shop": women's sphere of trade in eighteenth-century Philadelphia and New York', *Pennsylvania Magazine of History and Biography*, 119:3 (1995), pp. 181–6; Cathy Matson, 'Women's economies in North America before 1820', *Early American Studies*, 4:2 (2006), p. 272.

4 Peter Earle, *The Making of the English Middle Class: Business, Society, and Family Life in London, 1660–1730* (Berkeley: University of California Press, 1989), pp. 167–8; Lisa Wilson, *Life After Death: Widows in Pennsylvania, 1750–1800* (Philadelphia: Temple University Press, 1992).
5 Margaret Hunt, 'Wives and marital "rights" in the Court of Exchequer in the early eighteenth century', in Paul Griffiths and Mark Jenner (eds), *Londinopolis: Essays in the Social and Cultural History of Early Modern London* (Manchester: Manchester University Press, 2000), p. 111; Earle, *The Making of the English Middle Class*, pp. 159–60.
6 Julia Rudolph, *Common Law and Enlightenment in England, 1689–1750* (Woodbridge: Boydell Press, 2013), pp. 175–7; Susan Staves, *Married Women's Separate Property in England, 1660–1833* (Cambridge, MA: Harvard University Press, 1990), p. 15.
7 Wilfrid Prest, 'Law reform in eighteenth-century England', in Peter Birks (ed.), *Life of the Law: Proceedings of the 10th British Legal History Conference* (London: Hambledon, 1993), pp. 113–20.
8 William Searle Holdsworth, *A History of English Law*, 18 vols (London: Methuen, 1903–72), vol. 1, pp. 252–3.
9 Amy Erickson, 'Coverture and capitalism', *History Workshop Journal*, 59 (2005), pp. 3–5.
10 Hunt, 'Wives and marital "rights" in the Court of Exchequer', p. 119; Joanne Bailey, 'Favoured or oppressed? Married women, property, and "coverture" in England, 1660–1800', *Continuity and Change*, 17:3 (2002), pp. 353–6; Margot Finn, 'Women, consumption, and coverture in England, c. 1760–1860', *Historical Journal*, 39:3 (1996), pp. 703–9; Craig Muldrew, '"A mutual assent of her mind"? Women, debt, litigation, and contract in early modern England', *History Workshop Journal*, 55:1 (2003), pp. 47–9; Susan Staves, *Married Women's Separate Property in England*, p. 131; J. H. Baker, *An Introduction to English Legal History*, 3rd edn (London: Butterworths, 1990), p. 488.
11 Salmon, *Women and the Law of Property*, p. 54; Haggerty, *The British-Atlantic Trading Community*, pp. 6–7, 216–17.
12 Marjorie K. McIntosh, 'The benefits and drawbacks of *femme sole* status in England, 1300–1630', *Journal of British Studies*, 44:3 (2005), pp. 414–15; Muldrew, '"A mutual assent of her mind"?', p. 49; Earle, *The Making of the English Middle Class*, p. 160.
13 Elizabeth Chudleigh, Countess of Bristol, *The Laws Respecting Women* (London: J. Johnson, 1777), p. 177; Salmon, *Women and the Law of Property*, p. 45.
14 David McCord and Thomas Cooper (eds), *Statutes at Large of South Carolina*, vol. 2 (Columbia, SC: A. S. Johnston, 1836–98), p. 593; Salmon, *Women and the Law of Property*, p. 46.
15 McCord and Cooper (eds), *Statutes at Large of South Carolina*, vol. 3, p. 620; Cynthia Kierner, *Beyond the Household: Women's Place in the Early South, 1700–1835* (Ithaca: Cornell University Press, 1998), pp. 23–5; Salmon, *Women and the Law of Property*, p. 46.
16 *Laws of the Commonwealth of Pennsylvania*, vol. 1 (Philadelphia: J. Bioren, 1810), pp. 99–100; Salmon, *Women and the Law of Property*, p. 49.

17 Salmon, *Women and the Law of Property*, pp. 48–53; Patricia Cleary, *Elizabeth Murray: A Woman's Pursuit of Independence in Eighteenth-Century America* (Amherst: University of Massachusetts Press, 2000), p. 71.
18 Rudolph, *Common Law and Enlightenment in England*, pp. 131, 146–7; Hunt, *The Middling Sort*, pp. 158–60.
19 Henry Horwitz (ed.), *Exchequer Equity Records and Proceedings, 1649–1841* (London: Public Record Office, 2001), pp. 1–3.
20 Hunt, 'Wives and marital "rights" in the Court of Exchequer', p. 112.
21 J. Hall Pleasants (ed.), *Proceedings of the Court of Chancery of Maryland, 1669–1679*, vol. 51 (Baltimore: Maryland State Archives, 1934), pp. xxxv–xxxvii, accessed 11 October 2018 through https://msa.maryland.gov/megafile/msa/speccol/sc2900/sc2908/000001/000051/html/am51p-35.html; Anne King Gregorie (ed.), *Records of the Court of Chancery of South Carolina, 1671–1779* (Binghamton: Vail-Ballou Press, 1950), pp. 5–7, 25–6, 30–6; Marylynn Salmon, 'Women and property in South Carolina: the evidence from marriage settlements, 1730–1830', *William and Mary Quarterly*, 3rd series, 39:4 (1982), p. 659; Stanley Katz, 'The politics of law in colonial America: controversies over chancery courts and equity law in the eighteenth century', in Donald Fleming and Bernard Bailyn (eds), *Perspectives in American History*, vol. 5 (Cambridge, MA: Harvard University Press, 1971), p. 273.
22 Even after Virginia had declared itself separate from the British, it freely adopted England's model of the equity jurisdiction. Marvin K. Singleton, 'The chancery side of Virginia's evolution to statehood', *Journal of American Studies*, 2:2 (1968), p. 159; Linda Sturtz, *Within Her Power: Propertied Women in Colonial Virginia* (New York: Routledge, 2002), pp. 20–3.
23 Henry Horwitz and Patrick Polden, 'Continuity or change in the Court of Chancery in the seventeenth and eighteenth centuries?', *Journal of British Studies*, 35:1 (1996), pp. 44–5; Henry Horwitz, 'Chancery's "younger sister": the Court of Exchequer and its equity jurisdiction, 1649–1841', *Historical Research*, 72:178 (1999), p. 173.
24 Based on estimate that 135,000 of the 290,000 cases heard before these courts between 1700 and 1800 included at least one woman. Hunt, 'Wives and marital "rights" in the Court of Exchequer', p. 111.
25 Baker, *Introduction to English Legal History*, pp. 313–15; Rudolph, *Common Law and Enlightenment in England*, pp. 146–7.
26 Henry Horwitz (ed.), *Samples of Exchequer Equity Pleadings and Suits* (Kew: List and Index Society, 2000), p. 65.
27 Edward Papenfuse (ed.), *A Biographical Dictionary of the Maryland Legislature, 1635–1789* (Baltimore: Johns Hopkins University Press, 2010), pp. 172–3.
28 Gregorie (ed.), *Records of the Court of Chancery of South Carolina*, pp. 539, 550, 561–5.
29 Anglo-American Legal Tradition, Chancery Final Decrees, C78/1725, 14 December 1725, accessed 11 October 2018 through www.uh.edu/waalt/index.php/C78_1725; William Peere Williams, *Reports of Cases Argued and Determined in the High Court of Chancery, and of Some Special Cases Adjudged in the Court of King's Bench*, vol. 2 (Dublin: J. Moore, 1790), pp. 316–18; Susan Staves, *Married Women's Separate Property*

    in England, p. 133 n. 4; Marylynn Salmon, 'The legal status of women in early America: a reappraisal', *Law and History Review*, 1:1 (Spring 1983), pp. 147–8.
30 Gregorie (ed.), *Records of the Court of Chancery of South Carolina*, pp. 507–11; Salmon, 'Women and Property in South Carolina', p. 675; Salmon, *Women and the Law of Property*, pp. 82, 90–3, 112–13.
31 Eileen Spring, *Law, Land, and Family: Aristocratic Inheritance in England, 1300–1800* (Chapel Hill: University of North Carolina Press, 1993), p. 115; Baker, *Introduction to English Legal History*, p. 486.
32 Rippon v. Dawding (1767), Charles Ambler, *Reports of Cases Argued and Determined in the High Court of Chancery* (London: A. Strahan and W. Woodfall, 1790), p. 565; Max A. Robertson and Geoffrey Ellis (eds), *The English Reports (Full Reprint)*, vol. 27: *Chancery* (Getzville: HeinOnline, n.d.), pp. 363–5, accessed 5 October 2018 through https://heinonline.org/HOL/P?h=hein.engrep/engrc0027&i=371.
33 Salmon, *Women and the Law of Property*, pp. 114–15.
34 Margaret Hunt found that less than 5 per cent of married female litigants took action against their husbands. See Hunt, 'Wives and marital "rights" in the Court of Exchequer', p. 111. In my sample of three hundred cases from the Maryland Court of Chancery, only five cases involved a wife suing her husband.
35 Sara Butler, *Divorce in Medieval England: From One to Two Persons in Law* (New York: Routledge, 2013), p. 8; Martin Ingram, *Church Courts, Sex and Marriage in England, 1570–1640* (Cambridge: Cambridge University Press, 1987), p. 181–2.
36 Baker, *Introduction to English Legal History*, p. 486; Staves, *Married Women's Separate Property*, pp. 140–141.
37 Moore v. Moore (1737), John Tracy Atkyns, *Reports of Cases Argued and Determined in the High Court of Chancery*, vol. 1 (London: A. Strahan and W. Woodfall, 1794), pp. 272–8.
38 Salmon, *Women and the Law of Property*, p. 62; Mary Beth Sievens, *Stray Wives: Marital Conflict in Early National New England* (New York: New York University Press, 2005), p. 9.
39 Maryland State Archives, *Chancery Court, Chancery Record, 1671–1712*, 748, pp. 578–81, accessed 11 October 2018 through https://msa.maryland.gov/megafile/msa/speccol/sc2900/sc2908/000001/000748/html/am748-578.html.
40 Debbie Hooper (ed.), *Abstracts of Chancery Court Records of Maryland, 1669–1792* (Westminster, MD: Family Line Publications, 1996), p. 77. This case is also discussed in Alan Kulikoff, *Tobacco and Slaves: The Development of Southern Cultures in the Chesapeake, 1600–1800* (Chapel Hill: University of North Carolina Press, 1986), pp. 181–2.
41 Hooper, *Abstracts of Chancery Court Records of Maryland*, p. 98; Papenfuse (ed.), *A Biographical Dictionary of the Maryland Legislature*, p. 369; Theodorick Bland, *Reports of Cases Decided in the High Court of Chancery of Maryland [1811–1832]* (Baltimore: J. Neal, 1836), p. 570–5; Karen A. Lubieniecki, '"Scarce any ways or means": the separated woman in colonial Maryland, 1634–1776' (MA thesis, University of Maryland, Baltimore, 2007), pp. 29–32.
42 King (ed.), *Records of the Chancery of South Carolina*, pp. 322, 327, 329–30.

43 King (ed.), *Records of the Chancery of South Carolina*, pp. 381-2; Carl. J. Vipperman, 'The brief and tragic career of Charles Lowndes', *South Carolina Historical Magazine*, 70:4 (1969), pp. 211-25.

44 Salmon, *Women and the Law of Property*, pp. 120-1; William J. Curran, 'The struggle for equity jurisdiction in Massachusetts', *Boston University Law Review*, 31:3 (1951), pp. 269-74; Phyllis Maloney Johnson, 'No adequate remedy at law: equity in Massachusetts, 1692-1877', *Student Legal History Papers*, paper 2 (unpublished, Yale Law Library, 2012).

45 Salmon, *Women and the Law of Property*, pp. 91-2; William M. Offutt, Jr., *Of 'Good Laws' and 'Good Men': Law and Society in the Delaware Valley, 1680-1710* (Urbana: University of Illinois Press, 1995); Spencer Liverant and Walter Hitchler, 'A history of equity in Pennsylvania', *Dickinson Law Review*, 37:156 (1933), pp. 156-61.

46 Joseph Smith and Leo Hershkowitz, 'Courts of equity in the province of New York: the Cosby Controversy, 1732-1736', *American Journal of Legal History*, 16:1 (1972), pp. 6-10, 49-50; Rosen, *Courts and Commerce*, pp. 115-16; Mary Beth Debicki, 'Themis in the Empire State: the Supreme Court of Judicature and the Court of Chancery in the lives of New York women, 1783-1847' (PhD thesis, University of Kansas, 2004).

47 Debicki, 'Themis in the Empire State', p. 290; Rosen, *Courts and Commerce*, pp. 115-16.

48 William E. Nelson, *The Common Law in Colonial America*, vol. 2 (Oxford: Oxford University Press, 2013), pp. 88-9.

49 Finn, 'Women, consumption, and coverture in England', p. 718.

50 Horwitz and Polden, 'Continuity or change in the Court of Chancery', p. 45.

51 Debicki, 'Themis in the Empire State', p. 290; Rosen, *Courts and Commerce*, pp. 115-16.

Bibliography

The bibliography includes the main web addresses for the online databases used in this project in the 'Online primary source databases' section. Full URLs for individual sources can be found in the endnotes.

Manuscript sources

British Library
    Egerton Manuscripts
Essex Record Office
    Archdeaconry of Essex Depositions
    Barrington Family Papers
    Colchester Quarter Sessions Depositions
London Metropolitan Archives
    London Commissary Court Depositions
    London Consistory Court Depositions
    Middlesex Quarter Sessions Depositions
    Middlesex Quarter Sessions Petitions
    City of London Sessions Depositions
    Westminster Quarter Sessions Depositions
    Mayor's Court Original Bills
The National Archives, UK
    Records of the Court of Chancery
Henry E. Huntington Library
    Stowe Manuscripts, Temple Papers
    Ellesmere Manuscripts
    Hastings Manuscripts
Phillips Library
    Essex County Quarterly Courts, File Papers
    Essex County Quarterly Courts, Waste Books

Printed editions of primary manuscript sources

Browne, William Hand (ed.), *Proceedings and Acts of the General Assembly, January 1637/8 – September 1664* (Baltimore: Maryland State Archives, 1883).

Dow, George Francis (ed.), *Records and Files of the Quarterly Courts of Essex County, 1636–1686*, 9 vols (Salem: Essex Institute, 1911).

Essex Institute, *Essex Institute Historical Collections* (Salem: Essex Institute 1885).

Gregorie, Anne King (ed.), *Records of the Court of Chancery of South Carolina, 1671–1779* (Binghamton: Vail-Ballou Press, 1950).

Hardy, W. J. (ed.), *Middlesex County Records: Calendar of the Sessions Books, 1689–1709* (London: R. Nicholson, 1905).

Hooper, Debbie (ed.), *Abstracts of Chancery Court Records of Maryland, 1669–1792* (Westminster, MD: Family Line Publications, 1996).
Horwitz, Henry (ed.), *Samples of Exchequer Equity Pleadings and Suits* (Kew: List and Index Society, 2000).
────── (ed.), *Exchequer Equity Records and Proceedings, 1649–1841* (London: Public Record Office, 2001).
Laws of the Commonwealth of Pennsylvania (Philadelphia: J. Bioren, 1810).
McCord, David and Thomas Cooper (eds), *Statutes at Large of South Carolina* (Columbia, SC: A. S. Johnston, 1836–1898).
Mendelson, Sara and Laura Gowing (eds), *Women's Worlds in Seventeenth-Century England: A Sourcebook* (London: Routledge, 2000).
Salley, A. S., 'Abstracts from the records of the Court of Ordinary of the province of South Carolina, 1692–1700', *South Carolina Historical and Genealogical Magazine*, 8:3 (1907).
Shurtleff, Nathaniel B., *Records of the Governor and Company of the Massachusetts Bay in New England*, 6 vols (Boston: W. White, 1853).
Skinner, Vernon (ed.), *Abstracts of the Testamentary Proceedings of the Prerogative Court of Maryland*, vol. 4: *1677–1682, 1702–1704* (Baltimore: Clearfield Company, 2006).
Suffolk County Wills: Abstracts of the Earliest Wills Upon Record in the County of Suffolk, Massachusetts (Boston: New England Historical and Genealogical Society, 1984).

Online primary source databases

Anglo-American Legal Tradition, http://aalt.law.uh.edu.
Archives of Maryland Online, http://aomol.msa.maryland.gov.
Cause Papers in the Diocesan Courts of the Archbishopric of York, 1300–1858, www.dhi.ac.uk/projects/cause-papers.
Records and Files of the Quarterly Courts of Essex County, http://salem.lib.virginia.edu/Essex/index.html.

Printed primary works

Ambler, Charles, *Reports of Cases Argued and Determined in the High Court of Chancery* (London: A. Strahan and W. Woodfall, 1790).
Atkyns, John Tracy, *Reports of Cases Argued and Determined in the High Court of Chancery*, vol. 1 (London: A. Strahan and W. Woodfall, 1794).
Blackstone, William, *Commentaries on the Laws of England*, 4 vols (Oxford: Clarendon Press, 1765–69).
The Book of the General Lawes and Libertyes Concerning the Inhabitants of Massachusetts (Cambridge, MA: Matthew Day, 1648).
Coke, Edward, *Reports* (London: W. Lee, M. Walbanck, D. Pakeman and G. Bedell, 1600–58).
Chudleigh, Elizabeth, Countess of Bristol, *The Laws Respecting Women* (London: J. Johnson, 1777).
Dalton, Michael, *Countrey Justice* (London: The Company of Stationers, 1655 [1618]).

Leonard, William, *Reports and Cases of Law Argued and Adjudged in the Courts of Law at Westminster* (London: Thomas Roycroft, 1658).
Secker, William, *A Wedding Ring for the Finger* (Boston: Samuel Green, 1690).
Webster, John, *The Devil's Law-Case: or When Women goe to Law, the Devill is full of Businesse* (London, John Grismand: 1623).
Williams, William Peere (ed.), *Reports of Cases Argued and Determined in the High Court of Chancery, and of Some Special Cases Adjudged in the Court of King's Bench*, vol. 2 (Dublin: J. Moore, 1790).

Secondary works

Allen, David Grayson, *In English Ways: The Movement of Societies and the Transferral of English Local Law and Custom to Massachusetts Bay in the Seventeenth Century* (Chapel Hill: University of North Carolina Press, 1981).
Bailey, Joanne, 'Voices in court: lawyers' or litigants'?', *Historical Research*, 74:186 (2001).
———, 'Favoured or oppressed? Married women, property, and "coverture" in England, 1660–1800', *Continuity and Change*, 17:3 (2002).
Baker, J. H., *An Introduction to English Legal History*, 3rd edn (London: Butterworths, 1990).
———, *The Oxford History of the Laws of England*, vol. 6: *1483–1558* (Oxford: Oxford University Press, 2003).
Beard, Mary, *Woman as a Force in History: A Study in Traditions and Realities* (New York: Macmillan, 1946).
Beattie, Cordelia and Matthew Stevens (eds), *Married Women and the Law in Premodern Northwest Europe* (Woodbridge: Boydell Press, 2013).
Beimer, Linda Briggs, *Women and Property in Colonial New York: The Transformation from Dutch to English Law, 1643–1727* (Ann Arbor: UMI Research Press, 1983).
Billings, Warren, 'English legal literature as a source of law and legal practice for seventeenth-century Virginia', *Virginia Magazine of History and Biography*, 87:4 (1979).
———, 'The law of servants and slaves in seventeenth-century Virginia', *Virginia Magazine of History and Biography*, 99:1 (1991).
———, '"Send us … what other lawe books you shall thinke fitt": books that shaped the law in Virginia, 1600–1860', *Virginia Magazine of History and Biography*, 120:4 (2012).
Black, Barbara, 'Judicial power and the General Court in early Massachusetts, 1634–1686' (unpublished PhD thesis, Yale University, 1975).
Blaine, Marcia Schmidt, 'The power of petitions: women and the New Hampshire provincial government, 1695–1770', *International Review of Social History*, 46 (2001).
Bland, Theodorick, *Reports of Cases Decided in the High Court of Chancery of Maryland [1811–1832]* (Baltimore: J. Neal, 1836).
Bonfield, Lloyd, 'Testamentary causes in the Prerogative Court of Canterbury, 1660–96', in Christopher Brooks and Michael Lobban (eds), *Communities and the Courts in Britain, 1150–1900* (London: Hambledon, 1997).
Boyer, Allen D., 'Coke, Sir Edward (1552–1634)', *Dictionary of National Biography Online* (Oxford: Oxford University Press, 2009), accessed 4 October 2018 through

www.oxforddnb.com/view/10.1093/ref:odnb/9780198614128.001.0001/odnb-9780198614128-e-5826.

Brewer, John, *The Sinews of Power: War, Money, and the English State, 1688–1783* (London: Unwin Hyman, 1989).

Brooks, Christopher, *Pettyfoggers and Vipers of the Commonwealth: The 'Lower Branch' of the Legal Profession in Early Modern England* (Cambridge: Cambridge University Press, 1986).

——, *Lawyers, Litigation, and English Society Since 1450* (London: Hambledon, 1998).

Brooks, Christopher and Michael Lobban (eds), *Communities and Courts in Britain, 1150–1900* (London: Hambledon, 1997).

Brown, Kathleen, *Good Wives, Nasty Wenches, and Anxious Patriarchs: Gender, Race, and Power in Colonial Virginia* (Chapel Hill: University of North Carolina Press, 1996).

Brundage, James, 'Juridical space: female witnesses in canon law', *Dumbarton Oaks Papers*, 52 (1998).

——, *The Medieval Origins of the Legal Profession: Canonists, Civilians, and Courts* (Chicago: University of Chicago Press, 2008).

Bryson, William Hamilton, 'English common law in Virginia', *Journal of Legal History*, 6:3 (1985).

Butler, Sara, *Divorce in Medieval England: From One to Two Persons in Law* (New York: Routledge, 2013).

Canny, Nicholas (ed.), *The Origins of Empire: British Overseas Enterprise to the Close of the Seventeenth Century* [vol. 1 of William Roger Louis (ed.), *The Oxford History of the British Empire*] (Oxford: Oxford University Press, 1998).

Carr, Lois Green and Lorena S. Walsh, 'The planter's wife: the experience of white women in seventeenth-century Maryland', *William and Mary Quarterly*, 3rd series, 34:4 (1977).

Chu, Jonathan, 'Nursing a poisonous tree: litigation and property law in seventeenth-century Essex County, Massachusetts, the case of Bishop's Farm', *American Journal of Legal History*, 31:3 (1987).

Churches, Christine, 'Women and property in early modern England: a case-study', *Social History*, 23:2 (1998).

——, 'Putting women in their place: female litigants at Whitehaven, 1660–1760', in Nancy Wright, Margaret Ferguson and A. R. Buck (eds), *Women, Property, and the Letters of the Law in Early Modern England* (Toronto: University of Toronto Press, 2004).

Cioni, Maria, 'The Elizabethan Chancery and women's rights', in D. J. Guth and J. W. McKenna (eds), *Tudor Rule and Revolution* (Cambridge: Cambridge University Press, 1982).

——, *Women and Law in Elizabethan England, with Particular Reference to the Court of Chancery* (New York: Garland, 1985).

Cleary, Patricia, '"She will be in the shop": women's sphere of trade in eighteenth-century Philadelphia and New York', *Pennsylvania Magazine of History and Biography*, 119:3 (1995).

——, *Elizabeth Murray: A Woman's Pursuit of Independence in Eighteenth-Century America* (Amherst: University of Massachusetts Press, 2000).

Cohen, Sheldon, 'What man hath put asunder: divorce in New Hampshire, 1681–1784', *Historical New Hampshire*, 41:3 (1986).

BIBLIOGRAPHY

Conger, Vivian Bruce, *The Widow's Might: Widowhood and Gender in Early British America* (New York: New York University Press, 2009).

Cott, Nancy, 'Divorce and the changing status of women in eighteenth-century Massachusetts', *William and Mary Quarterly*, 3rd series, 33:4 (1976).

Crawford, Patricia, 'From the woman's view: pre-industrial England, 1500–1750', in Patricia Crawford (ed.), *Exploring Women's Past: Essays in Social History* (London: George Allen & Unwin, 1984).

Curran, William J., 'The struggle for equity jurisdiction in Massachusetts', *Boston University Law Review*, 31:3 (1951).

Daniels, Christine, '"Liberty to complain": servant petitions in Maryland, 1652–1797', in Christopher Tomlins and Bruce Mann (eds), *The Many Legalities of Early America* (Chapel Hill: University of Norton Carolina Press, 2001).

Daybell, James, 'Scripting a female voice: women's epistolary rhetoric in sixteenth-century letters of petition', *Women's Writing*, 13:1 (2006).

Dayton, Cornelia Hughes, *Women Before the Bar: Gender, Law, and Society in Connecticut, 1639–1789* (Chapel Hill: University of North Carolina Press, 1995).

——, 'Was there a Calvinist type of patriarchy? New Haven colony reconsidered in the early modern context', in Christopher Tomlins and Bruce Mann (eds), *The Many Legalities of Early America* (Chapel Hill: Omohundro Institute of Early American History and Culture, 2001).

——, 'Rethinking patriarchy, recovering voices', *American Historical Review*, 109:3 (2004).

Debicki, Mary Beth, 'Themis in the Empire State: the Supreme Court of Judicature and the Court of Chancery, 1783–1847' (PhD thesis, University of Kansas, 2004).

Ditz, Toby L., *Property and Kinship, Inheritance in Early Connecticut, 1750–1820* (Princeton: Princeton University Press, 1986).

Dodd, Gwilym, 'The hidden presence: Parliament and the private petition in the fourteenth century', in Anthony Musson (ed.), *Expectations of the Law in the Middle Ages* (Woodbridge: Boydell Press, 2001).

——, 'Reason, conscience, and equity: bishops as the king's judges in later medieval England', *History*, 99 (2014).

Dodd, Gwilym and Sophie Petit-Renaud, 'Grace and favour: the petition and its mechanisms', in Christopher Fletcher *et al.* (eds), *Political Life in England and France, c. 1300–c. 1500* (Cambridge: Cambridge University Press, 2015).

Dolan, Frances, *True Relations: Reading, Literature, and Evidence in Seventeenth-Century England* (Philadelphia: University of Pennsylvania Press, 2013).

Donahue, Charles, 'Proof by witnesses in the church courts of medieval England: an imperfect reception of the learned law', in Morris Arnold, Thomas Green, Sally Scully and Stephen White (eds), *On the Laws and Customs of England: Essays in Honor of Samuel E. Thorne* (Chapel Hill: North Carolina University Press, 1981).

Earle, Peter, *The Making of the English Middle Class: Business, Society, and Family Life in London, 1660–1730* (Berkeley: University of California Press, 1989).

Erickson, Amy, 'Common law versus common practice: the use of marriage settlements in early modern England', *Economic History Review*, 43:1 (1990).

——, *Women and Property in Early Modern England* (London: Routledge, 1993).

———, 'Coverture and capitalism', *History Workshop Journal*, 59 (2005).
Finn, Margot, 'Women, consumption, and coverture in England, c. 1760–1860', *Historical Journal*, 39:3 (1996).
Fletcher, Anthony, *Gender, Sex, and Subordination in England, 1500–1800* (New Haven: Yale University Press, 1995).
Gallup-Diaz, Ignacio, Andrew Shankman and David Silverman (eds), *Anglicizing America: Empire, Revolution, Republic* (Philadelphia: University of Pennsylvania Press, 2015).
Gay, E. F., 'The Temples of Stowe and their debts: Sir Thomas Temple and Sir Peter Temple, 1603–1653', *Huntington Library Quarterly*, 2:4 (1939).
———, 'Sir Richard Temple: the debt settlement and estate litigation, 1653–1675', *Huntington Library Quarterly*, 6:3 (1943).
Gowing, Laura, *Domestic Dangers: Women, Words, and Sex in Early Modern London* (Oxford: Oxford University Press, 1996).
———, 'Ordering the body: illegitimacy and female authority in seventeenth-century England', in Michael Braddick and John Walter (eds), *Negotiating Power in Early Modern Society: Order, Hierarchy, and Subordination in Britain and Ireland* (Cambridge: Cambridge University Press, 2000).
———, 'The haunting of Susan Lay: servants and mistresses in seventeenth-century England', *Gender and History*, 14:2 (2002).
———, 'Girls on forms: apprenticing young women in seventeenth-century London', *Journal of British Studies*, 55 (July 2016).
Graham, Michael, 'Meetinghouse and chapel: religion and community in seventeenth-century Maryland', in Lois Green Carr, Philip D. Morgan and Jean B. Russo (eds), *Colonial Chesapeake Society* (Chapel Hill: University of North Carolina Press, 1988).
Gundersen, Joan R. and Gwen Victor Gampel, 'Married women's legal status in eighteenth-century New York and Virginia', *William and Mary Quarterly*, 3rd series, 39:1 (1982).
Haggerty, Sheryllynne, *The British-Atlantic Trading Community, 1760–1810: Men, Women, and the Distribution of Goods* (Boston: Brill, 2006).
———, '"Ports, petticoats, and power?" Women and work in early-national Philadelphia', in Douglas Catterall and Jodi Campbell (eds), *Women in Port: Gendering Communities, Economics, and Social Networks in Atlantic Port Cities, 1500–1800* (Boston: Brill, 2012).
Hambleton, Else, *Daughters of Eve: Pregnant Brides and Unwed Mothers in Seventeenth-Century Massachusetts* (New York: Routledge, 2004).
Hancock, David, *Citizens of the World: London Merchants and the Integration of the British Atlantic Community, 1735–1785* (Cambridge: Cambridge University Press, 1995).
Harris, Barbara, *English Aristocratic Women, 1450–1550: Marriage and Family, Property and Careers* (Oxford: Oxford University Press, 2002).
Haskins, George, *Law and Authority in Early Massachusetts: A Study in Tradition and Design* (New York: Macmillan, 1960).
Helmholz, R. H., 'Debt claims and probate jurisdiction in historical perspective', *The American Journal of Legal History*, 23:1 (1979).
———, *The Canon Law and Ecclesiastical Jurisdiction from 597 to the 1640s* [vol. 1 of *The Oxford History of the Laws of England*] (Oxford: Oxford University Press, 2004).

Hening, William Waller (ed.), *Statutes at Large: Being a Collection of all the Laws of Virginia from the First Session of the Legislature, in the Year 1619* (New York: R. W. G. Bartow, 1808).

Herrup, Cynthia, *The Common Peace: Participation and the Criminal Law in Seventeenth-century England* (Cambridge: Cambridge University Press, 1987).

Hogrefe, Pearl, 'Legal rights of Tudor women and the circumvention by men and women', *Sixteenth Century Journal*, 3:1 (1972).

Holdsworth, William Searle, *A History of English Law*, 18 vols (London: Methuen, 1903–72).

Horn, James, 'Servant emigration to the Chesapeake in the seventeenth century', in Thad W. Tate and David L. Ammerman (eds), *The Chesapeake in the Seventeenth Century: Essays on Anglo-American Society* (New York: Norton, 1979).

——, *Adapting to a New World: English Society in the Seventeenth-century Chesapeake* (Chapel Hill: University of North Carolina Press, 1994).

Horwitz, Henry, 'Chancery's "younger sister": the Court of Exchequer and its equity jurisdiction, 1649–1841', *Historical Research*, 72:178 (1999).

Horwitz, Henry and Patrick Polden, 'Continuity or change in the Court of Chancery in the seventeenth and eighteenth centuries?', *Journal of British Studies*, 35:1 (1996).

Hubbard, Eleanor, *City Women: Money, Sex, and the Social Order in Early Modern London* (Oxford: Oxford University Press, 2012).

Hunt, Margaret, *The Middling Sort: Commerce, Gender, and the Family in England, 1680–1780* (Berkeley: University of California Press, 1996).

——, 'Wives and marital "rights" in the Court of Exchequer in the early eighteenth century', in Paul Griffiths and Mark Jenner (eds), *Londinopolis: Essays in the Cultural and Social History of Early Modern London* (Manchester: Manchester University Press, 2000).

Ingram, Martin, *Church Courts, Sex and Marriage in England, 1570–1640* (Cambridge: Cambridge University Press, 1987).

Johnson, Herbert Alan, 'The Prerogative Court of New York, 1686–1776', *American Journal of Legal History*, 17:2 (1973).

Johnson, Phyllis Maloney, 'No adequate remedy at law: equity in Massachusetts, 1692–1877', *Student Legal History Papers*, paper 2 (unpublished, Yale Law Library, 2012).

Johnson, Walter, 'On agency', *Journal of Social History*, 37:1 (2003).

Kane, Bronach and Fiona Williamson (eds), *Women, Agency, and the Law, 1300–1700* (London: Pickering and Chatto, 2013).

Katz, Stanley, 'The politics of law in colonial America: controversies over chancery courts and equity law in the eighteenth century', in Donald Fleming and Bernard Bailyn (eds), *Perspectives in American History*, vol. 5 (Cambridge, MA: Harvard University Press, 1971).

Kendall, John, *A Blessed Company: Parishes, Parsons, and Parishioners in Anglican Virginia, 1690–1776* (Chapel Hill: University of North Carolina Press, 2001).

Kerber, Linda, *Women of the Republic: Intellect and Ideology in Revolutionary America* (Chapel Hill: University of North Carolina Press, 1980).

Kierner, Cynthia, *Beyond the Household: Women's Place in the Early South, 1700–1835* (Ithaca: Cornell University Press, 1998).

King, Walter, 'Punishment for bastardy in early seventeenth-century England', *Albion*, 10:2 (1978).
Kittel, Ruth, 'Women under the law in medieval England, 1066-1485', in Barbara Kanner (ed.), *The Women of England: Interpretive Bibliographical Essays* (Hamden: Archon, 1979).
Konig, David Thomas, *Law and Society in Puritan Massachusetts: Essex County, 1629-1692* (Chapel Hill: University of North Carolina Press, 1979).
Kulikoff, Allan, *Tobacco and Slaves: The Development of Southern Cultures in the Chesapeake* (Chapel Hill: University of North Carolina Press, 1986).
Lebsock, Suzanne, *The Free Women of Petersburg: Status and Culture in a Southern Town, 1784-1860* (New York: Norton, 1984).
Lemmings, David, 'Women's property, popular cultures, and the Consistory Court', in Nancy Wright, Margaret Ferguson and A. R. Buck (eds), *Women, Property, and the Letters of the Law in Early Modern England* (Toronto: University of Toronto Press, 2004).
——, *Law and Government in England During the Long Eighteenth Century* (New York: Palgrave and Macmillan, 2011).
Lightfoot, Dana Wessell, *Women, Dowries and Agency: Marriage in Fifteenth-Century Valencia* (Manchester: Manchester University Press, 2013).
Liverant, Spencer and Walter Hitchler, 'A history of equity in Pennsylvania', *Dickinson Law Review*, 37:156 (1933).
Lubieniecki, Karen A., '"Scarce any ways or means": the separated woman in colonial Maryland, 1634-1776' (MA thesis, University of Maryland, Baltimore, 2007).
MacQueen, Edith E., 'The commissary in colonial Maryland', *Maryland Historical Magazine*, 25 (Baltimore: Maryland Historical Society, 1930).
Main, Gloria, *Tobacco Colony: Life in Early Maryland, 1650-1720* (Princeton: Princeton University Press, 1982).
Matson, Cathy, 'Women's economies in North America before 1820', *Early American Studies*, 4:2 (2006).
Mayo, Lawrence, *John Endecott: A Biography* (Cambridge, MA: Harvard University Press, 1936).
McInnis, L. R., 'Michael Dalton: the training of the early modern justice of the peace and the Cromwellian Reforms', in Jonathan Bush and Alain Wijffels (eds), *Learning the Law: Teaching and the Transmission of Law in England, 1150-1900* (London: Hambledon, 1999).
McIntosh, Marjorie K., 'The benefits and drawbacks of *femme sole* status in England, 1300-1630', *Journal of British Studies*, 44:3 (2005).
Meldrum, Tim, 'London domestic servants from depositional evidence, 1660-1750: servant-employer sexuality in the patriarchal household', in Tim Hitchcock, Peter King and Pamela Sharpe (eds), *Chronicling Poverty: The Voices and Strategies of the English Poor, 1640-1840* (London: Macmillan, 1997).
——, *Domestic Service and Gender, 1660-1750: Life and Work in the London Household* (Harlow: Pearson, 2000).
Menard, Russell, 'From servant to freeholders: status mobility and property accumulation in seventeenth-century Maryland', *William and Mary Quarterly*, 3rd series, 30:1 (1973).
——, 'From servants to slaves: the transformation of the Chesapeake labor system', *Southern Studies*, 16 (1977).

Mendelson, Sara and Patricia Crawford, *Women in Early Modern England* (Oxford: Clarendon Press, 1998).

Meyers, Debra, *Common Whores, Vertuous Women, and Loveing Wives: Free Will Christian Women in Colonial Maryland* (Bloomington: Indiana University Press, 2003).

Morgan, Edmund, *The Puritan Family: Religion and Domestic Relations in Seventeenth-century New England* (Westport: Greenwood Press, 1980).

Morris, Richard, *Studies in the History of American Law: With Special Reference to the Seventeenth and Eighteenth Centuries* (New York: Octagon Books, 1930).

Morris, Thomas D., *Southern Slavery and the Law, 1619-1860* (Chapel Hill: University of North Carolina Press, 1996).

Mosley, Charles (ed.), *Burke's Peerage and Baronetage*, vol. 2, 106th edn (London: Routledge, 1999).

Muldrew, Craig, "'A mutual assent of her mind"? Women, debt, litigation, and contract in early modern England', *History Workshop Journal*, 55:1 (2003).

Murrin, John, 'Anglicizing an American colony: the transformation of provincial Massachusetts' (PhD thesis, Yale University, 1966).

——, 'The legal transformation: the bench and bar of eighteenth-century Massachusetts', in Stanley Katz and John Murrin (eds), *Colonial America: Essays in Politics and Social Development* (Boston: Little, Brown, 1971).

Newbold, David, *Notes on the Introduction of the Equity Jurisdiction into Maryland, 1634-1720* (Boston: Curlander, 1906).

Nelson, William E., 'The utopian legal order of the Massachusetts Bay colony, 1630-1686', *American Journal of Legal History*, 47:2 (2005).

——, *The Common Law in Colonial America*, 2 vols (Oxford: Oxford University Press, 2008, 2013).

Norton, Mary Beth, *Liberty's Daughters: The Revolutionary Experience of American Women, 1750-1800* (Boston: Little, Brown, 1980).

——, 'Gender and defamation in seventeenth-century Maryland', *William and Mary Quarterly*, 3rd series, 44:1 (1987).

——, 'Gender, crime and community in seventeenth-century Maryland', in James Henretta, Michael Kammen and Stanley Katz (eds), *The Transformation of Early American History: Society, Authority, and Ideology* (New York: Knopf, 1991).

——, *Founding Mothers and Fathers: Gendered Power and the Forming of American Society* (New York: Knopf, 1996).

——, '"The ablest midwife that wee knowe in the land": Mistress Alice Tilly and the women of Boston and Dorchester, 1649-1650', *William and Mary Quarterly*, 3rd series, 55:1 (1998).

Oberholzer, Emile, *Delinquent Saints: Disciplinary Action in the Early Congregational Churches of Massachusetts* (New York: Columbia University Press, 1955).

O'Day, Rosemary, *Women's Agency in Early Modern Britain and the American Colonies: Patriarchy, Partnership and Patronage* (London: Pearson, 2007).

Offutt, William M., Jr., *Of 'Good Laws' and 'Good Men': Law and Society in the Delaware Valley, 1680-1710* (Urbana: University of Illinois Press, 1995).

Papenfuse, Edward (ed.), *A Biographical Dictionary of the Maryland Legislature, 1635-1789* (Baltimore: Johns Hopkins University Press, 2010).

Perley, Sidney, *The Essex Antiquarian*, vol. 9 (Salem: The Essex Antiquarian, 1905).
Pollack, Linda, 'Rethinking patriarchy and the family in seventeenth-century England', *Journal of Family History*, 23:3 (1998).
Poos, L. R., 'Sex, lies, and the church courts of pre-Reformation England', *Journal of Interdisciplinary History*, 25 (1995).
Pound, Roscoe, *The Formative Era of American Law* (Boston: Little, Brown, 1938).
Prest, Wilfrid R., 'Law and women's rights in early modern England', *Seventeenth Century*, 6:2 (1991).
——, 'Law reform in eighteenth-century England', in Peter Birks (ed.), *Life of the Law: Proceedings of the 10th British Legal History Conference* (London: Hambledon, 1993).
——, 'The experience of litigation in eighteenth-century England', in David Lemmings (ed.), *The British and Their Laws in the Eighteenth Century* (Woodbridge: Boydell Press, 2005).
Reis, Elizabeth, *Damned Women: Sinners and Witches in Puritan New England* (Ithaca: Cornell University Press, 1997).
Robertson, Max A. and Geoffrey Ellis (eds), *The English Reports (Full Reprint)*, vol. 27: *Chancery* (Getzville: HeinOnline, n.d.), accessed 5 October 2018 through https://heinonline.org/HOL/P?h=hein.engrep/engrc0027&i=371.
Rogers, Kim, 'Relics of the New World: conditions of widowhood in seventeenth-century New England', in Mary Kelley (ed.), *Woman's Being, Woman's Place: Female Identity and Vocation in American History* (Boston: G. K. Hall, 1979).
Rosen, Debra, *Courts and Commerce: Gender, Law, and the Market Economy in Colonial New York* (Columbus: Ohio State University Press, 1997).
Rudolph, Julia, *Common Law and Enlightenment in England, 1689–1750* (Woodbridge: Boydell Press, 2013).
Rutman, Darrett B. and Anita H. Rutman, '"Now wives and sons-in-law": parental death in a seventeenth-century Virginia county', in Thad W. Tate and David L. Ammerman (eds), *The Chesapeake in the Seventeenth Century: Essays on Anglo-American Society* (New York: Norton, 1979).
——, *A Place in Time: Middlesex County, Virginia, 1650–1760* (New York: Norton, 1984).
Salmon, Marylynn, 'Women and property in South Carolina: the evidence from marriage settlements, 1730–1830', *William and Mary Quarterly*, 3rd series, 39:4 (1982).
——, 'The legal status of women in early America: a reappraisal', *Law and History Review*, 1:1 (Spring 1983).
——, 'The court records of Philadelphia, Bucks, and Berks counties in the seventeenth and eighteenth centuries', *Pennsylvania Magazine of History and Biography*, 107:2 (1983).
——, *Women and the Law of Property in Early America* (Chapel Hill: University of North Carolina Press, 1986).
Scott, Henry Wilson, *The Courts of the State of New York: Their History, Development, and Jurisdiction* (New York: Wilson, 1909).
Scott, Joan, 'Gender: a useful category of historical analysis', *American Historical Review*, 91:5 (1986).
Shammas, Carole, 'English inheritance law and its transfer to the colonies', *American Journal of Legal History*, 31:2 (1987).
——, 'Anglo-American household government in comparative perspective', *William and Mary Quarterly*, 3rd series, 52:1 (1995).

Shapiro, Barbara, 'Law reform in seventeenth-century England', *American Journal of Legal History*, 19:4 (1975).
———, *A Culture of Fact, 1550–1720* (Ithaca: Cornell University Press, 2000).
Sharpe, J. A., *Defamation and Sexual Slander in Early Modern England: The Church Courts at York* (York: Borthwick Institute of Historical Research, 1980).
———, *Crime in Seventeenth-century England: A County Study* (Cambridge: Cambridge University Press, 1983).
Sheehan, Michael, 'The influence of canon law on the property rights of married women in England', in James Farge (ed.), *Marriage, Family, and Law in Medieval Europe: Collected Studies* (Toronto: Toronto University Press, 1997).
Shepherd, Alexandra, *Accounting for Oneself: Worthy, Status, and the Social Order in Early Modern England* (Oxford: Oxford University Press, 2015).
Sievens, Mary Beth, *Stray Wives: Marital Conflict in Early National New England* (New York: New York University Press, 2005).
Singleton, Marvin, 'The chancery side of Virginia's evolution to statehood', *Journal of American Studies*, 2:2 (1968).
Smith, Hilda, 'The foundation of law in Maryland', in George Athan Billias (ed.), *Law and Authority in Colonial America: Selected Essays* (Barre: Barre Publishers, 1965).
Smith, Joseph, *Colonial Justice in Western Massachusetts, 1639–1702* (Cambridge, MA: Harvard University Press, 1961).
Smith, Joseph and Leo Hershkowitz, 'Courts of equity in the province of New York: the Cosby Controversy, 1732–1736', *American Journal of Legal History*, 16:1 (1972).
Snyder, Terri, *Brabbling Women: Disorderly Speech and the Law in Early Virginia* (Ithaca: Cornell University Press, 2003).
Spring, Eileen, *Law, Land, and Family: Aristocratic Inheritance in England, 1300–1800* (Chapel Hill: University of North Carolina Press, 1993).
Surrency, Erwin C., 'The courts in the American colonies', *The American Journal of Legal History*, 11:3 (1967).
———, 'The beginnings of American legal literature', *American Journal of Legal History*, 31:3 (1987).
Staves, Susan, *Married Women's Separate Property in England, 1660–1833* (Cambridge, MA: Harvard University Press, 1990).
Stretton, Tim, *Women Waging Law in Elizabethan England* (Cambridge: Cambridge University Press, 1998).
Stretton, Tim and Krista Kesselring, *Married Women and the Law: Coverture in England and the Common Law World* (Montreal: McGill-Queen's University Press, 2013).
Sturtz, Linda L., '"As though I my self was pr[e]sent": Virginia women with power of attorney', in Christopher Tomlins and Bruce Mann (eds), *The Many Legalities of Early America* (Chapel Hill: University of North Carolina Press, 2001).
———, *Within Her Power: Propertied Women in Colonial Virginia* (New York: Routledge, 2002).
Tannenbaum, Rebecca Jo, *The Healer's Calling: Women and Medicine in Early New England* (Ithaca: Cornell University Press, 2002).
Taylor, Alan, *American Colonies: The Settling of North America* (London: Penguin, 2002).
Thompson, Roger, *Women in Stuart England and America: A Comparative Study* (Boston: Routledge, 1974).

———, *Sex in Middlesex: Popular Mores in a Massachusetts County, 1649–1699* (Amherst: University of Massachusetts Press, 1986).

Tolley, Michael, 'Maryland and its Anglo-American legal inheritance', *Journal of Legal History*, 11:3 (1990).

Tomlins, Christopher, and Bruce Mann (eds), *The Many Legalities of Early America* (Chapel Hill: Omohundro Institute of Early American History and Culture, 2001).

Towner, Lawrence, '"A fondness for freedom": servant protest in Puritan society', *William and Mary Quarterly*, 3rd series, 19:2 (1962).

Ulrich, Laurel Thatcher, 'Vertuous women found: New England ministerial literature, 1668–1735', *American Quarterly*, 28:1 (1976).

Vipperman, Carl J., 'The brief and tragic career of Charles Lowndes', *South Carolina Historical Magazine*, 70:4 (1969).

Walsh, Lorena, 'Servitude and opportunity in Charles County Maryland, 1658–1705', in Aubrey Land, Lois Green Carr and Edward Papenfuse (eds), *Law, Society, and Politics in Early Maryland* (Baltimore: Johns Hopkins University Press, 1974).

———, '"Til death us do part": marriage and family in seventeenth-century Maryland', in Thad W. Tate and David L. Ammerman (eds), *The Chesapeake in the Seventeenth Century: Essays on Anglo-American Society* (New York: Norton, 1979).

———, *Motives of Honor, Pleasure, and Profit: Plantation Management in the Colonial Chesapeake, 1607–1763* (Chapel Hill: University of North Carolina Press, 2010).

Wawrzyczek, Irmina, 'The women of Accomack versus Henry Smith: gender, legal recourse, and the social order in seventeenth-century Virginia', *Virginia Magazine of History and Biography*, 105:1 (1997).

Wilson, Lisa, *Life After Death: Widows in Pennsylvania, 1750–1800* (Philadelphia: Temple University Press, 1992).

Wrightson, Keith, 'The nadir of English illegitimacy in the seventeenth century', in Peter Laslett, Karla Oosterveen and Richard M. Smith (eds), *Bastardy and Its Comparative History* (Cambridge, MA: Harvard University Press, 1980).

———, *English Society, 1580–1680* (New Brunswick: Rutgers University Press, 1982).

———, *Earthly Necessities: Economic Lives in Early Modern Britain* (New Haven: Yale University Press, 2002).

Wulf, Karin, *Not All Wives: Women in Colonial Philadelphia* (Ithaca: Cornell University Press, 2000).

———, 'Women and families in early (North) America and the wider (Atlantic) world', in 'Rethinking gender, family, and sexuality in the early modern Atlantic world', *History Compass*, 8:3 (2010).

Index

adultery
  marital separation and 82–4
  moral offences and 29, 31, 82
  paternity suits and 98–100

Barrington, Lady Judith Smith 112–16
Bateman, Mary Perry 119–21

Chesapeake
  illegitimacy 92–4, 100–1
  inheritance 108, 116, 125
  marital separation 82, 84
  marriage 43, 84, 108, 116–17, 118, 125
  New England and 14, 43–4, 60, 76–7, 82–4, 93–4, 96, 101, 106, 108, 123, 125
  religious diversity 82, 121–2
  patriarchy 60, 67, 76–7, 101
  servants 60, 67–9, 76, 92–4, 100–1
  slaves 60, 76
  widows 7, 44, 106, 108, 116–18, 125
  women as estate executors 106, 108, 116–22, 125
  women's property and demography 7, 14, 43–4, 106, 108, 116, 118, 125
  see also Maryland; Virginia
Connecticut 133, 153
  common law 5, 28, 133, 153
  ecclesiastical law 5
  equity law 5, 28, 122
  inheritance 109, 122, 150
  marital separation 84
  New Haven (colony) 6
  women's separate estates 28, 122, 150

common law
  anglicisation 133, 152
  comparison of England and colonies 3–7, 21–3, 25–9, 33, 39–44, 52, 84, 106, 108–9, 122, 125, 133–5, 139–40, 150–1
  Dissenters and 6, 21–2, 28, 51, 84, 106, 122, 150–1
  ecclesiastical law and 21–2, 30–3. 47–8, 52
  equity law and 7, 21–2, 25–9, 44–5, 52, 107, 134–6, 139–40, 150–1
  female litigants in courts 13, 39–44, 133
  feme sole traders 134, 137–9
  inheritance 106–9, 112–13, 116–17, 125, 150–1
  petitions and 64, 82–5
  wives 7, 9, 22–5, 28, 39–44, 51–2, 82–5, 109, 134–9, 140, 150–1
  see also coverture
  widows 24, 26, 40–3, 106–7, 116–17, 122–5, 140, 150
coverture
  commercial economy and 134–9
  common law 5, 7, 22–5, 33, 39–40, 52
  definition of 5, 23
  ecclesiastical law 22, 33, 39–40, 51–2, 152
  equity law 22, 26, 28, 33, 39–40, 45, 52
  feme sole traders and 7, 137–9
  limitations posed by 5, 9, 22–6, 33, 125,
  marital separation 85
  'unity of person' 23, 150
  wives' petitions while under 13, 82–5
  wives' power of attorney 25

wives' protection of property while
under 14, 33, 107–8, 110,
113–14

Dissenters 6, 23, 82, 121–2
  Puritans 4, 5, 6, 28, 31, 51, 84, 106
  Quakers 4, 28, 31, 50, 151
divorce *see* marital separation
dower rights 147, 149
  Chesapeake 108, 116, 149
  England 24, 26, 47, 107–8, 147
  jointures and 107–8, 116, 147
  New England 108, 122–5
  'pin money' 147–8

ecclesiastical law
  absence of in colonies 5–6, 22, 28,
    31–3, 46–7, 84, 106
  common law and 4–5, 7, 13, 22,
    30, 33, 51
  coverture and 29–30, 46–8
  Dissenters and 5, 51, 106
  England 29
  equity law and 4–7, 13, 22, 33, 39,
    152
  female litigants in 2, 13, 29, 33, 39,
    47–9, 52, 152
  inheritance 7, 22, 24, 29–33, 47,
    49–51
  marital separation 83–4, 146, 148
  moral offences 29, 31
  widows 47–8, 51
  wives 5, 7, 22, 30–1, 33, 39, 47–50,
    51–2
Eltonhead, Jane Fenwick Smith Taylor
  117–18
Endicott, Elizabeth 123–4
England
  Archdeacon's Court (Essex) 47–8
  commercial economy 14, 134–6,
    139–40
  Commissary Court (London) 47–8
  common law 3–4, 21–3, 24, 26,
    39–41, 52, 106–8, 134–6

Court of Chancery 4, 21, 26, 27,
  44, 45–6, 113, 115, 140, 144,
  146, 147
Court of Exchequer 26, 44, 140–1,
  142
Court of Requests 26, 44
Diocesan Court (York) 152–3
Dissenters in 28
dower rights 24, 26, 107–8
ecclesiastical law 5, 21–3, 24,
  29–32, 33, 39, 46–50, 52, 146,
  152
equity law 13, 21–3, 26, 27, 33, 39,
  44–5, 52, 134–6, 139–40, 144–8
female litigants in 39–42, 45, 47–8,
  141, 152–3
feme sole traders 14, 137–8
illegitimacy 81–2, 90–1, 95–6, 98,
  100–1
marital separation 13, 81–3, 85–6,
  135, 146–8
marriage settlements 107–8,
  109–111, 112–13, 112–14,
  134–5, 145–8
Mayor's Court (London) 40–1
midwives 90–1, 95–6, 98, 100–1
petitions 64–66, 82–3, 85–6
servants 59–62, 65–6, 72–3, 75–7
slaves 61, 66–7, 75–7
widows 24, 26, 46–9, 52, 105–8,
  109–10, 111–12, 114–16, 125,
  140
wives 22–3, 27, 29–31, 40, 45,
  47–50, 52, 81–3, 85–6, 98,
  100–1, 105–8, 109–11, 112–14,
  125, 134–6, 140, 145, 153
entails 26, 106–8
equity law
  colonial 3, 5–6, 14, 20–3, 26–9,
    39–40, 45–6, 134
  commercial economy and 3, 14–15,
    25–6, 134–6, 139
  common law and 4–6, 7, 13, 22,
    25–7, 39, 44, 45, 134–6, 151

coverture and 25–7, 45–6
Dissenters and 5–6, 21–2, 27–9, 134, 150–1
ecclesiastical law and 5, 7, 33, 39, 47, 52, 146, 152
'equity of redemption' 142–3
female litigants in 3–4, 13, 39, 45–6, 141
marital separation 135, 146–7
marriage settlements 4, 26–7, 44–5, 107, 134, 145–6
mortgages 142–3
'restraint upon anticipation' 145
trusts 4, 7, 26, 40–1, 45–6, 139, 144–5
wives 3, 5–6, 7–8, 14–15, 22, 25–8, 39, 44–5, 134–5, 140, 144–7, 151
see also England, Court of Chancery; Maryland, Court of Chancery; New York, Court of Chancery; South Carolina, Court of Chancery
estate administration
comparisons between colonies 40, 51, 106, 122, 125
ecclesiastical courts (England) 29–31, 32, 46–50, 152
equity law 140
female litigants in 41–4, 46–50, 105–6, 111–12, 116–25, 143
prerogative courts (colonial) 22, 32–3, 51

Flynt, Margery 124–5

illegitimacy 91–101
see also midwives; paternity suits
inheritance
entails 106–7, 108
laws of 24, 26, 39, 106–9
multigeniture 109
primogeniture 108, 125

jointures
definition of 26, 107
dower and 26, 107–8, 116, 147
equity law 45
litigation concerning 109–16
marriage settlements 26–8, 107–8
New England 125, 150

law of necessaries 136–7, 139

marital separation 13, 81–9, 98, 101, 108, 135, 146–8
marriage settlements
dower vs. jointure 107–9
equity law 4, 26–8, 44–5, 134, 141
family conflict 109–16,
litigation 88, 109–16, 119–22, 147
New England 122, 125
'restraint upon anticipation' 15, 145
wives' separate estates 134, 141, 145, 147
Maryland
Court of Chancery 21, 27, 31–2, 40, 44–6, 140–3, 146, 148
dower rights 24, 116, 118
equity jurisdiction 3–4, 5–6, 22–3, 26–7, 39, 45, 52, 140
female litigants in 41, 43–4, 45–6, 141–2
feme sole traders 134
General Assembly 92
illegitimacy 92–4, 100–1
marital separation 84, 89, 148
marriage settlements 27, 44, 119, 145–6
midwives 92–4, 99
patriarchy 60, 134
Prerogative Court 22–3, 32–3, 51
Provincial Court 26, 40–1, 43–4, 69, 120–1
religious diversity 4, 31, 82, 121–2
servants 60, 67–9, 70–2, 92–4, 100–1
slaves 60, 143

INDEX

widows 14, 24, 43–4, 106, 108, 116–18, 120–1, 143
wives 89, 100, 121–2, 134, 145–6, 148
see also Chesapeake
Massachusetts
  common law 5, 28, 51
  Court of Assistants 123
  Dissenters in 4, 5, 28, 31, 51, 84, 87, 101, 108, 122, 150
  dower rights 108–9, 122–4
  ecclesiastical law 5, 31, 51
  equity law 5, 28–9, 122, 150–1
  General Court 28, 86, 92, 123, 124
  female litigants in 40–1, 43–4, 51
  feme sole traders 139
  illegitimacy 91–2, 96–8
  inheritance 108–9, 122–4, 150–1
  Lawes and Libertyes (1648) 108
  marital separation 84, 86, 98
  marriage settlements 122, 150–1
  midwives 92, 96, 98
  moral offences 31, 91–2, 96–7
  Quarterly Courts 40–1, 43, 74, 87,
  servants 73–5, 96–8
  widows 43, 108, 122–4
  wives 28–9, 51, 86–7, 122, 139, 150–1
  see also New England
midwives 90–2
  testimonies of 93–6, 98–100
  see also illegitimacy; paternity suits

New England
  common law 5, 6, 22–3, 28
  coverture 9, 23, 85
  Dissenters 5, 6, 23, 28, 76–7, 83–4, 106, 122, 134
  ecclesiastical law 5, 106
  equity law 22, 27–8, 122, 134, 150–1
  illegitimacy 82, 92–3, 96, 101
  inheritance 108–9, 122–3

marital separation 14, 82–5, 86–8, 101
patriarchy 3, 23–4, 60, 82, 87, 101, 106, 122, 125, 134, 150
southern colonies and 14, 22, 60, 76–7, 82–4, 92–3, 101, 106, 108, 122–3, 125, 134, 150–1
widows 106, 108, 122–3, 125, 150–1
see also Connecticut; Massachusetts
New York
  anglicisation 133
  common law 40
  Court of Chancery 45, 151
  equity 39, 45, 151
  female litigants in 40, 153
  Mayor's Court 40
  Prerogative Court 22
    compared to England 32–3, 39

paternity suits 81–2, 90–101
  see also illegitimacy
patriarchy
  as basis of social order 8, 23–4, 81–2, 84, 89–90, 91, 100–1, 153–4
  Dissenters and 23–4, 106, 122, 125, 134
  men's responsibilities 8, 13–14, 23–4, 83, 85, 87, 90, 92, 101, 122, 134–5, 147–8, 149, 153–4
  servants and slaves 8, 59–60, 65–6, 67, 75–7
  undermining of 2, 8–9, 12–13, 15, 100–1, 109, 112, 116, 125, 134–5, 147–8, 153–4
  women's property and 3, 106, 109, 112, 122, 125, 134–5, 147–8
  women's support of 10, 90
Pennsylvania
  common law 22, 27–8, 151
  equity 27–8, 52, 151
  feme sole traders 138–9
  Quakers *see* Dissenters

174

INDEX

Puritans *see* Dissenters

Quakers *see* Dissenters

servants
  apprentices 25, 59–60, 61–2, 65–6, 75
  of colour 61–4, 66, 67–8, 75
  contracts 60–70
  illegitimacy 92–7
  indentured 60, 62–3, 66–9, 72, 75
  laws governing 61–2
  patriarchal family and 59–60, 65–6, 69
  petitions of 64–6, 68–9, 74–5
  as witnesses 69–74
slavery
  ambiguous status of in England 61, 66–7, 76
  laws governing 60, 63–4, 76
  patriarchy and 60
  testimonies of slaves 75
South Carolina
  Court of Chancery 45, 140–1, 143, 144, 149–50
  Court of Ordinary 32–33
  equity jurisdiction in 3–4, 5–6, 22–3, 33, 39, 45, 134, 140–3, 144, 149–50
  female litigants in 141–2
  feme sole traders 134, 138
  marriage settlements 27, 28, 150
  prerogative courts 22, 32–3, 51
  wives 33, 134, 138, 142, 144, 149–50

Temple, Lady Hester Sandys 110–12

Virginia
  common law 5–6, 23, 26, 28, 140
  coverture 28
  equity 3, 5–6, 23, 26, 28, 140
  General Court 26, 140

inheritance 108, 116, 140
  marriage settlements 27
  religion in 31
  servants 67–8
  slavery 63–4, 75
  widows 24
  wives' power of attorney 25
  see also Chesapeake

widows
  comparisons between England and colonies 3, 14, 24, 41–4, 52, 105–8, 122, 125
  credit market 135
  guardianship of minor children 14, 106, 112
  illegitimacy 97
  in litigation 40–4, 46–9, 50, 105, 109–10, 110–12, 114–16, 117–21, 123–4, 140, 143
  patriarchy 8, 109, 112, 116, 122, 125
  property and 3, 14, 24, 26, 32, 47–9, 105–9, 116–17, 150
wives
  as attorneys for husbands 25, 72
  comparisons between England and colonies 9, 100–1, 122, 150–1
  credit market 136–7
  feme sole traders 7, 14, 134, 136–9
  infidelity 98–100
  as litigants 46–7, 49–50, 51, 88–9, 109–16, 140, 144–50
  mistresses of servants 65, 70–2, 73–5
  petitions for financial maintenance 81–90
  separate estates 15, 25, 141, 145, 147, 150
  'unity of person' 23, 150
  see also coverture; marital separation

175

EU authorised representative for GPSR:
Easy Access System Europe, Mustamäe tee 50,
10621 Tallinn, Estonia
gpsr.requests@easproject.com

www.ingramcontent.com/pod-product-compliance
Lightning Source LLC
Chambersburg PA
CBHW070239240426
43673CB00044B/1850